DISCARDS

CAREER
OPPORTUNITIES
IN LIBRARY
AND INFORMATION SCIENCE

CAREER OPPORTUNITIES IN LIBRARY AND INFORMATION SCIENCE

LINDA P. CARVELL

Ferguson
An imprint of ☑® Facts On File

Career Opportunities in Library and Information Science

Copyright © 2005 by Linda P. Carvell

Ferguson
An imprint of Facts On File, Inc.
132 West 31st Street
New York NY 10001

Library of Congress Cataloging-in-Publication Data
Carvell, Linda P.
    Career opportunities in library and information science / Linda P. Carvell
        p. cm.
    Includes bibliographical references and index.
    ISBN 0-8160-5244-1 (hc. alk. paper)
    1. Library science—Vocational guidance—United States. 2. Librarians—Job descriptions—United States.
    3. Information science—Vocational guidance—United States. I. Title.
    Z682.35. V62C37 2004
    020′.023′73—dc22   2004004005

Ferguson books are available at special discounts when purchased in bulk quantities for businesses, associations, institutions, or sales promotions. Please call our Special Sales Department in New York at (212) 967-8800 or (800) 322-8755.

You can find Ferguson on the World Wide Web at http://www.fergpubco.com.

Cover design by Nora Wertz

Printed in the United States of America

VB Hermitage 10 9 8 7 6 5 4 3 2 1

This book is printed on acid-free paper.

CONTENTS

SPECIAL LIBRARIES

APPENDIXES

ACKNOWLEDGMENTS

I'd like to thank every person, corporation, association, agency, and library who provided information, assistance, or encouragement for this book.

Specifically, this includes the American Association of Law Libraries, American Association of Museums, American Association of School Librarians (AASL), American Institute for Conservation of Historic and Artistic Works, American Library Association, Asian/Pacific American Librarians Association, American Society for Information Science and Technology, American Society of Indexers, American Theological Library Association, Archivists and Librarians in the History of the Health Sciences, Art Libraries Society of North America, Association for Library and Information Science Education, Association for Library Collections and Technical Services, Association for Library Service to Children, Association for Library Trustees and Advocates, Association for Records Managers and Administrators, The Association of Academic Health Sciences Libraries, Association of Architecture School Librarians, Association of College and Research Libraries, Association of Independent Information Professionals, Association of Jewish Libraries, Association of Library Services to Children, Association of Part-Time Librarians, *Association of Research Libraries,* Association of Specialized and Cooperative Library Agencies, Association of Vision Science Librarians, Beta Phi Mu: The International Library and Information Studies Honor Society, Bibliographical Society of America, The Canadian Association for Information Science, Catholic Library Association, Chief Officers of State Library Agencies, Chinese American Librarians Association, Church and Synagogue Library Association, Council of Planning Librarians, Council on Library and Information Resources, Educause, Independent Curators International, Institute of Museum and Library Services, International Federation of Library Associations and Institutions, Library Administration and Management Association, Library and Information Technology Association, Library Assistants and Technicians Group, Lutheran Church Library Association, Medical Library Association, Music Library Association, The National Association of Government Archives and Records Administrators, National Association to Promote Library and Information Services to Latinos and the Spanish Speaking, National Commission on Libraries and Information Services, National Federation of Abstracting and Information Service, National Information Standards Organization, Public Library Association, Reference and User Services Association, Research Libraries Group, Society of American Archivists, The Special Libraries Association, Special Libraries Association: Legal Division, Theatre Library Association, Urban Libraries Council, and the Young Adult Library Services Association (YALSA).

My thanks also to The University of Alabama School of Library and Information Studies, University of Arizona School of Information Resources and Library Science, University of California, Los Angeles Department of Information Studies, Southern Connecticut State University School of Communication, Information and Library Science, The Catholic University of America School of Library and Information Science, Florida State University School of Information Studies, University of South Florida School of Library and Information Science, Clark Atlanta University School of Library and Information Studies, University of Hawaii Library and Information Science Program, Dominican University Graduate School of Library and Information Science, University of Illinois at Urbana-Champaign Graduate School of Library and Information Science, Indiana University School of Library and Information Science, University of Iowa School of Library and Information Science, Emporia State University School of Library and Information Management, University of Kentucky College of Communications and Information Studies, Louisiana State University School of Library and Information Science, University of Maryland College of Information Studies, Simmons College Graduate School of Library and Information Science, University of Michigan School of Information, Wayne State University Library and Information Science Program, University of Southern Mississippi School of Library and Information Science, University of Missouri-Columbia School of Information Science and Learning Technologies, Rutgers University Department of Library and Information Science, Long Island University Palmer School of Library and Information Science, Pratt Institute School of Information and Library Science, City University of New York Graduate School of Library and Information Studies, St. John's University Division of Library and Information Science, Syracuse University School of Information Studies, SUNY Albany School of Information Science and Policy, SUNY Buffalo Department of Library and Information Studies, North Carolina Central University School of Library and Information Sciences, University of North Carolina at Chapel Hill School of Information and Library Science, The University of North Carolina at Greensboro Department of Library and Information Studies, Kent State University

School of Library and Information Science, University of Oklahoma School of Library and Information Studies, Clarion University of Pennsylvania Department of Library Science, Drexel University College of Information Science and Technology, University of Pittsburgh School of Information Sciences, University of Puerto Rico Graduate School of Information Sciences and Technologies, University of Rhode Island Graduate School of Library and Information Studies, University of South Carolina College of Library and Information Science, University of Tennessee School of Information Sciences, Texas Woman's University School of Information, University of North Texas School of Library and Information Sciences, The University of Texas at Austin Graduate School of Library and Information Science, University of Washington The Information School, University of Wisconsin–Madison School of Library and Information Studies, University of Wisconsin–Milwaukee School of Information Studies, University of Alberta School of Library and Information Studies, The University of British Columbia School of Library, Archival and Information Studies, Dalhousie University School of Library and Information Studies, University of Toronto Faculty of Information Studies, The University of Western Ontario Graduate Programs in Library and Information Science, McGill University Graduate School of Library and Information Studies, and the Université de Montréal École de bibliothéconomie et des sciences de l'information.

My thanks also to my agent Gene Brissie of James Peter Associates, and to my editor at Facts On File, James Chambers.

HOW TO USE THIS BOOK

Purpose

When it comes to the job of "librarian," most Americans think of a career in public or school libraries. While this is certainly true, in fact there are far more varied types of careers open to people who major in library science. There are specialty libraries for maps, music, art, architecture, science, chemistry, psychology, and just about every other topic you can think of. Health librarians can work in a medical school library, a hospital or medical center library, a government health agency library, or a pharmaceutical company. Chemical librarians might work for the U.S. government, for a drug company, for industry, or for a university. Librarians are intricately involved in website management and design, information brokering, bibliography development, and publishing.

Organization of Material

Career Opportunities in Library and Information Science is divided into five sections representing general types of libraries (academic, government, K–12, public, and special) and one "other" category for job listings held by librarians outside the typical library environment. Within each of these sections are descriptions of individual careers.

Section 1: Academic Libraries Academic libraries nurture ideas, from technology development to education, research, writing, and business management, to national policy formulation on information access, government funding, and free speech. Academic librarians are involved in many aspects of intellectual freedom.

Section 2: Government Libraries Most U.S. federal information is available electronically, and there are currently more than 1,200 depository libraries helping to disseminate and ensuring free access to this information. More and more government libraries are recognizing the need to provide librarians and information specialists to help patrons locate statistical data sets, geographic information systems, and electronic access to government information. While there may be fewer positions specifically described as "government information librarians," positions are readily available for people qualified in the area of government information, especially if the librarian is familiar with the use of statistical data sets.

Section 3: K–12 Libraries Children's librarians work with schoolchildren to help them find the information they need, analyzing their needs to determine what information is appropriate, and searching for, acquiring, and providing that material. But working in a K–12 library also involves an instructional role, teaching the basics of library science and showing children how to access information, put together a bibliography, and write research papers. School librarians also commonly help users navigate the Internet, showing them how to most efficiently search for relevant information.

Section 4: Outside the Library Librarians aren't restricted to working within the confines of a library. Increasingly, they apply their information management and research skills to other areas, such as database development, reference tool development, information systems, publishing, Internet coordination, and training of database users. Entrepreneurial librarians may start their own consulting practices, acting as freelance librarians, data delivery specialists, or information brokers and providing services to other libraries, businesses, or government agencies.

Section 5: Public Libraries The public library is the only institution in American society whose purpose is to guard against ignorance and conformity, and whose existence advertises the extent to which a democratic society values knowledge and truth. Public librarians provide free family literacy programs for low-literate, illiterate, and non-English-speaking people. In addition, hundreds of librarians across America lead outreach programs that teach citizenship and develop multilingual and multicultural materials for their patrons. Libraries serve senior citizens, prisoners, the homeless, the blind, and the deaf.

Section 6: Special Libraries Special librarians are information resource experts dedicated to putting knowledge to work to attain the goals of the organizations for which they work. You'll find special librarians working in corporations, private businesses, government agencies, museums, colleges, hospitals, nonprofit associations, and information management consulting firms.

Although there is no specific degree in "special librarianship," library and information science degrees are offered by schools accredited by the American Library Association, which often offers courses on "special librarianship."

About Each Profile

As you reach each of the various sections of this book, keep in mind there are many ways you can use a master's degree in library science (MLS). Within each section of the book, you'll find information necessary to acquaint you with the important jobs in the field. There are two parts to each job profile. The first part contains job information in a chart form for easy identification; the second part outlines more detailed information in a narrative text.

Here's a key to the organization of each profile:

Career Profile This quick-reference section provides a general overview of the job, including duties, alternate titles, salary range, employment and advancement prospects, best geographical location, and prerequisites.

Career Ladder The career ladder illustrates a normal job progression, beginning with the entry-level job on the bottom rung, followed by the current job title in the middle and jobs to which one may advance in the top rung.

Position Description This section provides a detailed description of all the duties connected with the job, although of course the exact job description may differ from one library to the next. The position description offers a general sense of what the average person in this position can expect on a day-to-day basis.

Salaries Salary ranges for the jobs in this book are as accurate as possible. Many are based on the U.S. *Occupational Outlook Handbook* estimates, surveys conducted by national library organizations, and information from library sources. Most salary ranges are also checked against actual classified ads for different parts of the country as listed on the Internet. Readers should keep in mind that salaries for any particular job will depend on the size and location of the library, as well as the candidate's experience and responsibilities.

Employment Prospects A job carrying an "excellent," "good," or "fair" rating means that it should not be too difficult to find a job in this field. This section also discusses how many opportunities there may be, and why they may be increasing or decreasing. Industry trends are also discussed here. This information is based in part on the U.S. Occupational Outlook Handbook, as well as library association information.

Advancement Prospects Once you've gotten your first job, this section will discuss how easy it will be to advance and what positions might be available to you. Any special skills or talents that may be required for advancement will be noted here.

Education and Training With very few exceptions (for entry-level clerk and assistant jobs), every librarian position requires at minimum a master's degree in information or library science from a school accredited by the American Library Association (ALA). Some positions also require further degrees, such as a Ph.D. for faculty or dean positions in university libraries. Many library programs also offer special certifications in certain fields.

Special Requirements In some cases, states require certification for certain positions, such as librarians in public libraries. In these cases, information about licensure or certification is included here.

Experience, Skills, and Personality Traits These traits tend to differ from job to job, but in general almost all library positions require good interpersonal and communication skills and computer literacy. Many administrative positions also require supervisory and/or budgeting experience. Typical personality traits for these positions include the ability to work independently, love of books and learning, and attention to detail.

Unions and Associations There are a huge number of professional organizations available for just about any specialty in which a librarian might be interested. Joining an appropriate professional association offers a number of important benefits to the job hunter, including the chance to make vital contacts and attend workshops or conferences (where jobs may be advertised on a job board). All have Internet websites and most include at least one page of classified ads or "job lines" in which current jobs are listed. Most of these are free to anyone surfing the Internet.

Tips for Entry This section gives readers a variety of tips on how to break into the field of library and information science, including information on helpful career websites, industry magazines or journals, and other inside tips.

Appendixes

Seven appendixes provide additional detailed information, including:

- names and contact information for professional associations
- federal libraries, with contact information
- presidential libraries, with contact information
- state libraries, with contact information
- accredited library and information science degree programs, by state
- U.S. library technician programs
- the 2005 "best library science master's degree programs" as ranked by *U.S. News & World Report*.

INTRODUCTION

Since the establishment of the very first library, these institutions have been the official repository of the record of the evolution of humankind. From the Library at Alexandria to the Internet, the library is where we have gone to research and to learn. Libraries make democracy work by providing access to information so that citizens can make the decisions necessary to govern themselves. Libraries preserve the record of a culture and a nation, enabling us to communicate through distance and time with those who have gone before. It is a miracle kept available by the meticulous sorting, storing, indexing, and preservation that still characterizes library work.

While patrons tend to think of libraries as a collection of books and manuscripts, libraries are far more than just a cozy place to read. Your library is the place to find exhibitions of valuable prints, author or poet readings, conferences, and collaborative brainstorming on the development of information technologies and how best to use them. Libraries also are storehouses for a variety of cultural artifacts—everything from coins to postage stamps, maps, records, and films to the latest CDs and DVDs.

Over the years, the types of materials on the library shelves have largely remained unchanged, but the nature of library services and the relationship between librarians and patrons has been profoundly altered by the onset of modern technology. In fact, the profession of library science has evolved into a more complex, more varied field now known as "information science." The traditional concept of a library is being redefined from a place to locate books and records to a place that houses the most advanced media—CD-ROMs, the Internet, virtual libraries, and remote access to a wide range of resources.

As a result, librarians are beginning to combine traditional duties with tasks involving ever-changing technology. Librarians help people find information and use it effectively for personal and professional purposes. They must be familiar with a wide variety of scholarly and public information sources, and follow trends related to publishing, computers, and the media to effectively oversee the selection and organization of library materials. They manage staff and develop and direct information programs and systems for the public to ensure information is organized to meet users' needs.

Most librarian positions incorporate three aspects of library work: user services, technical services, and administrative services. Even librarians specializing in one of these areas perform other responsibilities. Librarians in user services work with the public to help them find the information they need.

Librarians in technical services, such as acquisitions and cataloging, acquire and prepare materials for use and often do not deal directly with the public.

Librarians in administrative services oversee the management and planning of libraries, negotiate contracts for services, materials, and equipment, supervise library employees, perform public relations and fund-raising duties, prepare budgets, and direct activities to make sure everything works properly.

In small libraries or information centers, librarians usually handle all types of jobs, reading book reviews, publishers' announcements, and catalogs to keep up with current literature and other available resources, and selecting and purchasing materials from publishers, wholesalers, and distributors. To prepare new materials, librarians classify them by subject matter and describe books and other library materials so they are easy to find. They supervise assistants who prepare cards, computer records, or other access tools that direct users to resources. In large libraries, librarians often specialize in a single area, such as acquisitions, cataloging, bibliography, reference, special collections, or administration.

Librarians also compile lists of books, periodicals, articles, and audiovisual materials on particular subjects; analyze collections; and recommend materials. They collect and organize books, pamphlets, manuscripts, and other materials in a specific field, such as rare books, genealogy, or music. In addition, they coordinate programs such as storytelling for children and literacy skills and book talks for adults, conduct classes, publicize services, provide reference help, write grants, and oversee other administrative matters.

Librarians are classified according to the type of library in which they work—public libraries, school library media centers, academic libraries, and special libraries. Some librarians work with specific groups, such as children, young adults, adults, or the disadvantaged.

Increasingly, librarians also apply their information management and research skills to arenas outside libraries—for example, database development, reference tool development, information systems, publishing, Internet coordination, marketing, and training of database users. This new breed can be found working in publishing or for companies that supply goods and services to libraries. Some become webmasters, independent information consultants, or start their own information-related business. They may hold management positions in associations or corporate positions such as electronic image manager or risk management researcher. The possibilities are always expanding, as emerging information technologies create a need for more information.

Entrepreneurial librarians sometimes start their own consulting practices, acting as freelance librarians or information brokers and providing services to other libraries, businesses, or government agencies.

There are more than 117,000 libraries in the United States. In addition to public libraries in almost every community, there are thousands of libraries in schools, colleges and universities, hospitals, law firms, businesses, the armed forces, and more. Because libraries offer free access to all, they bring opportunity to all. And the greatest resources in each of these libraries are the librarians and library workers—almost 400,000 people who make libraries work for you every day.

ACADEMIC LIBRARIES

ACADEMIC LIBRARY CLERK

CAREER PROFILE

Duties: Compile records, sort and shelve books, and issue and receive library materials, register students and faculty patrons

Alternate Title(s): Library Aide or Circulation Assistant

Salary Range: $14,800 to $20,000

Employment Prospects: Excellent

Advancement Prospects: Good

Best Geographical Location(s): Larger cities may offer more possibilities, but academic libraries throughout the country use Library Clerks

Prerequisites:

Education or Training—High school diploma

Experience—Secretarial experience helpful

Special Skills and Personality Traits—Good people skills; attention to detail; neatness; organizational skills; aptitude for computers; good English writing and speaking skills; willingness to learn new skills

CAREER LADDER

```
┌─────────────────────────────┐
│   Library Assistant or      │
│   Library Technician        │
└─────────────────────────────┘

┌─────────────────────────────┐
│      Library Clerk          │
└─────────────────────────────┘

┌─────────────────────────────┐
│       Entry Level           │
└─────────────────────────────┘
```

Position Description

Library Clerks perform routine tasks such as shelving books and periodicals, signing out material, and maintaining books and equipment. Many clerks use their typing and computer skills to process material orders and to update library catalogs. They work under the direction of staff trained in the library and information profession.

Library Clerks compile records, sort and shelve books, and issue and receive library materials such as pictures, cards, slides, and microfilm. They locate library materials for loan and replace material in shelving areas, stacks, or files according to identification number and title. Library Clerks also work with patrons, registering them so that they may borrow books, periodicals, and other library materials. They record the borrower's name and address from an application and then issue a library card. Most Library Clerks enter and update patron records using computer databases.

Salaries

Salaries for this position vary a great deal depending on the location and size of the academic library, but they range from a low of $14,800 to $20,000 and above.

Employment Prospects

This work is attractive to retirees and others who want a part-time schedule, and for this reason, there is a lot of movement into and out of the occupation, reflecting the limited investment in training and subsequent weak attachment to this occupation. Opportunities should be good for people interested in jobs as Library Clerks through 2012, according to the U.S. Bureau of Labor Statistics, since many openings will become available each year to replace workers who transfer to another occupation. Some positions become available as Library Clerks move upward within the library.

Efforts to contain costs in the university may mean more hiring of support staff such as Library Clerks over librarians, which also means Library Clerks are taking on more responsibility. While academic libraries are not usually directly affected by the ups and downs of the business cycle, some clerks may lose their jobs if there are cuts in the university budget.

Because many academic library support positions are advertised only locally, it's worth checking the classified ad sections of newspapers. Many times, the on-line version will be more convenient than the print, because you can frequently search the classifieds by keyword. Ads are usually posted whenever a job comes open, and will mention a title and brief description of the position.

Advancement Prospects

A Library Clerk can usually advance by transferring to a position with more responsibilities. Library Clerks can be promoted to library assistants or library technicians. Advancement opportunities are better in larger academic libraries and may be more limited in smaller ones. Most libraries fill office and administrative support by promoting individuals within their organization, so Library Clerks who acquire new skills, experience, and training improve their advancement opportunities.

Education and Training

A high school diploma is generally required for a position as a Library Clerk, and standard secretarial and computer skills are highly desirable. Library Clerks often learn the skills they need in high schools, business schools, and community colleges. Business education programs offered by these institutions typically include courses in typing, word processing, shorthand, business communications, records management, and office systems and procedures.

Additional training for Library Clerks usually takes place on the job under the guidance of a supervisor or an experienced library assistant or technician. Most Library Clerks continue to receive instruction on new procedures and library policies after their initial training ends.

Experience, Skills, and Personality Traits

Experience with computers and good interpersonal skills are equally important to employers. Many Library Clerks deal directly with patrons, so a professional appearance and pleasant personality are important. A clear speaking voice and fluency in the English language also are essential, because Library Clerks frequently use the telephone or public address systems. Library Clerks work in areas that are clean, well lit, and relatively quiet, although their work may be repetitious and stressful.

Unions and Associations

Library Clerks working in academic libraries may belong to a variety of trade associations that provide educational guidance, support, conferences, and information to members. These might include the American Library Association, the Library Assistants and Technicians Group, the American Society for Information Science, or the Special Libraries Association.

Tips for Entry

1. Library Clerk jobs may be found in the classified section of your local newspaper, in either the print or on-line versions.
2. Visit your local academic library and speak with the director about possible jobs.
3. Take every opportunity available to get experience; volunteer in a college or university library (although any library experience is good). Library administrators are likely to prefer a candidate with some relevant experience.
4. Make contacts. Join various professional organizations for librarians and keep in touch with your library friends to provide a network through which you may hear about job opportunities.
5. Send out your résumé. Find out the name and address of every academic library in your area where you might like to work (the telephone book is helpful; call to find out to whom to address your cover letter). When openings occur, administrators often pull out their collection of unsolicited résumés and contact the candidates.

ACADEMIC LIBRARY ASSISTANT

CAREER PROFILE

Duties: Provide highly skilled reference service either directly to library users or in service support, helping librarians and library technicians

Alternate Title(s): None

Salary Range: $16,800 to $30,000

Employment Prospects: Excellent

Advancement Prospects: Good

Best Geographical Location(s): Larger cities may offer more possibilities, but academic libraries throughout the country use Library Assistants

Prerequisites:

Education or Training—High school diploma, with Library Technology Certificate or equivalent academic library experience; college degree helpful

Experience—Experience working in an academic library is helpful; computer skills are needed for many jobs

Special Skills and Personality Traits—Good people skills; attention to detail; neatness; organizational skills; aptitude for computers; good English writing and speaking skills; willingness to attend conferences and workshops; willingness to learn new skills

CAREER LADDER

```
┌─────────────────────────────────────┐
│  Library Technician or Supervisor    │
└─────────────────────────────────────┘

┌─────────────────────────────────────┐
│          Library Assistant           │
└─────────────────────────────────────┘

┌─────────────────────────────────────┐
│            Library Clerk             │
└─────────────────────────────────────┘
```

Position Description

The position of Library Assistant requires the application of basic professional knowledge and techniques of library science to a variety of assignments, including descriptive cataloging, acquisition of library materials, and response to information requests from library users. Employees work independently under the general supervision of a librarian. Assistants supervise shelving and general stack maintenance, and oversee maintenance of the periodical collection.

Library Assistants retrieve information from on-line computer catalogs or find information from written documents in order to help library users find books or information, and help train students to use the on-line computer catalog system. They may answer questions and provide service for routine reference requests, referring complex reference questions to the appropriate specialized librarian. In larger academic libraries, Assistants may help students

with disabilities use specialized equipment, such as magnifiers, computerized personal readers with synthesized speech, and Braille embossers.

Assistants may read computer cataloging information from a screen or printout, reconciling information with material being cataloged or acquired in the library. They may also help order, process, and catalog materials or work in charging out or receiving materials.

They may work at the circulation desk, lending and collecting books, periodicals, videotapes, and other materials; they also may inspect returned materials for damage and check due dates. Handling overdue material is another responsibility of Assistants, who may review records to compile a list of overdue materials, send out notices, and collect fees.

Throughout the library, Assistants sort and reshelve returned books, periodicals, and other items; locate materials to be loaned out; and try to repair damaged items.

Salaries

Salaries for this position vary a great deal depending on the responsibilities and location of the academic library, although workers with college degrees are likely to start at higher salaries and advance more easily than those without degrees. Average annual earnings of Library Assistants range from $16,800 to more than $30,000.

Employment Prospects

Opportunities should be good for people interested in jobs as Academic Library Assistants, especially if the Assistant is interested in a flexible schedule (more than half of all Library Assistants have part-time schedules). One reason that there are so many opportunities in this field is because there is a high turnover rate, reflecting the limited investment in training for these jobs.

As the university tries to contain costs, it is likely to cut more professional librarian positions, which opens up jobs and responsibilities for library support staff such as Library Assistants. Although universities are not directly affected by the ups and downs of the business cycle, some Assistants may lose their jobs if the school requires budgetary cuts.

Because many academic library support positions are advertised only locally, it's worth checking the classified ad sections of newspapers and their on-line versions.

Advancement Prospects

Library Assistants at academic libraries can be promoted to library technicians and eventually reach supervisory positions in technical service areas. Advancement opportunities are better in larger academic libraries, which usually fill office and administrative support positions by promoting individuals within the university. This means that Library Assistants who acquire new skills, experience, and training improve their advancement opportunities. In some academic libraries, a college degree may be required for advancement to management.

Education and Training

A high school diploma is all the specialized training needed by Library Assistants, since training for these jobs usually takes place on the job, and new employees learn tasks under the guidance of a supervisor or an experienced library technician. Most Library Assistants can expect to continually learn new procedures and library policies on the job, along with formal classroom training in some areas such as computer software.

Experience, Skills, and Personality Traits

Library Assistants need to be familiar with computers and library automated systems, such as OCLC (Online Computer Library Center) and Docline, and be able to work cooperatively with other faculty members and students. They need to be able to learn job-related material primarily through oral instruction and observation, which takes place mainly on the job.

Because many Library Assistants deal directly with students and faculty, a professional appearance and pleasant personality are important. A clear speaking voice and fluency in the English language also are essential, because these employees frequently use the telephone or public address systems. Good spelling and computer literacy often are needed, particularly because most work involves considerable computer use. Library Assistants work in areas that are clean, well lit, and relatively quiet, although their work may be repetitious and stressful.

Unions and Associations

Library Assistants working in academic libraries may belong to a variety of associations that provide educational guidance, support, conferences, and information to members. These might include the American Library Association, the Library Assistants and Technicians Group, the American Society for Information Science, or the Special Libraries Association.

Tips for Entry

1. Jobs in this field may be found in the classified section of your local newspaper.
2. Take every opportunity available to get experience. Volunteer in a university library, since administrators are likely to select a candidate with some relevant experience over one with none.
3. Make contacts. Join various professional organizations for librarians and keep in touch with your library friends to provide a network through which you may hear about job opportunities.
4. Send out your résumé. Find out the name and address of every college or university library in your area where you might like to work (the telephone book is helpful; call to find out to whom to address your cover letter). When openings occur, administrators often pull out their collection of unsolicited résumés and contact the candidates.
5. If you're targeting a specific institution or geographic area, take a look at individual academic library websites for postings.

ACADEMIC LIBRARIAN

CAREER PROFILE

Duties: Provide public and technical services, instruction, collection development, and library automation in college and university libraries

Alternate Title(s): College Librarian, University Librarian

Salary Range: $24,510 to $66,590+

Employment Prospects: Good

Advancement Prospects: Good

Best Geographical Location(s): Positions are available at colleges and universities throughout the United States

Prerequisites:

Education or Training—Master of library science; an additional master's degree in a specialty area is desirable; librarians who want to teach or hold top administrative positions will find it helpful to have a Ph.D. in library or information science

Experience—Teaching and computer experience can be very helpful

Special Skills and Personality Traits—Leadership ability; communication skills; ability to work in a team environment; good technical skills; people skills; above-average academic ability; love of books and learning; flexibility

CAREER LADDER

```
┌─────────────────────────┐
│  Academic Librarian in  │
│   a Larger Institution  │
└─────────────────────────┘

┌─────────────────────────┐
│   Academic Librarian    │
└─────────────────────────┘

┌─────────────────────────┐
│ Assistant Academic Librarian │
└─────────────────────────┘
```

Position Description

Academic Librarians work with students and professors in college and university libraries, where they are an essential component in the culture of higher education. Unlike public libraries, which must appeal to all their patrons, academic libraries are free to focus on meeting specialized needs of teachers and students. Academic Librarians often specialize in one subject area, such as history, biology, or art.

All accredited institutions have libraries, ranging from small to large, old-fashioned or high tech, largely dependent upon the size of the campus and the commitment to funding by the institution's administration. Many campuses (particularly at universities) offer multiple libraries to serve different academic communities, and they build their collections to match the goals of the school they serve. Academic libraries may be oriented primarily to research, or more dedicated to the needs of students—or some combination of the two.

On some campuses, Academic Librarians are appointed faculty and are able to secure tenure. As faculty members, these Librarians are expected to pursue further formal education, to do research, and to publish. Whatever the venue, Academic Librarians usually work side by side with paraprofessionals and student workers.

Academic libraries primarily serve the academic community, including undergraduates, graduate students, faculty, administration, and staff. Librarians in academic settings often focus on instruction, teaching students how to synthesize information. They help students (especially entering freshmen) polish their research skills by conducting group classes and holding tutoring sessions. In order to keep students current with the newest technology, Academic

Librarians also must learn about the newest technological advances. In addition, an Academic Librarian must select from all new book titles those that are relevant to his or her library. The Librarian must know the curriculum, types of assignments given, and the courses required by all students. The Librarian must also be aware of changes in curriculum, so one of the important jobs of an Academic Librarian is to maintain close ties with faculty members. Faculty library committees are one good way of doing this.

A small college may focus on serving the student body by concentrating on supporting the curriculum. At larger universities, the academic library not only supports the school's curriculum, but provides graduate students and faculty with material to support their research. Some academic libraries also serve the needs of the general population; as the cost of services outstrips increases in funding, some communities and colleges have joined together to provide library service for the entire population. By creating formal or informal networks, they can make interlibrary loans and help keep collection development more efficient.

In addition, many academic libraries (especially those at large universities) often maintain rare, specialized collections, such as oral histories of Native Americans or rare art prints.

An Academic Librarian may work among several areas or be expected to rotate through several areas during the course of a year. Academic librarianship encompasses public and technical services, instruction, collection development, and library automation. The size of operations varies from a one-person branch operation to a major research library. The focus ranges from undergraduate students to research professors.

Salaries

Salaries for this position vary a great deal depending on specific job responsibilities and the location of the library. Starting salaries for professional librarians in the United States range from $24,510 to $40,000 a year, but experienced librarians can expect a salary ranging from $25,000 to more than $66,590. The median salary for Academic Librarians is $43,090.

Employment Prospects

Employment of Academic Librarians is expected to continue to grow steadily as technological advances continue through 2012, and new positions will continue to be available. The increasing use of computerized information storage and retrieval systems means slower growth in the demand for Academic Librarians, because computers make cataloging easier so that library technicians can now handle this part of the job. In addition, many students and faculty members can now access library computers directly from their homes or offices, which allows users to bypass librarians and conduct research on their own.

However, Academic Librarians are still needed to manage staff, help users develop database searching techniques, address complicated reference requests, and define users' needs. The need to replace Librarians as they retire means there will still be many new job openings.

Advancement Prospects

Opportunities vary according to the interests and expertise of the individual librarian. Librarians can use a particular subject background to develop collections and provide specialized services, or devote a career to technical services or library automation. The more time, experience, and additional education an individual has, the better the advancement prospects.

Education and Training

The master of library science (M.L.S.) degree from a graduate program accredited by the American Library Association (ALA) is the appropriate professional degree for employment as an Academic Librarian. Many colleges and universities also require Academic Librarians to have an additional master's degree in a particular subject area of importance to the institution; those Librarians with faculty status may be required to have a Ph.D.

Experience, Skills, and Personality Traits

Academic Librarians should have leadership ability, strong communication skills, ability to work in a team environment, good technical skills, and knowledge of the issues facing libraries and higher education. A broad understanding of all aspects of librarianship from reference work to technical services is useful. Experiences in teaching and Web development also are important. Flexibility to both lead and adjust to change throughout your career is critical.

Unions and Associations

At some universities, Librarians are tenured; at other institutions, Academic Librarians are unionized. Academic Librarians also can belong to a variety of trade associations that provide educational guidance, support, conferences and information to members. These might include the American Library Association, the Association of College and Research Libraries, or the Library Administration and Management Association (the latter two are divisions of the American Library Association [ALA]).

Tips for Entry

1. For entry-level positions, get work in an academic library—even an unpaid internship or volunteer job is a good start. Internships at well-known libraries, such as the Library of Congress or the National Library of Medicine, may lead to a future job.

2. College placement services can be great resources for help in finding a job. Check out the placement service bulletin board and talk to faculty members for advice and job leads.

3. Vary your experience as much as possible—teach library instruction sessions or courses, develop or contribute to Web services, supervise students, work at the reference desk, work in technical services.

4. Join various professional librarian organizations and keep in touch with your library friends to provide a network through which you may hear about job opportunities.

5. The American Library Association can provide numbers from state, regional, and association hotlines.

6. The e-mail discussion groups LIBJOBS and LIS-JOBS are a good source for job postings. Topical groups are also a good place for finding advertisements in a particular field of librarianship.

7. Look for jobs on the Internet, such as on www.Lisjobs.com, the daily job postings on "Hot Jobs Online" at the website of the American Library Association (www.ala.org), the American Society of Information Science website job line (www.asis.org/Jobline), or www.libraryjobpostings.org. Or visit the ALISE website (www.alise.org), which has links to all library schools, each of which has state and national employment listings. If you're targeting a specific institution or geographic area, take a look at individual websites for postings.

8. Check out *Jobs for Librarians and Information Professionals,* a comprehensive guide to on-line job resources for librarians and information professionals.

9. Subscribe to major library trade publications, such as *Library Journal* or *American Libraries.*

10. Attend library conventions or conferences, check job boards, and check out the placement service that lists library-related jobs at annual ALA conventions.

11. Check out the *American Library Directory,* which lists a wide variety of libraries in its two-volume directory, or the *Guide to Employment Sources in the Library and Information Professions,* which is available on-line at the ALA website.

ASSISTANT ACADEMIC LIBRARY DIRECTOR

CAREER PROFILE

Duties: Assist the academic library director with hiring and training staff, attending meetings, scheduling, and handling public relations

Alternate Title(s): Associate Library Director

Salary Range: $42,629 to $100,000+

Employment Prospects: Good

Advancement Prospects: Good

Best Geographical Location(s): Positions are available at colleges and universities throughout the United States

Prerequisites:

Education or Training—Master's degree in library or information science (M.L.S.)

Experience—Teaching assistant and computer experience is helpful

Special Skills and Personality Traits—Good people skills; communications skills; organizational ability

CAREER LADDER

```
┌─────────────────────────────────────┐
│      Academic Library Director       │
└─────────────────────────────────────┘

┌─────────────────────────────────────┐
│  Assistant Academic Library Director │
└─────────────────────────────────────┘

┌─────────────────────────────────────┐
│          Academic Librarian          │
└─────────────────────────────────────┘
```

Position Description

Depending on the size of the library, the Assistant Academic Library Director spends most hours on administrative tasks, although at smaller college libraries the person may also fill in on the reference desk or helping students. The Assistant Director helps oversee the management of the library; performs public relations and fund-raising duties; and helps direct activities to make sure the library functions properly.

In addition to helping to run the library, an important part of the Assistant Director's day is to manage library employees, help evaluate new employees, and attend meetings, workshops, seminars, and conferences. The Assistant Director may be required from time to time to represent the director at state, regional, and national professional organizations.

Assistant Academic Library Directors may need to work more than a standard 40-hour week, including some weekend and evening hours, and must be able to use the library's computers, printers, copiers, typewriters, microfilm readers, and fax machines. Assistant Academic Library Directors also need to create and follow budgets, and they must work with university trustees and faculty leaders to seek the funding required for a robust academic library.

Salaries

Salaries for this position vary a great deal depending on the responsibilities and location of the university library. The average salary for Assistant Library Directors and those who supervise support staff is $42,629, but can top $100,000 at a large academic library.

Employment Prospects

Employment prospects for Assistant Library Directors continue to be good as technological advancement opens up new opportunities in academic libraries. Librarians' technological skills have improved their employment prospects and should continue to make this a strong career choice through 2012.

Advancement Prospects

After a few years of working as a librarian and then Assistant Academic Library Director, the logical next step on the library career ladder is to move into a directorship. Assistant Library Directors who pursue continuing education and technological advancement will find plenty of opportunities to move into more responsible administrative positions in larger public libraries. Promotions usually come with the acquisition of experience and administrative skills, knowledge of automated systems, and additional training. Advancement opportunities are greater in the larger library systems.

Education and Training

Most academic library positions require a master of library science (M.L.S.) degree, preferably from a school accredited by the American Library Association (ALA). Undergraduate degrees in almost any subject area are appropriate. Several years of experience as a librarian are usually required.

Experience, Skills, and Personality Traits

Assistant Academic Directors should possess strong interpersonal and communication skills, excellent organizational and computer skills, managerial skills, and be capable of dealing with employees, supervisors, students, trustees, and faculty. In addition, individuals are often required to have at least three years of professional library experience.

Unions and Associations

Assistant (or Associate) Academic Library Directors may belong to a variety of trade associations that provide educational guidance, support, conferences, and information to members. These might include the American Library Association, the American Society for Information Science, the Association for Library Collections and Technical Services, Association for Records Managers and Administrators, and the Library Administration and Management Association.

Tips for Entry

1. Join various professional organizations to provide a network through which you may hear about job opportunities.
2. Visit e-mail discussion groups such as LIBJOBS and LIS-JOBS, which are a good source for job postings. Topical groups are also a good place for finding advertisements in a particular field of librarianship.
3. Look for jobs on the Internet, at sites such as www.Lisjobs.com; the daily job postings on "Hot Jobs Online" at the website of the American Library Association (www.ala.org); the American Society of Information Science website job line (www.asis.org/ Jobline); or www.libraryjobpostings.org. Or visit the ALISE website, which has links to all library schools, each of which has state and national employment listings (www.alise.org). If you're targeting a specific institution or geographic area, take a look at individual websites for postings.
4. Check out *Jobs for Librarians and Information Professionals,* a comprehensive guide to on-line job resources for librarians and information professionals.
5. Subscribe to major library trade publications, such as *Library Journal* and *American Libraries.*
6. Attend library conventions or conferences, check job boards, and check out the placement service that lists library-related jobs at annual ALA conventions.
7. Check out the *American Library Directory,* which lists a wide variety of libraries in its two-volume directory, or the *Guide to Employment Sources in the Library and Information Professions,* which is available on-line at the American Library Association website.

ACADEMIC LIBRARY DIRECTOR

CAREER PROFILE

Duties: Significant management responsibilities, including hiring and training staff, maintaining the facility, attending meetings, scheduling, budgeting, and handling public relations

Alternate Title(s): Library Administrator or Head Librarian

Salary Range: $72,384 to $274,519+

Employment Prospects: Good

Advancement Prospects: Good

Best Geographical Location(s): Academic libraries throughout the country have positions for director

Prerequisites:

Education or Training—Master's degree in library or information science (M.L.S.); a Ph.D. or D.L.S. (doctor of library science) may be necessary to obtain a director position in a top academic library

Experience—Professional library experience, preferably in an administrative or managerial capacity in an academic library

Special Skills and Personality Traits—Good people skills; administrative skills; communications skills and organizational ability; good computer and technology skills; intellectual curiosity; above-average academic ability; a desire for continuing education; ability to make decisions

CAREER LADDER

```
┌─────────────────────────────────┐
│   Academic Library Director of   │
│          Larger Library          │
└─────────────────────────────────┘

┌─────────────────────────────────┐
│     Academic Library Director    │
└─────────────────────────────────┘

┌─────────────────────────────────┐
│ Assistant Academic Library Director │
└─────────────────────────────────┘
```

Position Description

The Academic Library Director plans, coordinates, and supervises all aspects of the library, and is usually responsible to the university library board of trustees for implementing policies and services. A large part of the Director's job is administrative, and involves working with university trustees and the development office to obtain the funding required for a robust academic library. The Director must oversee the management and planning of the library; negotiate contracts for services, materials, and equipment; perform public relations and fund-raising duties; prepare budgets; and direct activities to make sure the library functions properly.

In addition to running the library, an important part of the Director's day is managing library employees and adminis-

tering the library personnel policy, including evaluation of current employees. The Director must replace and add new staffers, while scheduling current employees for either refresher training or training for new responsibilities.

The increased use of automated information systems means that Academic Library Directors can focus on administrative and budgeting responsibilities, grant writing, and specialized research requests, while delegating more technical and user services responsibilities to librarians or technicians.

Academic Library Directors are also involved in planning new buildings or alterations and improvements in existing buildings throughout the campus library system.

The duties of a Library Director may require working beyond the standard 40-hour week, and involve some weekend and evening work. The Director also attends workshops, seminars, and conferences, and is active in state, regional, and national professional organizations.

The Academic Library Director must draft proposals for library grants and must be able to use library equipment, including computers, printers, copiers, typewriters, microfilm readers, and fax machines.

In addition, the Academic Library Director is responsible for the overall maintenance of the library collection, keeping it current, attractive, and useful by setting up a schedule of replacement for encyclopedias; placing standing orders for annuals and irregular publications needed in reference; and systematically checking bibliographies and selection aids for new editions, replacement titles, and subject area expansion. The Academic Library Director also must evaluate the current collection, maintain a continuous program of "weeding" to remove obsolete and worn-out materials, and conduct periodic inventory checks.

Salaries

Salaries for this position vary a great deal depending on the responsibilities and location of the university library; $72,384 is the average salary for an Academic Library Director in a suburban setting. Academic Library Directors at smaller colleges would average less. Salaries for Directors of very large libraries, who supervise an extensive support staff, may top $274,519.

Employment Prospects

Employment prospects for Library Directors in academic libraries are good, since every school of higher learning in the United States has its own library, and each of these libraries needs a Director.

Advancement Prospects

As the explosion of technology continues, opportunities continue to improve for Library Directors educated in technological areas. If the individual continues to keep up with his or her education, it should be possible to move into larger and more responsible administrative positions in larger academic libraries. Library Directors often are required to have between three and five years of professional library experience as some type of librarian.

Education and Training

Most academic library positions require a master of library science (M.L.S.) degree, preferably from a school accredited by the American Library Association (ALA). (Although many colleges and universities offer M.L.S. programs, employers often prefer graduates of the approximately 56 schools accredited by the ALA). Undergraduate degrees in almost any subject area are appropriate. However, individuals interested in obtaining some of the top director positions in the larger universities may find it helpful to have a Ph.D. or L.L.S. in library science, or an advanced business degree.

Experience, Skills, and Personality Traits

Library Directors should be skilled in analyzing and resolving complex problems in a wide variety of areas, and be capable of dealing with employees, supervisors, patrons, trustees, and news media. Directors should have good people skills, and be able to maintain effective working relationships with the library board, staff, faculty, students, and private agencies and organizations. They should be flexible, adaptable, and comfortable with both the academic and technical aspects of the library.

In addition, a Library Director should be able to evaluate financial data and understand budgets; analyze the needs of the library; and maintain a collection of books, periodicals, and other documents in a variety of formats, including electronic ones, to meet those needs.

Unions and Associations

Library Directors working in academic libraries can belong to a variety of trade associations that provide educational guidance, support, conferences, and information to members. These might include the American Library Association, the American Society for Information Science, the Association for Library Collections and Technical Services, Association for Records Managers and Administrators, the Association for Library Trustees and Advocates, or the Library Administration and Management Association.

Tips for Entry

1. Join various professional organizations for Library Directors to provide a network through which you may hear about job opportunities.
2. The e-mail discussion groups LIBJOBS and LISJOBS are a good source for job postings. Topical groups are also a good place for finding advertisements in a particular field of librarianship.
3. Look for jobs on the Internet, such as on www. Lisjobs.com, the daily job postings on "Hot Jobs Online" at the website of the American Library Association (www.ala.org), the American Society of Information Science website job line (www.asis.org/Jobline), or www.libraryjobpostings.org. Or visit the ALISE website, which has links to all library schools, each of which has state and national employment listings (www.alise.org). If you're targeting a specific institution or geographic area, take a look at individual academic library websites for postings.
4. Check out *Jobs for Librarians and Information Professionals,* a comprehensive guide to on-line job resources for librarians and information professionals.

5. Subscribe to major library trade publications, such as *Library Journal* and *American Libraries.*
6. Attend library conventions or conferences, check job boards, and check out the placement service that lists library-related jobs at annual ALA conventions.

7. Check out the *American Library Directory,* which lists a wide variety of libraries in its two-volume directory, or the *Guide to Employment Sources in the Library and Information Professions,* which is available online at the American Library Association website.

ACADEMIC CATALOGER

CAREER PROFILE

Duties: Describe library materials (usually in computerized catalogs) by author, title, subject, or keyword so users will know whether they want to see that particular item

Alternate Title(s): None

Salary Range: $42,730 to $55,000

Employment Prospects: Good

Advancement Prospects: Good

Best Geographical Location(s): Most positions are available in larger academic libraries

Prerequisites:

Education or Training—Master's degree in library or information science

Experience—Experience as a volunteer in a library, archive, or museum is helpful

Special Skills and Personality Traits—Attention to detail; ability to work independently; foreign language skills; communications skills; organizational ability

CAREER LADDER

```
┌─────────────────────────────────────┐
│  Cataloger in Larger Academic Library │
└─────────────────────────────────────┘

┌─────────────────────────────────────┐
│             Cataloger                │
└─────────────────────────────────────┘

┌─────────────────────────────────────┐
│      Assistant Cataloger or          │
│      Entry-Level Position            │
└─────────────────────────────────────┘
```

Position Description

Catalogers classify books, videos, CD-ROMs, and other material so students and faculty can find what they are looking for. The Cataloger describes materials by subject discussed, date published, format, author, title, and many other characteristics, completing a record for each item. Catalogers spend all their time acquiring and preparing materials for use, and often do not deal directly with students or faculty.

A Cataloger takes each new item that arrives at the library and, using digital technology to preserve and organize information, records the title, author's name, publication information, and a short summary of the item ("nonfiction reference," "children's fiction," "classical music recording," and so on). Cataloging new materials is not simply a matter of figuring out the title and the author; however, Catalogers must make constant distinctions and decisions about materials, such as whether to omit a dated or misleading term.

Certain items that are valuable or important may be photographed and assigned a code that explains where to find the items in the library. The codes and other relevant information are then recorded in a computerized reference database. These codes help librarians locate lost or stolen items,

charge late fees, and ensure they don't order too many of one item for the library collection.

In the past, Catalogers recorded all their information on cards that were kept in card files. Today Catalogers use computerized database retrieval systems, which means that keeping track of the library collection is only a mouse click away.

Catalogers who work in academic libraries keep regular business hours unless a large number of books are acquired that need to be stored or displayed immediately, which requires overtime and weekend work. It is typical for a Cataloger in a large academic library to supervise one or two beginning librarians and several technicians, assistants, or clerks.

Because of on-line access, making catalogs easy to use is even more important than before. More and more, Catalogers share catalogs with a database. For example, cataloging information may come from networks such as the Online Computer Library Center (OCLC), the Western Library Network, or the Research Libraries Information Network. When a library acquires new material, Catalogers can search for it in the shared catalog. If a record exists, they can verify and customize the data without having to create a brand new record. Today, only about 10 percent of new material in most academic libraries needs to have a new record created by a Cataloger.

The sheer volume of their tasks can be overwhelming, as materials often come into the library faster than they can be cataloged; this type of library job can be highly stressful.

Salaries

Salaries for this position vary a great deal depending on the responsibilities and location of the library, but the average is about $42,730. Catalogers in large academic libraries can expect to earn more than those employed in smaller institutions.

Employment Prospects

The number of jobs is projected to grow about as fast as the average through 2012. Cataloging has become even more important as searchers log on to on-line catalogs from home.

Advancement Prospects

Catalogers can become archivists, reference librarians, or take on administrative positions, or they can apply their methodical and analytical skills to other fields, such as history, bibliography, and data entry. Promotions usually come with experience and administrative skills, knowledge of automated systems, and additional training. Advancement opportunities are greater in larger library systems.

Education and Training

Catalogers generally need a master's degree in library or information studies (although many colleges and universities offer M.L.S. programs, employers often prefer graduates of the approximately 56 schools accredited by the American Library Association), along with a bachelor's degree in general arts. Prospective Catalogers should supplement this education with courses in computers and business studies. It is also a good idea to volunteer with a library, archive, or museum, as any experience in the field will be beneficial in the long run.

Experience, Skills, and Personality Traits

Catalogers in academic libraries need to be patient and decisive, with good communication and organizational skills. They should enjoy research, love books, and be comfortable working alone. An analytical mind and a thorough, methodical approach to tasks are important qualities. In addition, Catalogers should be able to skim reading material quickly to decide how it should be organized, recognizing its general theme and content, have a reading knowledge of at least one foreign language, and develop skills in special knowledge areas. They also need to be comfortable with a variety of other materials, such as recordings, photographs, slides, films, videotapes, and computer software. A love of sorting and classification is important in a successful Cataloger.

Unions and Associations

Catalogers working in academic libraries can belong to a variety of associations that provide educational guidance, support, conferences, and information to members. These might include the Association of College and Research Libraries, the American Library Association, the American Society for Information Science, the American Association of School Librarians (AASL), the Association for Library Collections and Technical Services (ALCTS), the Association of Research Libraries, or the Special Libraries Association.

Tips for Entry

1. Get experience. If you are attending library school, take every opportunity available to work as a student assistant in the university library, do a practicum or internship in another library, or volunteer in the cataloging department of the library. Library administrators are likely to select a candidate with some relevant experience over one with none.

2. Make contacts. Join professional organizations for librarians and keep in touch with your library friends to provide a network through which you may hear about job opportunities.

3. Send out your résumé. Find out the name and address of every academic library where you might like to work (the telephone book is helpful; call to find out to whom to address your cover letter). When openings occur, administrators often pull out their collection of unsolicited résumés and contact the candidates.

4. The e-mail discussion groups LIBJOBS and LISJOBS are a good source for job postings. Topical groups are also a good place for finding advertisements in cataloging.

5. Look for jobs on the Internet, such as on www.Lisjobs.com. Check daily job postings on "Hot Jobs Online" at the website of the American Library Association (www.ala.org). Investigate other Internet websites that list library job postings, such as www.libraryjobpostings.org. Or visit the ALISE website, which has links to all library schools, each of which has state and national employment listings (www.alise.org), or the American Society of Information Science website job line (www.asis.org/Jobline). If you're targeting a specific institution or geographic area, take a look at individual websites for postings.

6. Subscribe to major library trade publications, such as *Library Journal* and *American Libraries*.

7. *Jobs for Librarians and Information Professionals* is a comprehensive guide to on-line job resources for librarians and information professionals.

8. Attend library conventions or conferences and check job boards.

ACADEMIC ARCHIVIST

CAREER PROFILE

Duties: Search for, acquire, appraise, analyze, describe, arrange, catalog, restore, preserve, exhibit, maintain, and store valuable items that can be used by researchers or for exhibitions, publications, broadcasting, and other educational programs

Alternate Title(s): None

Salary Range: $20,010 to $66,050

Employment Prospects: Good

Advancement Prospects: Good

Best Geographical Location(s): Larger university libraries may offer more possibilities

Prerequisites:

Education or Training—Undergraduate and graduate degree in library science, political science, American history, or similar major

Experience—Many Archivists work in archives or museums while completing their formal education, to gain the hands-on experience that many employers seek when hiring; many jobs request three to five years of professional experience with project management experience

Special Skills and Personality Traits—Good organizational and people skills; computer capability; communication skills; attention to detail

CAREER LADDER

```
┌─────────────────────────────────────┐
│ Archivist for Larger University Library │
│     or Director of Archives          │
└─────────────────────────────────────┘

┌─────────────────────────────────────┐
│        Academic Archivist            │
└─────────────────────────────────────┘

┌─────────────────────────────────────┐
│        Archives Technician           │
└─────────────────────────────────────┘
```

Position Description

Archives are intended to be kept permanently, to preserve the past and allow others to discover it. It is the job of the Archivist to preserve this heritage by helping students and faculty members, doing promotional work (including exhibitions, presentations, or media work), as well as the curatorial skills of selecting, arranging, and cataloging archives.

The Archivist establishes and maintains physical and intellectual control over records of enduring value. He or she selects, arranges, describes, and ensures the long-term preservation of records, and helps researchers who wish to use them. These items may include historical documents, audiovisual materials, institutional records, works of art, coins, stamps, minerals, clothing, maps, living and preserved plants and animals, buildings, computer records, or historic sites. In addition, Archivists at a more senior level also carry out traditional management tasks such as those concerning budgets, staff, and strategy.

Archivists search for, acquire, appraise, analyze, describe, arrange, catalog, restore, preserve, exhibit, maintain, and store valuable items that can be used by students and researchers, or for exhibitions, publications, broadcasting, and other educational programs. Archivists plan and oversee the arrangement, cataloging, and exhibition of collections and, along with technicians and conservators, maintain collections. They may coordinate educational and public outreach programs, such as tours, workshops, lectures, and classes, and may work with government officials to administer plans and policies. They also may research topics or items relevant to their collections.

Archivists determine what portion of the vast amount of records maintained by the university library should be made part of permanent historical holdings, and which of these records should be put on exhibit. They maintain records in their original arrangement according to the creator's organizational scheme, and describe records to facilitate retrieval. Records may be saved on any medium, including paper, film, videotape, audiotape, electronic disk, or computer. They also may be copied onto some other format to protect the original, and to make them more accessible to researchers who use the records.

As computers and various storage media evolve, Archivists must keep abreast of technological advances in electronic information storage. Archivists consider any medium containing recorded information as documents, including letters, books, and other paper documents, blueprints, photos and audiovisual materials, and computer records.

Archivists often specialize in an area of history or technology so they can better determine what records in that area should become part of the university archives. Archivists also may work with specialized forms of records, such as manuscripts, electronic records, photographs, cartographic records, motion pictures, and sound recordings.

Computers are increasingly used to generate and maintain archival records. Professional standards for use of computers in handling archival records are still evolving, but computers are expected to transform many aspects of archival collections as computer capabilities, including multimedia and World Wide Web use, expand and allow more records to be stored and exhibited electronically.

The work of the Archivist is related to (but different from) a typical librarian position. Although both librarians and Archivists collect, preserve, and make accessible materials for research, there are significant differences in the way these materials are arranged, described, and used. The Archivist is concerned with relatively small quantities of records considered important enough to be retained for an extended period, and works with paper, film, electronic records, photographs, video and sound recordings, computer tapes, and video and optical disks, as well as the more traditional unpublished letters, diaries, and other manuscripts. Archival records are the products of everyday activity, and researchers use them both for their administrative value and for purposes other than those for which they were created.

Archives may be part of the university's library or museum, or they may exist as a distinct unit. Archives range from large, well-funded operations that offer various archival services to limited establishments dependent upon a part-time volunteer staff.

To preserve an archive for posterity, it has to be protected against theft and damage. For this reason, archives must be kept in secure rooms under optimal storage conditions. That means that Archivists have to know the latest techniques regarding preservation, pest control, and safeguards against fire and water damage. As a result of paper's high acidity, it is subject to natural disintegration, which requires continual restoration.

The working conditions of Archivists vary. Some spend most of their time working with students and faculty, providing reference assistance and educational services. Others perform research or process records, which often means working alone or in offices with only a few people. Those who restore and install exhibits or work with bulky, heavy record containers may climb, stretch, or lift.

Salaries

Salaries, benefits, and working conditions vary, depending on the size and nature of the university library. The average annual salary for Archivists ranges from a low of $20,010 to a high of $66,050 for nonsupervisory, supervisory, and managerial positions. Archivists may begin their careers on grant-funded projects; however, many ultimately achieve long-term job stability.

Employment Prospects

Competition for jobs as Archivists is expected to be keen as qualified applicants outnumber job openings. Graduates with highly specialized training, such as master's degrees in both library science and history, with a concentration in archives or records management, and extensive computer skills should have the best opportunities for jobs as Archivists.

Employment of Archivists is expected to increase about as fast as the average for all occupations through 2012. Job opportunities are expected to grow as public and private universities emphasize establishing archives and organizing records and information, and as public interest in science, art, history, and technology increases. Although the rate of turnover among Archivists is relatively low, the need to replace workers who leave the occupation or stop working will create some additional job openings.

Advancement Prospects

Many archives within a university are very small, with limited promotion opportunities. Archivists typically advance by transferring to a larger unit with supervisory positions. A doctorate in history, library science, or a related field may be needed for some advanced positions, such as director of a state archive. Continuing education, which enables Archivists to advance, is available through meetings, conferences, and workshops sponsored by archival, historical, and museum associations.

Education and Training

Most entry-level archival positions require an undergraduate and a graduate degree, in addition to archival coursework and a practicum. Many Archivists work in archives or museums while completing their formal education, to gain the hands-on experience that many employers seek when hiring.

Typically, there are three routes to becoming an Archivist. The first is to have a background in history (usually an

M.A.) with practical training or course work offered by a professional archival association. The second is to have a master's degree in library and information science with an archives specialization (although many colleges and universities offer M.L.S. programs, employers often prefer graduates of the approximately 56 schools accredited by the American Library Association). The third is to have a master's degree in archival science/studies (M.A.S.).

Special knowledge of certain subjects may be important for work in archives that have specialized collections, such as business or medicine. Training and experience in conducting research in primary and secondary sources are also helpful.

The number of archival education programs has expanded in recent years, and a few institutions now offer master's degrees in archival studies. Graduate archival programs may offer a variety of courses that include basic archival theory, methods, and/or practice of appraisal, arrangement, description, preservation, reference services, outreach, legal concerns, and ethics. Programs may also offer courses that include records management, aspects of library and information science, management, and historical and research methods.

An increasing number of Archivists have a double master's degree in history and library science. While there are currently no programs offering bachelor's or master's degrees in archival science, about 65 colleges and universities offer courses or practical training in archival science as part of history, library science, or another discipline. The Academy of Certified Archivists offers voluntary certification for Archivists. Certification requires the applicant to have experience in the field and to pass an examination offered by the academy.

Experience, Skills, and Personality Traits

Archivists need research and analytical ability to understand the content of documents and the context in which they were created, and to decipher deteriorated or poor-quality printed matter, handwritten manuscripts, or photographs and films. A background in preservation management is often required because Archivists are responsible for taking proper care of their records. Archivists also must be able to organize large amounts of information and write clear instructions for its retrieval and use. In addition, computer skills and the ability to work with electronic records and databases are increasingly important. Archivists must be committed to customer service as well as heritage and information management. Although Archivists are not researchers, they may occasionally need to do research in order to interpret archives; an understanding of research skills is also helpful for advising users.

Unions and Associations

University Archivists may belong to a variety of associations that provide educational guidance, support, conferences, and information to members, such as the Society of American Archivists (SAA).

Tips for Entry

1. Look for job ads in the SAA on-line employment bulletin (www.archivists.org/employment/index.asp).
2. Check daily job postings on "Hot Jobs Online" at the website of the American Library Association (www.ala.org) or other Internet websites that list library job postings, such as: http://www.libraryjobpostings.org.
3. Subscribe to archival journals and periodicals to keep current with the latest classified ads and trends, such as the SAA *Employment Bulletin, Archival Outlook, American Archivist,* or *American Libraries* magazine.
4. Attend the annual SAA convention in late summer, or check job boards at the placement service that list library-related jobs at annual ALA conventions.
5. Visit the ALISE website, which has links to library schools, with state and national employment listings (www.alise.org).

CONSERVATOR

CAREER PROFILE

Duties: Search for, acquire, appraise, preserve, and maintain items, documents, and buildings for exhibits and educational programs

Alternate Title(s): Preservation Specialist, Conservation Scientist, Conservation Administrator, Conservation Educator

Salary Range: $20,010 to $66,050

Employment Prospects: Fair

Advancement Prospects: Fair

Best Geographical Location(s): Larger cities are more likely to have opportunities for jobs at larger university collections

Prerequisites:

Education or Training—Master's degree in conservation or library science; Ph.D. desirable.

Experience—For most positions, experience in a full-time internship is required

Special Skills and Personality Traits—Detail oriented; organization; ability to work alone or with minimal interaction with others

CAREER LADDER

```
┌─────────────────────────────────────┐
│  Conservator for Larger Institution │
└─────────────────────────────────────┘

┌─────────────────────────────────────┐
│            Conservator              │
└─────────────────────────────────────┘

┌─────────────────────────────────────┐
│  Conservator Assistant or Entry Level │
└─────────────────────────────────────┘
```

Position Description

Conservators search for, acquire, appraise, preserve, and maintain items, documents, and buildings for exhibits and educational programs. Conservators care for and preserve documents, works of art, artifacts, and buildings, and manage, care for, and preserve the items that curators collect. Their work involves historical, scientific, and archeological research.

Using X-rays, chemical testing, microscopes, special lights, and other sophisticated laboratory techniques, Conservators examine objects and determine their condition, the need for treatment or restoration, and the appropriate method for preservation. They then document their findings and treat items to minimize deterioration or restore items to their original state.

Conservators also specialize in a particular material or type of object, such as documents and books, paintings, decorative arts, textiles, metals, or architectural material. Although much of their work takes place inside the univer-

sity, Conservators can spend a good amount of time traveling to other locations to identify and find new objects for exhibit.

Conservators normally do not work with the public. They spend their days evaluating and treating valuable objects to preserve them for the future, usually working in laboratories and historical buildings. Although many work normal 40-hour weeks, some concentrating on special projects can work every day of the week.

They may work as freelancers under contract to treat particular items, rather than as regular employees of a university. These Conservators may work on their own as private contractors, or as employees of a conservation laboratory or regional conservation center that contracts their services to universities.

Salaries

Salaries for Conservators can vary greatly depending on experience, specialty, region, job description, and employer. Salaries of Conservators in large, well-endowed university museums can be significantly higher than those in smaller institutions; salaries range from $20,010 to $66,050.

Employment Prospects

Competition for Conservator positions remains fierce, both to get into conservator programs in universities and afterward in the academic world. Employment prospects are best for those who have completed graduate work in conservation, speak another language, and are willing to relocate or travel abroad. The small size of the conservation community makes it relatively easy to keep abreast of job openings.

Employment of conservators is expected to increase about as fast as the average for all occupations through 2012. Jobs are expected to grow as universities emphasize establishing archives and organizing records and information, and as public interest in science, art, history, and technology increases.

Advancement Prospects

Conservation, curatorial, and registration responsibilities are intermingling and producing new hybrid conservation professions such as collections care, environmental monitoring, and exhibits specialists.

In order to be promoted, Conservators must participate in continuing education programs, which are available through meetings, conferences, and workshops sponsored by archival, historical, and museum associations. Some larger organizations, such as the National Archives, offer such training in-house.

Education and Training

Employment as a Conservator usually requires graduate education and related work experience. Many work as interns while completing their formal education, to gain the hands-on experience that many employers seek when hiring. Before the establishment of graduate degree programs in conservation, apprenticeships were the primary method of training. A student may still choose to pursue a series of apprenticeships and independent educational opportunities as an alternative to a formal graduate program. This approach takes longer than the degree program to acquire comparable education, and professional recognition may be less certain. Apprenticeships vary a great deal, and less emphasis may be placed on important theoretical, philosophical, and scientific aspects of conservation. Today, the apprenticeship remains an important part of every conservator's practical education, but graduate education has become the more recognized route into the profession.

When hiring conservators, employers look for a master's degree in conservation or in a closely related field and substantial experience. Conservators should have a bachelor's degree in art history, history, archeology or a related field; most universities require a master's degree in museum studies, conservation, library science, or an appropriate specialty. A Ph.D. in museum studies or a specialty is frequently preferred.

Only a few graduate programs in conservation exist in the United States, and competition for places in these schools is fierce. To qualify, a student must have a background in chemistry, archaeology, or studio art and art history, as well as work experience. For some programs, knowledge of a foreign language is also helpful. Conservation apprenticeships or internships as an undergraduate can also improve one's admission prospects. Graduate programs last two to four years; the latter years include internship training. A few students enter conservation through apprenticeships with museums, nonprofit organizations, and Conservators in private practice. Apprenticeships should be supplemented with courses in chemistry, studio art, and history. Apprenticeship training instead of university training is accepted, although it is a more difficult route into the conservation profession.

Experience, Skills, and Personality Traits

Conservators do not work with the public, and should be content in working alone or with very little contact with others. Attention to detail and organizational skills are important. Conservators must have an appreciation and respect for cultural property, an aptitude for scientific and technical subjects, patience for meticulous and tedious work, good manual dexterity and color vision, intelligence and sensitivity, and the ability to communicate effectively. Conservators should be comfortable using high-tech equipment, including high-powered microscopes and even CAT scan machines. Substantial work experience in collection management, exhibit design, or restoration, as well as database management skills, are required to obtain and keep permanent status with an institution.

Unions and Associations

Conservators in academic situations do not usually belong to unions, but they can belong to a variety of trade associations that provide educational guidance, support, conferences, and information to members. These might include the American Association of Museums, the American Institute for Conservation of Historic and Artistic Works, Independent Curators International, Institute of Museum and Library Services, and the Society of American Archivists.

Tips for Entry

1. Check job ads in the bimonthly *AIC News,* published by the American Institute for Conservation of Historic and Artistic Works.
2. Check job ads in the monthly *Aviso,* published by the American Association of Museums.
3. Check job ads in other museum, library, and archival publications, such as *Library Journal* and *American Libraries.*
4. Attend library conventions or conferences, check job boards, and check out the placement service that lists library-related jobs at annual ALA conventions.

ACADEMIC CURATOR

CAREER PROFILE

Duties: Search for, acquire, appraise, analyze, describe, arrange, catalog, restore, preserve, exhibit, maintain, and store valuable items used by scholars and students, and for exhibitions, publications, and other educational programs

Alternate Title(s): Exhibitions Officer

Salary Range: $35,000 to $61,490+ for nine- or 12-month positions

Employment Prospects: Fair

Advancement Prospects: Fair

Best Geographical Location(s): Larger universities are more likely to provide more types of varied collections

Prerequisites:

Education or Training—Master's degree in library science from an ALA-accredited library and information studies program

Experience—Several years of professional library experience in archives in an academic research library

Special Skills and Personality Traits—Flexibility; objective, methodical approach; good written and verbal communication skills; interest and ability in working with students and scholarly researchers

CAREER LADDER

```
┌─────────────────────────────────────────┐
│  Academic Museum or Library Director     │
└─────────────────────────────────────────┘

┌─────────────────────────────────────────┐
│                 Curator                  │
└─────────────────────────────────────────┘

┌─────────────────────────────────────────┐
│   Curator of Smaller Academic Museum     │
└─────────────────────────────────────────┘
```

Position Description

Curators search for, acquire, appraise, analyze, describe, arrange, catalog, restore, preserve, exhibit, maintain, and store valuable items that can be used by students or academic researchers or for exhibitions, publications, broadcasting, and other educational programs at the university. Items in the collection may include historical documents, audiovisual materials, institutional records, works of art, coins, stamps, minerals, clothing, maps, living and preserved plants and animals, buildings, computer records, or historic sites.

Academic Curators plan and oversee the arrangement, cataloging, and exhibition of collections and, along with technicians and conservators, maintain university collections. Curators also may coordinate educational and public outreach programs, such as tours, workshops, lectures, and classes, and may work with the university boards to administer plans and policies.

Curators who work in large universities may travel extensively to evaluate potential additions to the collection, organize exhibitions, and conduct research in their area of expertise. They generally work in restricted-access museum collection storage areas at least 40 hours a week. They may work with toxic materials such as paint, wood preservatives, sealants, and Plexiglas.

Salaries

Earnings of Curators vary considerably by type and size of university. University Curators are often 12-month, tenure track faculty positions. Professional achievement, service, and research or creative activity are required for tenure and promotion. Annual earnings of Curators range from a low of $35,000 to a high of more than $61,490. Median annual earnings of Academic Curators are $40,000.

Employment Prospects

Competition for jobs as Academic Curators is tight as qualified applicants outnumber job openings. Many candidates may have to work part time, as an intern, or even as a volunteer assistant curator or research associate after completing their formal education before finding a permanent academic job. Experience in collection management, exhibit design, or restoration, as well as database management skills, can help improve employment prospects. Job opportunities for Curators should be best in university art and history museums.

Advancement Prospects

In large university collections, Curators may advance through several levels of responsibility, eventually to director. Individual research and publications are important for advancement in larger universities.

Education and Training

A master's degree in an appropriate discipline of the museum's specialty (art, history, or archaeology) or museum studies is required, and many universities prefer a doctoral degree, particularly for Curators specializing in natural history or science. Earning two graduate degrees—in museum studies (museology) and a specialized subject—gives a candidate a distinct advantage in this competitive job market. Many universities require at least five years of professional library experience in archives in an academic research library, together with formal education or training in archival theory and practice.

In small university collections, curatorial positions may be available to individuals with a bachelor's degree. For some positions, an internship of full-time museum work supplemented by courses in museum practices is needed.

Technology is important in this field, and Curators are expected to have significant knowledge of digital technology and experience creating and maintaining web pages. In addition, Curators are often expected to be familiar with MARC (machine-readable cataloging) format; Archives, Personal Papers, and Manuscripts Cataloging Manual (APPM) standards for describing manuscript and archival materials; and familiarity with digital encoding of archival finding aids.

Academic Curator positions often require knowledge in a number of fields. For historic and artistic conservation, courses in chemistry, physics, and art are desirable. Since Curators may have administrative and managerial responsibilities, courses in business administration, public relations, marketing, and fund-raising also are recommended.

Experience, Skills, and Personality Traits

Curators should have a strong service orientation and the ability to interact effectively and work productively in a complex and rapidly changing university environment. They should be well organized and work independently, and be able to supervise the work of others, including student interns. A working knowledge of at least one foreign language is usually preferred.

Curators need computer skills and the ability to work with electronic databases, and should be familiar with digital imaging, scanning technology, and copyright infringement, since many are responsible for posting information on the Internet.

Unions and Associations

Academic Curators can belong to a variety of trade associations that provide educational guidance, support, conferences, and information to members. These might include the Association of College and Research Libraries, the Institute of Museum and Library Services, the American Institute for Conservation of Historic and Artistic Works, or the Independent Curators International.

Tips for Entry

1. Get experience. Take every opportunity available to work as a student curator assistant in the university libraries or do a practicum or internship.
2. Make contacts. Join various professional organizations for Curators to provide a network through which you may hear about job opportunities.
3. Send out your résumé. Find out the name and address of every academic museum in your area where you might like to work (the telephone book is helpful; call to find out to whom to address your cover letter). When openings occur, administrators often pull out their collection of unsolicited résumés and contact the candidates.
4. Visit the ALISE website, which has links to all library schools, each of which has state and national employment listings (www.alise.org) or the American Society of Information Science website job line (http://www.asis.org/Jobline).
5. Attend library conventions or conferences, check job boards, and check out the placement service that lists library-related jobs at annual ALA conventions.

ACADEMIC GOVERNMENT DOCUMENTS LIBRARIAN

CAREER PROFILE

Duties: Work with students and faculty to locate, evaluate, and organize information published by government agencies and sources

Alternate Title(s): Government Documents Information Specialist

Salary Range: $30,126 to $66,590+ in nine- or 12-month appointments

Employment Prospects: Good

Advancement Prospects: Good

Best Geographical Location(s): Large university libraries throughout the country offer the best chance for a job as Government Documents Librarian

Prerequisites:

Education or Training—Master of library science degree is required

Experience—Several years of direct working experience with federal government information at the professional level is often required; internship is helpful

Special Skills and Personality Traits—Interest in working with students and faculty; flexibility; patience; attention to detail; statistical ability; computer skills

CAREER LADDER

```
┌─────────────────────────────────────┐
│ Government Documents Librarian       │
│ in a Larger Academic Library         │
└─────────────────────────────────────┘

┌─────────────────────────────────────┐
│ Academic Government Documents        │
│ Librarian                            │
└─────────────────────────────────────┘

┌─────────────────────────────────────┐
│ Assistant Government Documents       │
│ Librarian                            │
└─────────────────────────────────────┘
```

Position Description

Government Documents Librarians who work in academic libraries specialize in handling both published and unpublished government information in print, CD-ROM, on-line, and multimedia formats. Most government documents are not included in commercial reference works, so the Academic Government Documents Librarian is responsible for providing an invaluable reference service including reference desk, telephone, and electronic mail services, as well as user and staff education classes.

An important aspect of the Academic Government Documents Librarian's job is to design and implement educational and outreach programs to let students and faculty know about available government document services and resources.

Government documents are obtained by a number of means, including the Internet, government printing offices or commercial book dealers, or through membership in depository library programs that acquire government information for free. (The Federal Depository Library Program is the depository program of the U.S. government.)

Academic Government Documents Librarians also coordinate and oversee the daily operations of the government documents department, create procedures for support staff and students, and keep appropriate statistics and write reports. Other aspects of administering the documents collection include acquiring monographs and serials and managing databases and stacks.

Salaries

Salaries for this position vary a great deal depending on the responsibilities and location of the library. Beginning full-time Academic Government Documents Librarians with a master's degree in library and information studies accredited by the ALA but with no professional experience can expect a salary range of $30,126 to $37,580; with experience, the salary may surpass $66,590.

Employment Prospects

Employment of Academic Government Documents Librarians in universities is expected to grow about as fast as the average for all occupations through 2012, with about a 5 percent growth through 2008. The increasing use of computerized information storage and retrieval systems means that librarians trained in these technologies will become more valuable. Academic Government Documents Librarians will still be needed to help users search relevant databases, address complicated reference requests, and define users' needs.

The need to replace Librarians as they retire will result in numerous additional job openings, and the continuing demand for accurate computer-delivered information will increase the need for Librarians with information management skills. Most opportunities will occur in larger libraries in metropolitan areas.

Advancement Prospects

Academic Government Document Librarians can advance to administrative positions in a university library, such as department head, library director, or chief information officer, with more experience and administrative skills, knowledge of automated systems, and additional training. Advancement opportunities are better in larger university libraries.

Education and Training

Most Academic Government Documents Librarian positions require a master of library science (M.L.S.) degree from a school accredited by the American Library Association (ALA). Additional on-the-job training in government documents is helpful.

Experience, Skills, and Personality Traits

Several years of experience working with federal government information at the professional level is often required. Knowledge of emerging technologies in libraries and their applications for government information resources and services is helpful, as is teaching or training experience in a classroom setting. The ability to accept and work with change is one of the most important characteristics of an Academic Government Documents Librarian. Other characteristics include patience, the ability to work with details, statistical ability, people skills, and computer knowledge.

Unions and Associations

Academic Government Documents Librarians may belong to a variety of trade associations that provide educational guidance, support, conferences, and information to members, including the American Library Association, the American Society for Information Science, or the Special Libraries Association.

Tips for Entry

1. Get experience. If you are attending library school, take every opportunity available to work as a student assistant in the university library, or do a practicum or internship in another library. Library administrators are likely to select a candidate with some relevant experience.
2. Make contacts. Join professional organizations for Librarians and keep in touch with your library friends to provide a network through which you may hear about job opportunities.
3. Send out your résumé. Find out the name and address of every library in your area where you might like to work (the telephone book is helpful; call to find out to whom to address your cover letter). When openings occur, administrators often pull out their collection of unsolicited résumés and contact the candidates.
4. The e-mail discussion groups LIBJOBS and LIS-JOBS are a good source for job postings. Topical groups are also a good place for finding advertisements in a particular field of librarianship. For example, Web4Lib often receives library webmaster-type job postings.
5. Look for jobs on the Internet, such as on www. Lisjobs.com. Check daily job postings on "Hot Jobs Online" at the website of the American Library Association (www.ala.org). Investigate other Internet websites that list library job postings, such as www.libraryjobpostings.org. Or visit the ALISE website, which has links to all library schools, each of which has state and national employment listings (www.alise.org), or the American Society of Information Science website job line (www.asis.org/Jobline). If you're targeting a specific institution or geographic area, take a look at individual websites for postings.
6. *Jobs for Librarians and Information Professionals* is a comprehensive guide to on-line job resources for librarians and information professionals.
7. Subscribe to major library trade publications, such as *Library Journal* and *American Libraries*.
8. Attend library conventions or conferences and check job boards.
9. Check out the placement service that lists library-related jobs at annual ALA conventions.

UNIVERSITY LIBRARY DIRECTOR

CAREER PROFILE

Duties: Manage university library and staff and provide information to professors and students

Alternate Title(s): University Library Head

Salary Range: $47,689 to $274,519+

Employment Prospects: Good

Advancement Prospects: Good

Best Geographical Location(s): Larger universities may offer more possibilities, but college and university libraries throughout the country have positions for director

Prerequisites:

Education or Training—Graduate degree in library or information science; a doctoral degree may be required in many large university libraries

Experience—Professional library experience, preferably in an administrative or managerial capacity

Special Skills and Personality Traits—Strong oral and written communication skills, good interpersonal skills, and solid computer skills; strong academic background; attention to detail; ability to manage others; good administrative skills; ability to make decisions

CAREER LADDER

```
┌─────────────────────────────────────────┐
│   Director of Larger University Library  │
└─────────────────────────────────────────┘

┌─────────────────────────────────────────┐
│      Director of University Library      │
└─────────────────────────────────────────┘

┌─────────────────────────────────────────┐
│           University Librarian           │
└─────────────────────────────────────────┘
```

Position Description

A University Library Director is responsible for the entire workings of the school library, including purchasing, selecting, organizing, and disseminating information to students and professors alike. They may evaluate advanced information technologies; plan, budget, and manage programs and services; develop, design, and manage digital access and content; teach users how to find information relevant to the university curriculum; develop content and design materials for instructional purposes; and design and manage digital access.

A large part of the Director's job is administrative, and involves working with upper-level university employees, trustees or board members, and professors. The Director must oversee the management and planning of the library; negotiate contracts for services, materials, and equipment; perform public relations duties; prepare budgets; and in general make sure the library functions properly.

In addition to running the library, an important part of the Director's day is to manage library employees and evaluate current employees. The Director must replace personnel and keep the staff well trained, including scheduling employees for either refresher training or training for new responsibilities.

The increased use of automated information systems enables Library Directors to focus on administrative and budgeting responsibilities, grant writing, and specialized research requests, while delegating more technical and user services responsibilities to technicians.

The duties of a Library Director may require working beyond the standard 40-hour week, and involve some weekend and evening work, although the Director's schedule may in part be tied into the academic year (with workload being lighter during the summer months).

The Director may need to attend workshops, seminars, and conferences, and represent his or her university in state, regional, and national professional organizations. He or she also must be able to use library equipment, including computers, printers, copiers, typewriters, microfilm readers, and fax machines.

In addition, the Library Director is responsible for the overall maintenance of the collection, keeping it current, attractive, and useful by setting up a schedule of replacement; placing standing orders for reference materials; and systematically checking bibliographies and selection aids for new editions, replacement titles, and subject area expansion. The Director also must evaluate the current collection, maintain a continuous program of "weeding" to remove obsolete and worn-out materials, and make sure current inventory matches the university's curriculum needs.

Salaries

Salaries vary according to the size and location of the school and its library, the individual's experience, and the length of employment; $72,384 is an average salary for a medium-sized University Library Director; small University Library Directors would average less, about $65,127. The upper end of salary for Library Directors of very large libraries who supervise an extensive support staff may top $274,519.

Employment Prospects

Because there are only so many university libraries in any one state, a willingness to relocate could be crucial in landing a job as an assistant director or Director of a university library. Employment of university librarians is expected to grow steadily, by at least 5 percent through 2008; continual attrition leads to openings for Library Director positions. The technological explosion that shows no signs of abating means that university libraries will continue to require well-educated Directors to manage the ever-increasing resources.

Advancement Prospects

At any one time, there are a limited number of directorships at university libraries around the country, but as the explosion of technology continues, opportunities continue to improve for University Library Directors with experience in technology. With hard work and continuing education in the field of information science, it should be possible to move from librarian positions into larger and more responsible administrative positions, beginning with assistant director and then Director at larger and larger university libraries.

Education and Training

Master's degrees in library and information science—and often doctoral degrees—from an ALA-accredited school are usually required. A doctoral degree may be either a Ph.D. in library science, a D.L.S. (doctorate in library science), or a doctor of arts in library science.

Experience, Skills, and Personality Traits

Directors of university libraries are expected to combine strong administrative skills with solid training in library science, and should be able to juggle all kinds of details without getting flustered. The Director should be comfortable expressing himself or herself both orally and in writing. Since staff management is such an important aspect of this job, good interpersonal skills and the ability to manage others are crucial. In addition, the Director of a university library must have solid computer skills, a strong academic background, and the ability to make decisions. Since budget responsibilities are also a part of this job, a sound background in finance or business is helpful.

Unions and Associations

Library Directors working in university libraries do not usually belong to unions, but they can belong to a variety of trade associations that provide educational guidance, support, conferences, and information to members. These might include the American Library Association, the American Society for Information Science, the Association for Library and Information Science Education, or the Association of College and Research Libraries.

Tips for Entry

1. Join various professional organizations to provide a network through which you may hear about job opportunities, such as the American Library Association, the American Society for Information Science, the Association for Library and Information Science Education, or the Association of College and Research Libraries.

2. The e-mail discussion groups LIBJOBS and LIS-JOBS are a good source for job postings. Topical groups are also a good place for finding advertisements in a particular field of librarianship. For example, Web4Lib often receives library webmaster-type job postings.

3. Look for jobs on the Internet, such as on www. Lisjobs.com. *Jobs for Librarians and Information Professionals* is a comprehensive guide to on-line job resources for librarians and information professionals. Check daily job postings on "Hot Jobs Online" at the website of the American Library Association (www.ala.org).

4. Investigate other Internet websites that list library job postings, such as http://www.libraryjobpostings.org. Visit the ALISE website, which has links to all

library schools, each of which has state and national employment listings (www.alise.org), or the American Society of Information Science website job line (http://www.asis.org/Jobline).

5. Subscribe to major library trade publications, such as *Library Journal* and *American Libraries*.

6. Attend library conventions or conferences and check job boards, including the placement service that lists library-related jobs at annual ALA conventions.

7. Read related publications, such as the *Chronicle of Higher Education* or the *College & Research Libraries News*.

MEDICAL SCHOOL LIBRARIAN

CAREER PROFILE

Duties: Provide health information about new medical treatments, clinical trials and standard trials procedures, tests, and equipment to professors and medical students

Alternate Title(s): Librarian

Salary Range: $31,000 to $100,000+

Employment Prospects: Good

Advancement Prospects: Good

Best Geographical Location(s): Major cities are usually the primary location for large medical schools with good medical libraries

Prerequisites:

Education or Training—Graduate degree in library or information science

Experience—A background in science, health sciences, or allied health is helpful

Special Skills and Personality Traits—Strong oral and written communication skills; good interpersonal skills; solid computer skills

CAREER LADDER

```
┌─────────────────────────────────┐
│   Director of Medical School or  │
│     Nursing School Library       │
└─────────────────────────────────┘

┌─────────────────────────────────┐
│     Medical School Librarian     │
└─────────────────────────────────┘

┌─────────────────────────────────┐
│    Assistant Medical Librarian   │
└─────────────────────────────────┘
```

Position Description

A Medical Librarian at a medical school is responsible for retrieving, selecting, organizing, and disseminating health information to students and professors alike. The person may assess advanced information technologies, teach users how to find health care information, develop content and design materials for instructional purposes, and design and manage digital access.

The Medical School Librarian also provides general and subject reference assistance, and develops and manages the collection. Librarians provide faculty and students from a variety of disciplines with the latest information on diseases, procedures, treatments, and research, and ensure that the collection supports the medical school curricula. Medical school librarians also select and maintain medical books, journals, and audiovisual materials, and provide computer database searches for users. In addition, administrative responsibilities include supervising support staff.

Medical School Librarians also must be familiar with key databases that cover biomedical literature, such as MEDLINE, a huge index of some 7 million articles published since 1966 that is the standard searching tool for medical literature. Also commonly used is Dialog, a database vendor that allows a user to search through numerous databases such as Biosis (abstracts of scientific articles) and Science Citation Index (abstracts of articles in diverse magazines and journals). In addition, Medical Librarians train students and faculty to do their own searches and teach search strategies.

Salaries

Salaries vary according to the size and location of the medical school, the level of responsibility, and the length of employment. Average starting salary for a Medical School Librarian is $31,066. The average salary for Medical Librarians at medical schools was $45,016, but salaries for experienced library directors at large medical school libraries can top $100,000.

Employment Prospects

Employment of Medical School Librarians is expected to continue to grow steadily as technology advances and new positions continue to be available. The need to replace Librarians as they retire means there will still be many new job openings, but because there are only a limited number of medical schools in the country, flexibility and willingness to relocate are important characteristics for a Librarian to be successful in the job search.

Advancement Prospects

Opportunities vary according to the interests and expertise of the individual librarians. Medical School Librarians can use a particular subject background to develop collections and provide specialized services, or devote a career to technical services or library automation. The more time, experience, and additional education an individual has, the better the advancement prospects.

Because Medical School Librarians have a number of marketable skills, they can move on to a variety of positions such as Web manager for a medical center, medical informatics expert, or chief information officer. A Medical School Librarian may move into work as a community outreach coordinator for a public health agency, reference librarian at a hospital, electronic resources cataloger for an Internet startup company, director of a nursing school library, user education specialist at a consumer health library, or information architect for a pharmaceutical company.

Education and Training

A master's degree in library and information science from an ALA-accredited school is required for any position as a Medical School Librarian; many medical school libraries also require a background in science, health sciences, or allied health, or graduate courses in medical informatics or medical librarianship. The Medical School Librarian should gain extra knowledge related to the medical field; for example, understanding biomedical references, principles of organization of information in the biomedical sciences, and on-line computer databases such as MEDLINE from the National Library of Medicine.

Experience, Skills, and Personality Traits

Because Medical School Librarians spend most of their day working with people, strong interpersonal and communica-

tion skills are required. In addition, excellent organizational and computer skills are important, along with a solid basis and interest in medicine or health-related issues. Librarians working in medical libraries need to be well organized with strong attention to detail. Because the Medical School Librarian is expected to work with both faculty and students, the ability to communicate effectively with diverse clients, exercise discretion, and maintain clients' privacy is vital.

Unions and Associations

Medical Librarians working in medical school libraries do not usually belong to unions, but they can belong to a variety of trade associations that provide educational guidance, support, conferences, and information to members. These might include the Medical Library Association, the American Library Association, the American Society for Information Science, Archivists and Librarians in the History of the Health Sciences, or the Association of Academic Health Sciences Libraries.

Tips for Entry

1. Study the job listings on the Medical Librarian Association website (www.mlanet.org/jobs/index.html), "Hot Jobs Online" at the website of the American Library Association (www.ala.org), at http://www.libraryjobpostings.org, or the American Society of Information Science website job line (www.asis.org/Jobline).
2. Visit the ALISE website, which has links to all library schools, each of which has state and national employment listings: www.alise.org.
3. Attend the annual May convention of the Medical Librarian Association and check out the jobs listing.
4. Check out the placement service library job lists at the annual ALA conventions.
5. Assess the job ads in *American Libraries* magazine.
6. If you're targeting a specific institution or geographic area, take a look at individual websites for each medical school for job postings.
7. Check out the *American Library Directory,* which lists a wide variety of libraries in its two-volume directory, or the *Guide to Employment Sources in the Library and Information Professions,* which is available on-line at the American Library Association website.

ACADEMIC MUSIC LIBRARIAN

CAREER PROFILE

Duties: Responsible for the overall management of the university music library, including collection management and acquisition of printed music and special materials, policy formulation, budget preparation and implementation, and liaison with the school of music

Alternate Title(s): None

Salary Range: $32,500 to $60,000+

Employment Prospects: Good

Advancement Prospects: Good

Best Geographical Location(s): Music libraries in colleges and universities exist throughout the country; but in general, the larger the university and music department, the more positions and better chance of promotion

Prerequisites:

Education or Training—Master's degrees in both library science and music (preferably musicology)

Experience—At least five years' experience in a music library, preferably at an academic or research institution, with managerial and collection development experience

Special Skills and Personality Traits—Experience in music and libraries; attention to detail; interest in working with students; excellent verbal and communication skills

CAREER LADDER

```
┌─────────────────────────────────────┐
│         Music Librarian at          │
│     Larger Academic Library or      │
│ Director of Music at Academic Library│
└─────────────────────────────────────┘

┌─────────────────────────────────────┐
│      Academic Music Librarian       │
└─────────────────────────────────────┘

┌─────────────────────────────────────┐
│  Assistant Academic Music Librarian │
└─────────────────────────────────────┘
```

Position Description

An Academic Music Librarian specializes in music at the university level, working in the music section in libraries at universities, colleges, and conservatories. Specifically, this means that Music Librarians administer the university's music library collection, manage the music manuscript collections, and serve as bibliographer for the school's printed music and special materials. Typically, a Music Librarian will maintain a liaison with the university's school of music, and support activities with both local and national music library associations and organizations.

Administrative tasks are another important role for Music Librarians, who are responsible for soliciting gifts and bringing in donations, as well as management—formulating and implementing goals, objectives, policies, and procedures; setting priorities; and allocating financial, staff, and space resources.

Just like traditional librarians, most Music Librarians organize, catalog, and maintain collections in their music libraries. They also teach students how to use the music library; answer music-related reference questions; and select music, books, journals, recordings, microforms, and sometimes manuscripts and other rare materials for acquisition. Music Librarians also recommend ways of preserving and housing materials in their care.

In addition, Music Librarians may plan exhibits and concerts, and collaborate with other colleges and universities in reorganizing music-related lectures, classes, or other academic programs. In a conservatory or university school of music, Music Librarians may order or rent the music needed by student ensembles, orchestras, bands, opera workshops, and chamber groups.

In addition, Music Librarians may play an active role in music scholarship by compiling bibliographies, pursuing research, or writing reviews of new publications. They often teach music bibliography and other classroom subjects within their areas of specialization.

Music Librarians may perform original and copy cataloging and classification of musical scores, develop procedures and oversee the physical processing of these materials, and catalog sound recordings and other music resources.

Salaries

Salaries for this position vary a great deal depending on the responsibilities of the Academic Music Librarian and the location and size of the university. Beginning Music Librarians start at $32,500, while the average salary of a Music Librarian ranges between $42,704 and $50,000 and above.

Employment Prospects

Employment prospects are good for Academic Music Librarians, who may work full time in a large academic library, or in smaller college libraries on a part-time basis. Some Music Librarians combine this job with other work as a musician.

Advancement Prospects

Just as in traditional library positions, Music Librarians may seek promotion with a wide range of administrative and supervisory responsibilities. Music collections at smaller colleges are often administered by a single Music Librarian plus a small support staff, but in large academic libraries Music Librarians also may hold management positions as assistant heads or department heads, with budget, personnel, facilities, and collection management responsibilities.

Education and Training

A master's degree in music, in addition to a master's degree in library science (M.L.S.) is usually required for a job in the field of music librarianship, because Music Librarians need a thorough knowledge of music history and repertory. Although many colleges and universities offer M.L.S. programs, employers often prefer graduates of the approximately 56 schools accredited by the American Library Association.

Some schools offer a dual degree program for a master of library science–master of arts in music, and some library schools offer special courses or internships in music librarianship. Beyond this special training, education for music librarianship should include as broad an education as possible in both music and the liberal arts.

A strong background in the humanities is important for Music Librarians, since they need to understand the relationship of music to other disciplines. And because musicology literature is published throughout the world, Music Librarians need to have a working knowledge of German and at least one Romance language, such as French or Italian.

Training in ethnomusicology, archives management, and other languages is required for work in libraries specializing in folk music or music of non-Western cultures. In libraries where music is combined with other subjects, such as dance or fine arts, background in those subjects may also be expected.

Experience, Skills, and Personality Traits

Academic Music Librarians must have a broad musical background, thorough knowledge of music history, and an equal ability to understand both music and music publications. Music Librarians in a university library should have a substantial knowledge of music repertory, music bibliography, and music acquisitions, together with an awareness of current concerns and developments in music librarianship.

A practicum or internship in a music library is essential; many students gain experience by working in their university's music library. The best introduction to music librarianship as a career is to work in a music library as a volunteer.

Music Librarians in an academic setting need excellent organizational skills, written and verbal communication skills, initiative, accuracy, attention to detail, judgment, and the ability to work independently and collaboratively in a team environment. Knowledge of basic software applications, including Microsoft Word and Excel, is important. In addition, the ability to supervise and teach library instruction is also important. Music Librarians should be team oriented, innovative, and energetic, and possess excellent interpersonal skills.

Unions and Associations

Music Librarians can belong to a variety of professional associations that provide educational guidance, support, conferences, and information to members. These include the Music Library Association, the American Library Association, the American Society for Information Science, and the Special Libraries Association.

Tips for Entry

1. Joining the Music Library Association as a student member can open the door to making valuable contacts in the music library field.
2. Visit the placement service job list on the Music Library Association website (www.musiclibraryassoc.org).
3. Attend the annual MLA meeting in the late winter or early spring, or visit the nearest regional chapter (there are 12) that meet regularly. Job postings are often listed here.
4. E-mail discussion groups such as MLA-L, LIBJOBS, and LIS-JOBS are a good source for job postings. Topical groups are also a good place for finding advertisements in a particular field of librarianship.
5. Check out job lists on the Internet, such as www. Lisjobs.com, the daily job postings on "Hot Jobs Online" at the website of the American Library Association (www.ala.org); or the American Society of Information Science website job line (www.asis.org/

Jobline) or www.libraryjobpostings.org. Visit the ALISE website, which has links to all library schools, each of which has state and national employment listings (www.alise.org).

6. Check out *Jobs for Librarians and Information Professionals,* a comprehensive guide to on-line job resources for librarians and information professionals.

7. Another place to check is the major library trade publications, such as *Library Journal* (www.libraryjournal.com). There are also related publications, such as the *Chronicle of Higher Education* (http://chronicle.com/jobs) for academic library postings.

FINE ARTS LIBRARIAN

CAREER PROFILE

Duties: Direct an art library in an academic setting; provide visual art reference services and manage visual art collections

Alternate Title(s): Catalog Librarian, Visual Resources Librarian

Salary Range: $30,000 to $50,000+

Employment Prospects: Excellent

Advancement Prospects: Good

Best Geographical Location(s): Art libraries in colleges and universities exist throughout the country

Prerequisites:

Education or Training—Graduate degree in art history and a master's degree in library science from a school accredited by the American Library Association

Experience—The best introduction to art librarianship as a career is to work in an art library as a volunteer

Special Skills and Personality Traits—Aptitude and training in art, art history, and librarianship are necessary, together with attention to detail, love of books and art, love of learning, and willingness to work hard

CAREER LADDER

```
┌─────────────────────────────────────────┐
│   Fine Arts Librarian, Larger University  │
└─────────────────────────────────────────┘

┌─────────────────────────────────────────┐
│          Fine Arts Librarian             │
└─────────────────────────────────────────┘

┌─────────────────────────────────────────┐
│      Assistant Fine Arts Librarian       │
└─────────────────────────────────────────┘
```

Position Description

A Fine Arts Librarian directs the college or university art library, provides visual arts reference services, and organizes and manages visual arts collections, such as slides and photographs, or visual arts documentation.

The Fine Arts Librarian provides on-site and electronic reference services in fine arts and develops educational services that support research, teaching, and learning activities with a primary focus in the fine arts. The Fine Arts Librarian works closely with the faculty, students, and staff in the art history and studio art departments of the university. The Librarian also implements and evaluates programs to meet the needs of a diverse clientele, managing and developing a rich collection of art, architecture, and photography materials in all formats.

The Fine Arts Librarian also helps faculty, students, and staff develop research skills, and supervises or provides technical services such as cataloging, material processing, and equipment maintenance.

Many Fine Arts Librarians at larger universities also administer the school's art collections and its art galleries, guiding the development of collections in architecture and the fine arts.

Salaries

Salaries for this position vary a great deal depending on the responsibilities and location of the library. Although beginning Art Librarians begin at salaries around $30,000, the average salary of an Art Librarian ranges between $42,704 and $50,000 and above.

Employment Prospects

Employment prospects are excellent for Fine Arts Librarians who are willing to relocate, which increases the chance of obtaining a position in the contemporary world of art and visual reference librarianship.

Advancement Prospects

Fine Arts Librarians may move into a broad range of administrative and supervisory positions. While smaller art collections are administered and operated by a single professional Fine Arts Librarian plus a small support staff, in large art libraries Librarians may hold management positions as assistant heads or department heads, and have budget, personnel, facilities, and art collection management responsibilities.

Education and Training

A master's degree in library or information science is required (although many colleges and universities offer M.L.S. programs, employers often prefer graduates of the approximately 56 schools accredited by the American Library Association). A combined master of library science and master of arts in art or art history degree is often recommended. Such a program prepares students for professional library and information specialist positions in fine arts and related libraries and information centers. Some schools offer courses in fine arts librarianship specialization.

Experience, Skills, and Personality Traits

Fine Arts Librarians should have a strong art history background, knowledge of library automation and electronic resources in the art field, and knowledge of one or more foreign languages. The Fine Arts Librarian should have experience working in the fine arts library in an academic institution, with excellent oral and written communication skills, exceptional organizational skills, familiarity with collection development, and the ability to work effectively with faculty and students.

Unions and Associations

Fine Arts Librarians working in university arts libraries do not usually belong to unions, but they may belong to a variety of associations that provide educational guidance, support, conferences, and information to members. These might include the Art Libraries Society of North America (ARLIS/NA), the American Library Association, or the Special Libraries Association.

Tips for Entry

1. To learn about the profession's current activities and to make useful contacts, join the Art Libraries Society of North America.
2. Visit the job list on the Art Libraries Society of North America website (www.arlisna.org/jobs.html).
3. Consider attending the annual ARLIS conference in spring, where job postings are often listed. For this and other conferences, see the ARLIS conference website at www.arlisna.org/confsites.html.
4. E-mail discussion groups such as ARLIS-L, LIB-JOBS, and LIS-JOBS are a good source for job postings. Topical groups are also a good place for finding advertisements in art librarianship.
5. Look for jobs on the Internet, such as on www.Lisjobs.com, the daily job postings on "Hot Jobs Online" at the website of the American Library Association (www.ala.org), the American Society of Information Science website job line (www.asis.org/Jobline), or www.libraryjobpostings.org. Or visit the ALISE website, which has links to all library schools, each of which has state and national employment listings (www.alise.org).
6. Check out *Jobs for Librarians and Information Professionals,* a comprehensive guide to on-line job resources for librarians and information professionals.

RARE BOOKS LIBRARIAN

CAREER PROFILE

Duties: Preserve, handle, and manage rare book and artifact collections which, because of their physical format or rarity, cannot be shelved with the general collection in college and university libraries

Alternate Title(s): None

Salary Range: $44,819 to $200,000+

Employment Prospects: Good

Advancement Prospects: Good

Best Geographical Location(s): Academic libraries throughout the United States

Prerequisites:

Education or Training—Master of library science; an additional master's degree in a specialty area is desirable

Experience—Restoration skills can be very helpful

Special Skills and Personality Traits—Restoration skills; foreign language skills; leadership ability; communication skills; ability to work in a team environment; good technical skills; people skills; above-average academic ability; love of books and learning; flexibility

CAREER LADDER

```
┌─────────────────────────────┐
│   Rare Books Librarian      │
│   in a Larger Institution   │
└─────────────────────────────┘

┌─────────────────────────────┐
│    Rare Books Librarian     │
└─────────────────────────────┘

┌─────────────────────────────┐
│ Assistant Rare Books Librarian │
└─────────────────────────────┘
```

Position Description

Rare Books Librarians acquire, catalog, maintain, preserve, and restore rare manuscripts, books, and artifacts in college and university libraries, where they are an essential component in the culture of higher education. They are responsible for arrangement and describing the items in the collections, and managing the records and the archives of the university. To fulfill this mission, the rare books department collects, maintains, preserves, and makes available for use books, pamphlets, ephemera, and other materials which are considered rare, unique, or in some way extraordinary.

Rare Books Librarians primarily serve the academic community, including undergraduates, graduate students, faculty, administration, and staff. Under the direction of the director of the special collections department, the Rare Books Librarian is responsible for the acquisition of books and other printed materials through purchase, gift, or transfer. The Librarian also provides reference assistance and instruction to faculty, students, scholars, and other visitors in person and by telephone, mail, and e-mail; and maintains cordial relations with donors and antiquarian booksellers around the world. Rare Books Librarians may also supervise library assistants or clerks who carry out technical processing of acquisitions, fund management, and website maintenance duties. The Rare Books Librarian supervises materials that need repairs and protective cases and decides the kind and extent of work to be done. He or she participates in the exhibit program, which generally features one of the library's strengths or complements a campus program; and as appropriate, attends conferences, symposia, and book fairs.

Salaries

Starting salaries for Rare Books Librarians in the United States begin at $34,819 to $40,000 a year, but experienced Rare Books Librarians can expect a salary ranging from $45,000 to more than $200,000. The median salary for Rare Books Librarians is $55,775.

Employment Prospects

Rare Books Librarians continue to find employment in academic libraries around the country. Technological advancements have had less of an impact in this area of library work than in others, since the special skills of the Rare Books Librarian are not so easily managed by computer. Rare Books Librarians are still also needed to manage staff, address complicated reference requests, and restore and maintain fragile collections.

Advancement Prospects

Opportunities vary according to the interests and expertise of the individual Rare Books Librarian. The more time, experience, and additional education an individual has, the better the advancement prospects.

Education and Training

The master of library science (M.L.S.) from a graduate program accredited by the American Library Association (ALA) is the appropriate professional degree for a Rare Books Librarian. (Although many colleges and universities offer M.L.S. programs, employers often prefer graduates of the approximately 56 schools accredited by the American Library Association).

Many colleges and universities also require Rare Books Librarians to have an additional undergraduate or master's degree in European history and culture or a broad general educational background in the humanities and social sciences; those Librarians with faculty status may be required to have a Ph.D.

Rare Books Librarians should have a strong background in history and culture as well as knowledge of early printed books; printing history; Latin, Greek, and/or Romance languages; and book arts in general. The Rare Books Librarian should have a demonstrated ability to promote and develop collections of rare books, and an enthusiasm for and experience with rare books and the development of coherent rare books collections. Finally, the Rare Books Librarian should understand the application of information technology to rare books processing and access, especially multimedia and website expertise, and be familiar with national standards in handling books.

Experience, Skills, and Personality Traits

The Rare Books Librarian should be skilled in the care of old books and manuscripts, and have a commitment to the preservation of cultural heritage materials. The Rare Books Librarian should have leadership ability, communication skills, flexibility, good technical skills, above-average academic ability, love of books and learning, and the ability to maintain good relations with the rare book community.

Unions and Associations

Rare Books Librarians may belong to a variety of associations that provide educational guidance, support, conferences, and information to members. These might include the American Institute for Conservation of Historic and Artistic Works, the American Library Association, the Rare Books and Manuscripts Section of the Association of College and Research Libraries, the Preservation and Reformation Section of the Association for Library Collections and Technical Services (ALCTS), the Library Administration and Management Association (division of ALA), or the Society of American Archivists.

Tips for Entry

1. College placement services can be great resources for help in finding a job. Check out the placement service bulletin board and talk to faculty members for advice and job leads.
2. Join various professional rare books organizations and keep in touch with your library friends to provide a network through which you may hear about job opportunities.
3. The American Library Association can provide numbers from state, regional, and association hotlines.
4. E-mail discussion groups such as LIBJOBS and LISJOBS are a good source for job postings. Topical groups are also a good place for finding advertisements in a particular field of librarianship.
5. Look for jobs on the Internet, such as on www.Lisjobs.com, the daily job postings on "Hot Jobs Online" at the website of the American Library Association (www.ala.org), the American Society of Information Science website job line (www.asis.org/Jobline), or www.libraryjobpostings.org. Or visit the ALISE website, which has links to all library schools, each of which has state and national employment listings (www.alise.org).
6. Check out *Jobs for Librarians and Information Professionals,* a comprehensive guide to on-line job resources for librarians and information professionals.
7. Subscribe to major library trade publications, such as *Library Journal* and *American Libraries.*
8. Attend library conventions or conferences and check job boards, and check out the placement service which lists library-related jobs at annual ALA conventions.
9. Check out the *American Library Directory,* which lists a wide variety of libraries in its two-volume directory, or the *Guide to Employment Sources in the Library and Information Professions,* which is available on-line at the ALA website.

ACADEMIC SYSTEMS LIBRARIAN

CAREER PROFILE

Duties: Design, deliver, and maintain information technology at the university library, and help plan, develop, implement, and maintain an information technology platform

Alternate Title(s): Technology Librarian

Salary Range: $35,704 to $55,000+ for a 9- or 12-month year

Employment Prospects: Excellent

Advancement Prospects: Excellent

Best Geographical Location(s): Systems Librarian jobs can be found in academic libraries in colleges and universities throughout the country

Prerequisites:

Education or Training—Master's degree in library and information science from ALA-accredited institution; undergraduate degree in computer science is helpful

Experience—Knowledge of current and emerging library technology, including current and emerging content-linking and authentications standards, such as OpenURL, DOI, Z39.50

Special Skills and Personality Traits—Excellent planning and project management skills; superior organizational, analytical, troubleshooting, and communication skills; the ability to configure servers and to implement and manage network security

CAREER LADDER

```
┌─────────────────────────────────────┐
│      Director, Library Technology    │
└─────────────────────────────────────┘

┌─────────────────────────────────────┐
│      Academic Systems Librarian      │
└─────────────────────────────────────┘

┌─────────────────────────────────────┐
│  Assistant Academic Systems Librarian│
└─────────────────────────────────────┘
```

Position Description

Depending upon the size of the university and its dedication to modern technology, a Systems Librarian may mean a job as librarian with the addition of computer responsibilities, to (as is more common) a unique position focusing almost entirely on the responsibility for library technology.

In most large libraries, an Academic Systems Librarian may serve as the library webmaster, manage on-line databases, and manage and repair computers, printers, and copy machines. The Systems Librarian may have primary responsibility for implementing and managing improved services including e-serials management, metadata encoding, authentication, and related technical issues. The Systems Librarian may also be responsible for implementing and managing comprehensive content-linking/resolution service

technologies, and system administration of the Interlibrary Loan Servers. They may help in strategic planning and in evaluating and recommending services, products and projects, and help teach, provide student aids, and solve problems for library technology applications.

Most Systems Librarians on the library faculty are 12-month, nontenured professionals with academic rank and responsibilities for collection development, university service, and professional development.

Systems Librarians may oversee a few computer terminals in the university library with access limited only to the catalog, or they may supervise multiple computer labs with a wide range of equipment and applications.

The Systems Librarian often acts as a liaison between the library and the campus computing services department, monitoring the status of library computers and reporting problems to computing services. In some libraries, however, the Systems Librarian is the person responsible for managing and repairing computers, printers, and copiers. Because library workstations receive a lot of use and abuse, this creates a need for frequent maintenance. In addition, most academic library print systems have many points at which the process can break down: the printers, the network, the card reader, and the computer that controls the system. As a result, the Systems Librarian spends a great deal of time diagnosing and repairing malfunctions (both hardware and software), investigating network faults, answering complex technology questions, and averting printing disasters. At the same time, the person is usually expected to work at the reference desk and fulfill the many requirements of a tenure-track faculty position.

In addition to computers and their peripheral components, Systems Librarians often have responsibility for a host of software applications, e-mail functions, Web browsers, statistical and mathematical applications, programming languages, and sophisticated graphic design software. They also oversee a digital printing network, electronic classrooms, and public photocopiers.

Finally, Systems Librarians also often supervise staffs, including library clerks, technicians, and assistants.

Salaries
Salaries range from $35,704 to more than $55,000, depending on the Librarian's experience and the university library's size and reliance on technology. Positions in academic libraries are usually nontenured, faculty positions, and are usually (though not always) for 12-month positions.

Employment Prospects
As universities begin to evolve more completely into a highly technical world complete with library Web teams intent on developing digital initiatives, the Academic Systems Librarianship will become even more of a financially stable career choice. Those with the most varied and current knowledge of emerging library technologies will have the best chance of earning a position.

Advancement Prospects
While the technological needs of smaller academic libraries are often administered and operated by a single professional Systems Librarian plus a small support staff, in large academic libraries Systems Librarians may hold management positions as assistant heads or department heads, with budget, personnel, facilities, and hardware management responsibilities. Librarians looking for a Systems Librarian position should show strong evidence of their interest and ability in applying innovative technologies to enhance library services, together with experience in an academic library/information

technology setting and experience in administration and supporting networked information technology.

Education and Training
Academic Systems Librarianship is an ideal way to combine librarianship with a computer background. A master's degree in library or information studies from an ALA-accredited institution is required, together with a bachelor's degree in computer science. Alternatively, prospective Systems Librarians may enhance their M.L.S. degree with courses in computers, technology, and business studies. It is also a good idea to volunteer with a library, archive, or museum, as any experience in the field will improve job prospects.

Systems Librarians should be familiar with server administration and management experience, and current and emerging content-linking and authentications standards, including OpenURL, DOI, and Z39.50. They also should be familiar with ILLiad, SQL, IIS, EZProxy, Internet technologies, computer networks, library automation systems, server management, Win2000/NT/2003, HTML, Microsoft Office and Internet applications, OSI (Open Source Initiative), OAI (Open Archives Metadata Harvesting Protocol.), Shibboleth, LDAP, MetaData/Dublin Core, Marc21, and PURL.

Experience, Skills, and Personality Traits
Systems Librarians should have experience with both software and hardware, and must have excellent planning and project management skills; superior organizational, analytical, troubleshooting, and communication skills; the ability to configure servers and to implement and manage network security; a commitment to professional development; and an ability to work effectively in a collaborative environment as part of a team and with diverse groups, maintaining an environment of mutual respect. The Systems Librarian in a university setting should have proven data management skills in databases, spreadsheets, and office applications. These Librarians also should understand how students use information and how its effective organization and appropriate content can facilitate scholarly research. Academic Systems Librarians must be flexible, creative, and have initiative; they should have the ability to effectively communicate technical issues to colleagues, library patrons, and vendors, and have a demonstrated commitment to skills development for professional growth and position requirements.

Unions and Associations
Academic Systems Librarians may belong to a variety of trade associations that provide educational guidance, support, conferences, and information to members. These might include the American Society for Information Science and Technology; the Association for Library Collections and Technical Services (ALCTS); the Library and Information Technology Association (LITA); the American

Library Association; or the Association of College and Research Libraries.

Tips for Entry

1. To learn about the profession's current activities and to make useful contacts, consider joining a professional association such as the American Society for Information Science and Technology (www.asis.org).

2. Visit the placement service job list on the website of the American Society for Information Science and Technology (www.asis.org/Jobline).

3. E-mail discussion groups are a good source for job postings. LIBJOBS (www.ifla.org/II/lists/libjobs.htm) is one of the more popular ones. Topical groups are also a good place for finding advertisements in Systems Librarianship.

4. Look for jobs on the Internet, such as on www. Lisjobs.com or the daily job postings on "Hot Jobs Online" at the website of the American Library Association (www.ala.org). For academic library postings check the major library trade publications on-line, such as *Library Journal,* at: www.libraryjournal.com or the *Chronicle of Higher Education* (http://chronicle.com/jobs). Visit the ALISE website, which has links to all library schools, each of which has state and national employment listings (www.alise.org); Libweb (http://sunsite.berkeley.edu/Libweb) can help you locate library homepages.

5. Attend annual conferences of library associations, where job listings are often posted.

SERIALS AND ELECTRONIC ACQUISITIONS LIBRARIAN

CAREER PROFILE

Duties: Manage all aspects of electronic serials acquisition and oversee the efficient operation of the serials unit

Alternate Title(s): Serials Librarian

Salary Range: $37,000 to $43,000

Employment Prospects: Good

Advancement Prospects: Good

Best Geographical Location(s): University libraries exist throughout the country, but in general, the larger the university library, the more available jobs

Prerequisites:

Education or Training—Master's degrees in library and information science

Experience—Experience working in an academic library is helpful; computer skills are usually needed

Special Skills and Personality Traits—Aptitude and training in librarianship is necessary, together with attention to detail, love of books, computer skills, and willingness to work hard

CAREER LADDER

```
┌─────────────────────────────────────┐
│   Head of Acquisitions Department    │
└─────────────────────────────────────┘

┌─────────────────────────────────────┐
│      Serials and Electronic          │
│      Acquisitions Librarian          │
└─────────────────────────────────────┘

┌─────────────────────────────────────┐
│  Serials and Electronic Acquisitions │
│        Assistant Librarian           │
└─────────────────────────────────────┘
```

Position Description

The Serials and Electronic Acquisitions Librarian is responsible for coordinating the purchase and licensing of all electronic materials (such as e-magazines) overseeing all aspects of serials acquisition (including ordering of journals, magazine, and other periodicals), and receipt, invoicing, claiming, binding, vendor assessment, and other related functions. In addition, the Serials and Electronic Acquisitions Librarian coordinates the work of the serials unit with other appropriate library areas to ensure efficient workflow and communication.

Because this is often a faculty position, the Serials and Electronic Acquisitions Librarian often is expected to participate in university and professional activities, including conference presentations and research and publication. These positions often require regular reference desk coverage, including helping students and faculty access periodicals and electronic resources. The Librarian is also responsible for cataloging and maintaining the electronic databases.

Salaries

Salaries for this position vary a great deal depending on the responsibilities and location of the library, but in general, they range between $37,000 to $43,000 for a 12-month contract, depending on experience. Appointment is usually at a faculty rank, on a contract renewal basis.

Employment Prospects

Serials and Electronic Acquisitions Librarians continue to find employment in academic libraries around the country as technological advancements make their special skills vital in an ever-more-complex environment. Serials and Electronic Acquisitions Librarians are also needed to manage staff and maintain complicated technological systems.

Advancement Prospects

Opportunities vary according to the interests and expertise of the individual Librarians. In general, the more time, experience, and additional education an individual has, the better the advancement prospects.

Education and Training

A master's degree in library science from a program accredited by the American Library Association is required, in addition to several years of serials experience. The Serials and Electronic Acquisitions Librarian should also have excellent computer skills and experience supervising or organizing the work of others.

Many libraries also require experience with electronic resources, including negotiating contracts and licenses for electronic resources. Some budget management experience is usually desirable, as well as experience working in an integrated automated environment.

Experience, Skills, and Personality Traits

Serials and Electronic Acquisitions Librarians should have excellent communications skills, attention to detail, strong analytical and problem-solving skills, and a demonstrated interest in professional and research activities.

Unions and Associations

The Serials and Electronic Acquisitions Librarian may belong to a variety of trade associations that provide educational guidance, support, conferences, and information to members. These might include the North American Serials Interest Group, the American Library Association, the American Society of Information Science and Technology, the Association of Subscription Agents, the Reference and User Services Association, the Research Libraries Group, the Association of College and Research Libraries, or the Association for Library Collections and Technical Services.

Tips for Entry

1. Join various professional organizations such as the North American Serials Interest Group to provide a network through which you may hear about job opportunities.
2. E-mail discussion groups such as LIBJOBS and LIS-JOBS are a good source for job postings. Topical groups are also a good place for finding advertisements in a particular field of librarianship.
3. Look for jobs on the Internet, at such websites as: www.Lisjobs.com; the daily job postings on "Hot Jobs Online" at the website of the American Library Association (www.ala.org); the American Society of Information Science job line (www.asis.org/Jobline); North American Serials Interest Group (www.NASIG.org/jobs/index.htm); or www.libraryjobpostings.org. Or visit the ALISE website, which has links to all library schools, each of which has state and national employment listings (www.alise.org).
4. Check out *Jobs for Librarians and Information Professionals,* a comprehensive guide to on-line job resources for librarians and information professionals.
5. Subscribe to major library trade publications, such as *Library Journal* and *American Libraries.*
6. Attend library conventions or conferences, check job boards, and check out the placement service that lists library-related jobs at annual ALA conventions.
7. Check out the *American Library Directory,* which lists a wide variety of libraries in its two-volume directory, or the *Guide to Employment Sources in the Library and Information Professions,* which is available on-line at the American Library Association website.

ACADEMIC LAW LIBRARY CLERK

CAREER PROFILE

Duties: Prepare and shelve new materials, provide support to the librarian and offer secretarial support as needed

Alternate Title(s): None

Salary Range: $15,000 to 25,000+

Employment Prospects: Good

Advancement Prospects: Good

Best Geographical Location(s): Law schools throughout the United States may hold employment possibilities

Prerequisites:

Education or Training—High school diploma; diploma from library clerk course

Experience—Experience working in a law library and legal secretarial experience are helpful

Special Skills and Personality Traits—Attention to detail; flexibility; good computer skills; written and verbal communication skills

CAREER LADDER

```
┌─────────────────────────────────────┐
│  Academic Law Library Technician     │
└─────────────────────────────────────┘

┌─────────────────────────────────────┐
│  Academic Law Library Clerk          │
└─────────────────────────────────────┘

┌─────────────────────────────────────┐
│  Entry Level                         │
└─────────────────────────────────────┘
```

Position Description

Academic Law Library Clerks shelve books and periodicals, sign out materials, and maintain books and equipment. Many Clerks use their typing and computer skills to process materials orders and to update library catalogs. In addition, Law Library Clerks may serve as receptionist, taking incoming telephone calls, providing general information about the law library, and referring students to appropriate personnel for assistance. They may maintain copies of staff schedules and sort, process, and distribute incoming and outgoing mail and delivery, including daily check-in of periodicals.

Clerks also may sort the collection by subject category in preparation for shelving, process reserves, collect fines and fees, prepare deposit records and deposit money, and record daily statistics. They also may sort and file personnel information, correspondence, memoranda, reports, and other materials, some of which may be confidential, maintain a database of mailing lists, and prepare labels for newsletters or special events. They may enter information into the computer system and may review entries for accuracy. Clerks also operate the photocopier and other basic office machines.

Law Library Clerks work under the direction of staff trained in the library and information profession, and may help catalog and classify materials, produce graphic and display materials, and help develop circulation procedures.

Salaries

Salaries of Academic Law Library Clerks vary according to the individual's qualifications and the type, size, and location of the library, but generally range from $15,000 to $25,000.

Employment Prospects

Academic Law Library Clerks can apply for jobs in all parts of the country, but because these jobs are limited to law school libraries a person may have to move in order to find a job in this field. Employment of Law Library Clerks is expected to grow faster than the average for all occupations through 2012.

Advancement Prospects

With experience and a diploma from a library course at a technical school, Academic Law Library Clerks can advance to law library technician jobs. Armed with an advanced degree in library science, they could then move into positions at law libraries as librarian.

Education and Training

Law Library Clerks usually must be high school graduates with standard secretarial and computer skills. They should be familiar with standard office procedures and practices. Libraries often prefer Library Clerks to have one year of general clerical experience that includes public contact. With additional training, they can perform the specialized functions unique to an academic library, preparing them to support and assist law librarians and technicians.

Experience, Skills, and Personality Traits

Law library work is a service profession, so an aptitude for and a commitment to working with students and professors in a service environment is a strong asset. Law Library Clerks should be able to pay close attention to details; be neat and well-organized; enjoy working with computers; and have good typing, English writing and speaking skills; be willing to learn new skills; and be able to perform library clerical work quickly and accurately. Being personable and able to work well with others is a plus.

Unions and Associations

Law Library Clerks can belong to a variety of trade associations that provide educational guidance, support, conferences, and information to members. These might include the American Association of Law Libraries, the American Library Association, the American Society for Information Science, or the Special Libraries Association.

Tips for Entry

1. Clerk jobs in academic law libraries are almost always advertised locally, so check the classified section in your local daily paper.

2. The American Association of Law Libraries website maintains a job database that is updated regularly and includes jobs in all kinds of law libraries.

3. If you have an academic law library nearby, visit and ask to speak with the director about possible jobs. If there are no immediate openings, ask about volunteering. Library administrators are likely to prefer a candidate with some relevant experience.

4. Send out your résumé. Find out the name and address of every academic law library in your area where you might like to work (the telephone book is helpful; call to find out to whom to address your cover letter). When openings occur, administrators often pull out their collection of unsolicited résumés and contact the candidates.

ACADEMIC LAW LIBRARY TECHNICIAN

CAREER PROFILE

Duties: Provide reference help for professors and students, prepare and shelve new materials, and help take care of collections

Alternate Title(s): None

Salary Range: $16,800 to 30,000+

Employment Prospects: Excellent

Advancement Prospects: Excellent

Best Geographical Location(s): Academic libraries throughout the country need Library Technicians

Prerequisites:

Education or Training—High school diploma is required; associate's degree in liberal arts or library technical services with one or more years of library experience is preferred; diploma from library technician course acceptable

Experience—Experience working in a law library is helpful

Special Skills and Personality Traits—Good people skills; detail oriented; flexible; good written and verbal communication skills

CAREER LADDER

Academic Law Librarian

Academic Law Library Technician

Academic Law Library Clerk

Position Description

Academic Law Library Technicians cover all facets of library functions, including circulation, acquisitions, reference, and audiovisual. They usually work under the supervision of law librarians, but may also supervise other library or clerical staff. Some Law Library Technicians may be involved in working with patrons, handling the loan of books, films, and videotapes, and may collect and organize books, pamphlets, manuscripts, and other materials in specific areas of law.

Law Library Technicians also help care for the books in their care, organizing and maintaining periodicals and preparing volumes for binding. They also may help supervise support staff.

As law libraries begin to depend more completely on computerized information storage and retrieval systems, Law Library Technicians today are expected to be comfortable handling more technical jobs once performed by law librarians, such as entering catalog information into the library's com-

puter. Increasingly, Law Library Technicians are using computers to handle many routine library tasks, such as circulation control, and also for the storage and retrieval of information, both within the library and through the use of external databases. As recordkeeping has become more automated, Law Library Technicians have found they are spending less time performing clerical work and more time working with patrons.

Salaries

Salaries of Academic Law Library Technicians vary according to the individual's qualifications and the type, size, and location of the library, but range from a low of $16,000 to $35,660 and above.

Employment Prospects

Academic Law Library Technicians can apply for jobs in all parts of the country, but because these jobs are limited to law school libraries a person may have to move in order to find a good job in this field. Employment of Law Library Technicians is expected to grow about as fast as the average for all occupations through 2012. The increasing use of computerized information storage and retrieval systems continues to contribute to slow growth in these jobs, as fewer employees are needed to accomplish tasks; applicants for Law Library Technician jobs in large metropolitan areas, where most prefer to work, usually face tougher competition. However, the Bureau of Labor Statistics projects that the number of Law Library Technicians will grow faster than the number of law librarians through 2012.

Advancement Prospects

The position of Law Library Technician is an entry-level job; as Technicians begin to take on more responsibilities, it's possible to move into supervisory positions, becoming responsible for the day-to-day operation of a department. With experience and advanced degrees, an Academic Law Library Technician can be promoted to a variety of positions, such as law librarian, department head, library director, or chief information officer.

Education and Training

Community colleges and technical institutes often offer a library diploma program for Law Library Technicians. This training prepares individuals to perform the specialized functions unique to an academic law library, such as assisting the law librarian, coordinating the clerical staff, and assuming responsibility for a section or department in a larger library. In a small academic law library where the organizational duties are already established, the Law Library Technician may serve as the library manager.

Experience, Skills, and Personality Traits

An aptitude for and a commitment to working with law students and professors in a service environment is a strong asset. You should be able to pay close attention to details, be neat and well organized, enjoy working with computers, have good English writing and speaking skills, and be willing to learn new skills. Because providing reference help is an important part of their job, Academic Law Library Technicians must be able to communicate effectively with students and faculty members. Being personable and able to work well with others is a plus.

Unions and Associations

Law Library Technicians may belong to a variety of trade associations that provide support and information to members, such as the American Association of Law Libraries (AALL), the American Library Association, the American Society for Information Science, or the Special Libraries Association.

Tips for Entry

1. Jobs in academic law libraries are almost always advertised both locally and nationally.
2. Check out the American Association of Law Libraries website, at www.aallnet.org, which maintains a job database that is updated regularly and includes jobs in all types of law libraries.
3. Many jobs are posted on AALL chapter listservs and websites.
4. For additional jobs as an Academic Law Library Technician, check out ads on the websites of the Special Library Association and American Library Association.

ACADEMIC LAW LIBRARIAN

CAREER PROFILE

Duties: Develop and direct information programs and systems at the law school library to ensure information is organized to meet users' needs; provide reference help for professors and students; prepare and shelve new materials; supervise technicians

Alternate Title(s): None

Salary Range: $38,215 to $100,000+

Employment Prospects: Excellent

Advancement Prospects: Good

Best Geographical Location(s): All locations may hold employment possibilities

Prerequisites:

Education or Training—Master's degree in library science; a law degree is also helpful

Experience—Experience working in a law library is often as important as having a law degree

Special Skills and Personality Traits—Good people skills; detail oriented; flexible; good written and verbal communication skills

CAREER LADDER

```
┌─────────────────────────────────────┐
│   Academic Law Library Director      │
└─────────────────────────────────────┘

┌─────────────────────────────────────┐
│      Academic Law Librarian          │
└─────────────────────────────────────┘

┌─────────────────────────────────────┐
│   Academic Law Library Technician    │
└─────────────────────────────────────┘
```

Position Description

Law Librarians fill many of the same positions that can be found at other libraries. They are in technical services, cataloging, public services, collection development, and reference services.

The Academic Law Librarian serves the legal and teaching needs of an entire law school, and also may serve the needs of the institution's alumni, the local bar associations, and members of the community. The law librarian may conduct research for a professor or student, serve on a committee, edit a newsletter, and train technicians. Law Librarians also organize materials, information, people and projects, and (in some libraries) make decisions about personnel and resources. In addition, the Law Librarian may help maintain advanced media, including CD-ROMs, the Internet, virtual libraries, and remote access to a wide range of resources.

One of the primary duties of the Academic Law Librarian is to provide help to those doing legal research and, in turn, to instruct students in the methods of legal research.

The instructors for introductory and advanced legal research courses are generally Librarians. The future attorney should be able to locate information from a book as well as from the computer: their future law firm may only have access to one or the other. It is the Librarian's duty to help the student become proficient at both.

Law Librarians must be familiar with a wide variety of scholarly and public information sources, and follow trends related to publishing, the law, computers, and the media to effectively oversee the selection and organization of library materials. They manage staff and develop and direct information programs and systems to ensure that information is organized to meet users' needs.

Many law libraries have access to remote databases and maintain their own computerized databases. The widespread use of automation in libraries makes database searching skills important to Librarians. Librarians develop and index databases and help train users to develop searching skills for the information they need.

The Internet also is expanding the amount of available reference information. Librarians with computer and information systems skills can work as automated systems librarians, planning and operating computer systems, and information science librarians, designing information storage and retrieval systems and developing procedures for collecting, organizing, interpreting, and classifying information. These librarians analyze and plan for future information needs.

Salaries

Law Librarians make less than many lawyers, but salaries for law librarians are still on the high end of librarian salaries. The median salary for a Law Librarian in a one-person library is $45,000, but could top $100,000. Salaries for this position vary a great deal depending on the responsibilities and the type, size, and location of the library.

Employment Prospects

Academic Law Librarians can apply for (and might even be recruited for) jobs in all parts of the country. However, depending on the city, applicants might need to move in order to get a desired position. For example, if an individual wanted to work in an academic law library and the one law school in the person's area did not have any openings, it would be necessary to apply elsewhere. Law librarianship also has local job markets (for instance, most law firm library jobs are advertised and filled locally).

Employment of Law Librarians is expected to grow about as fast as the average for all occupations throughout the 2000–12 period. The increasing use of computerized information storage and retrieval systems continues to contribute to slow growth in the demand for Law Librarians. Computerized systems make cataloging easier, so that library technicians can now handle cataloging. In addition, many users can now access law library computers directly from their homes or offices. These systems allow users to bypass Librarians and conduct research on their own. However, Law Librarians are still needed to manage staff, help users develop database searching techniques, address complicated reference requests, and define users' needs.

Surveys suggest there are still twice as many openings as people looking for jobs, according to the American Association of Law Libraries. The need to replace Librarians as they retire means there will be many additional job openings because about 50 percent of the profession will retire in the next 10 to 15 years. Applicants for Law Librarian jobs in large metropolitan areas, where most graduates prefer to work, usually face competition.

Advancement Prospects

Experienced Academic Law Librarians can advance to administrative positions, such as department head, law library director, or chief information officer.

Education and Training

Many academic law libraries require law degrees for Librarians. Since academic law library directors are usually members of the law school faculty, almost all of them have law degrees. To qualify for virtually any professional job in an academic law library, a person must have a graduate degree in library science and may want to consider also earning a law degree. About 85 percent of those working as Law Librarians have a graduate degree in library science. Most jobs require a master's degree from an American Library Association (ALA)–accredited institution; the names of the degrees vary (B.M.L.S., M.L.I.S., M.S.I.S., M.L., M.A. in L.S.B.) but all reflect an appropriate entry-level educational requirement for careers in the law librarianship profession. Less than 20 percent of law librarian jobs require both an M.L.S. and a law degree.

Some jobs will state a preference for the law degree in addition to the graduate degree in library science, but law library work experience is often as important as having a law degree. Nearly 30 percent of all law librarians also have a J.D. or L.L.B. degree. Most employers seeking candidates with a law degree require that this degree be earned from a law school accredited by the American Bar Association (ABA). The candidate armed with both J.D. and M.L.S. degrees will be qualified for more positions in law librarianship.

Experience, Skills, and Personality Traits

Academic Law Librarians must be able to communicate effectively with students and faculty members, as they answer questions and provide reference help, and be friendly and work well with others. Academic Law Librarians usually work normal business hours, although they often work overtime, weekends, and evenings, and have to work some holidays. They usually have vacation schedules similar to those of professors.

Unions and Associations

Law Librarians do not usually belong to unions, but they can belong to a variety of trade associations that provide educational guidance, support, conferences, and information to members. These might include the American Library Association, the American Society for Information Science, the American Association of Law Libraries, or the Special Libraries Association.

Tips for Entry

1. Plan to attend the annual July meeting of the American Association of Law Libraries (AALL), which has a placement committee that coordinates job interviews.
2. The AALL website maintains a job database that is updated regularly and includes jobs in all kinds of law libraries. Many jobs are posted on AALL chapter listservs and websites, so visit them too.

3. Check out the two main publications of the AALL: the *AALL Spectrum* and the *Law Library Journal.*

4. Jobs are also advertised on the Special Library Association and American Library Association websites.

5. E-mail discussion groups such as LIBJOBS and LIS-JOBS are a good source for job postings. Topical groups are also a good place for finding advertisements in a particular field of librarianship.

6. Look for jobs on the Internet, such as on www.Lisjobs.com, the daily job postings on "Hot Jobs Online" at the website of the American Library Association (www.ala.org), the American Society of Information Science website job line (www.asis.org/Jobline) or www.libraryjobpostings.org. Or visit the ALISE website, which offers links to all library schools, each of which has state and national employment listings (www.alise.org).

7. Check out *Jobs for Librarians and Information Professionals,* a comprehensive guide to on-line job resources for librarians and information professionals.

ACADEMIC LAW LIBRARY DIRECTOR

CAREER PROFILE

Duties: Perform administrative work; conduct research for a professor or student; serve on a committee; train employees

Alternate Title(s): Law Librarian

Salary Range: $63,636 to $107,900+

Employment Prospects: Good

Advancement Prospects: Good

Best Geographical Location(s): All locations may hold employment possibilities

Prerequisites:

Education or Training—High school diploma; master's degree in library science; a law degree is also helpful

Experience—Experience working in a law library is often as important as having a law degree

Special Skills and Personality Traits—Good people skills; detail oriented; flexible; good written and verbal communication skills

CAREER LADDER

```
┌─────────────────────────────────┐
│  Consultant or Academic Law Library │
│  Director of Larger Law School   │
└─────────────────────────────────┘

┌─────────────────────────────────┐
│  Academic Law Library Director   │
└─────────────────────────────────┘

┌─────────────────────────────────┐
│  Academic Law Librarian          │
└─────────────────────────────────┘
```

Position Description

The Academic Director of a law library serves the entire law school, and may juggle many different duties and projects. In addition to administrative work (depending on the size of the library), the Library Director may do research for a professor or student, serve on a committee, edit a newsletter, or conduct a training session. They may instruct law students in the effective use of research tools in the library or the classroom.

Library Directors also organize materials, information, people, and projects, and tend to think institutionally about policies and procedures—for example, setting up a system for assigning study carrels that will be fair to all the law students, or setting up a check-out system for a library that is likely to be used by all the instructors.

Most Academic Law Library Directors are involved in setting library policy and making decisions about personnel and resources. The traditional concept of a library is being redefined from a place to access paper records or books, to one that also houses the most advanced media, including CD-ROMs, the Internet, virtual libraries, and remote access to a wide range of resources. Consequently, librarians increasingly are combining traditional duties with tasks involving quickly changing technology. Academic law librarians must be familiar with a wide variety of scholarly and public information sources, and follow trends related to publishing, computers, and the media to effectively oversee the selection and organization of library materials. They manage staff and develop and direct information programs and systems to ensure information is organized to meet users' needs. The Law Library Director oversees the management and planning of libraries, negotiates contracts for services, materials, and equipment, supervises employees, performs public relations and fund-raising duties, prepares budgets, and directs activities to ensure that everything functions properly.

The increased use of automated information systems enables Academic Law Library Directors to focus on administrative and budgeting responsibilities, grant writing, and specialized research requests, while delegating more technical and user services responsibilities to technicians. Academic Law Library Directors usually work normal business hours, although they often work overtime, weekends, and evenings, and have to work some holidays. They usually have vacation schedules similar to those of professors.

Salaries

Law Library Directors make less than many lawyers. The average for a Director/chief law librarian is $63,636, but can top $107,900. Salaries for this position vary a great deal depending on the responsibilities and the type, size, and location of the library.

Employment Prospects

Academic Law Library Directors may be recruited for jobs in all parts of the country. However, depending on the city, applicants might need to move in order to get a desired position. For example, if an individual wanted to work in an academic law library and the one law school in the person's area did not have any openings, it would be necessary to apply elsewhere. Still, law schools are found in almost every state, in both urban and rural areas. The average law school library has a collection of about 320,000 books with an annual budget of more than $1.5 million. There are, therefore, plenty of opportunities to find employment.

Employment of Law Library Directors is expected to grow about as fast as the average for all occupations throughout the 2000–12 period. Law Library Directors manage staff, help users develop database searching techniques, and address complicated reference requests.

The need to replace Law Library Directors as they retire means there will be many additional job openings. Applicants for law librarian jobs in large metropolitan areas, where most graduates prefer to work, usually face competition.

Advancement Prospects

Experienced academic law librarians can advance to administrative positions, such as department head, Law Library Director, or chief information officer. Some academic law librarians prefer to move from academia into heading law firm libraries in the corporate world.

Education and Training

To qualify for virtually any professional job in an academic law library, a person must have a graduate degree in library science and may want to consider also earning a law degree. Many academic law libraries require law degrees for librarians and management positions. Since Academic Law Library Directors are usually members of the law school faculty, almost all of them have law degrees. About 85 percent of those working as academic law librarians have a graduate degree in library science. Most jobs require a master's degree from an American Library Association (ALA)–accredited institution; the names of the degrees vary (B.M.L.S., M.L.I.S., M.S.I.S., M.L., M.A. in L.S.B.) but all reflect an appropriate entry-level educational requirement for careers in the law librari-anship profession. Although less than 20 percent of law librarian jobs require both degrees, the sectors where law degrees are rarely required most often do not search nationally, so few of those jobs are advertised through the national sources.

Although some jobs require the graduate degree in library science and state a preference for the law degree as well, experience working in a law library is often as important as having a law degree. Nearly 30 percent of all law librarians also have a J.D. or L.L.B. degree. Most positions require that this degree be earned from a law school accredited by the American Bar Association (ABA). The candidate armed with both J.D. and M.L.S. degrees will be qualified for more positions in law librarianship.

Experience, Skills, and Personality Traits

Academic Law Library Directors must be able to communicate effectively with students and faculty members, as they answer questions and provide reference help in addition to managing staff and directing the growth of the library. Being personable and able to work well with others is a plus, since directors typically work closely with staff, students, and faculty.

Unions and Associations

Law Library Directors do not usually belong to unions, but they can belong to a variety of trade associations that provide educational guidance, support, conferences, information to members. These might include the American Library Association, the American Society for Information Science, the American Association of Law Libraries, or the Special Libraries Association.

Tips for Entry

1. Jobs in academic law libraries are almost always advertised nationally. Check out the American Association of Law Libraries (AALL), which has a placement committee that coordinates personal interviews at its annual meeting, held in July each year.
2. Visit the AALL website, which maintains a job database that is updated regularly and includes jobs in all kinds of law libraries. Many jobs are posted on AALL chapter listservs and websites, so visit them, too.
3. Check out the two main publications of the AALL: the *AALL Spectrum* and the *Law Library Journal*.
4. Jobs are also advertised on the Special Library Association and American Library Association websites.
5. E-mail discussion groups such as LIBJOBS and LIS-JOBS are a good source for job postings. Topical groups are also a good place for finding advertisements in a particular field of librarianship.
6. Look for jobs on the Internet, such as on www. Lisjobs.com, the daily job postings on "Hot Jobs

Online" at the website of the American Library Association (www.ala.org), the American Society of Information Science website job line (www.asis.org/Jobline), or www.libraryjobpostings.org. Or visit the ALISE website, which has links to all library schools, each of which has state and national employment listings: www.alise.org.

7. Check out *Jobs for Librarians and Information Professionals,* a comprehensive guide to on-line job resources for librarians and information professionals.

DEAN, SCHOOL OF LIBRARY AND INFORMATION SCIENCE

CAREER PROFILE

Duties: Provide academic and administrative leadership; articulate a compelling vision of the school's role in information science education and research; understand national trends and issues in information science; oversee fund-raising; develop partnerships both internal and external to the university; take a national and international leadership role in shaping the future of library and information science

Alternate Title(s): None

Salary Range: $94,824 to $176,101

Employment Prospects: Fair

Advancement Prospects: Fair

Best Geographical Location(s): University schools of information science are found throughout the United States

Prerequisites:

Education or Training—A doctorate in library or information science or other doctoral degree appropriate for leadership in information studies, or a commensurate background

Experience—Administrative experience, teaching experience, library experience helpful

Special Skills and Personality Traits—A vision for the roles of information professions in a changing world; commitment to serving lifelong learning needs of practicing professionals; entrepreneurial spirit; excellent people and fund-raising skills

CAREER LADDER

```
┌─────────────────────────────────────┐
│  Dean, Larger School of Library and  │
│       Information Science            │
└─────────────────────────────────────┘

┌─────────────────────────────────────┐
│   Dean, School of Library and        │
│       Information Science            │
└─────────────────────────────────────┘

┌─────────────────────────────────────┐
│     Professor of Library and         │
│       Information Science            │
└─────────────────────────────────────┘
```

Position Description

The Dean of a school of library and information science is responsible for leading the faculty and student body, motivating and supporting a high level of faculty performance in teaching, scholarship, and service, and promoting faculty morale and cohesiveness. The Dean administers and coordinates the activities of the school and may be involved in maintaining and expanding distance education opportunities. The dean also must articulate a vision of the school's role in information science education and research.

An important aspect of the job as Dean is to maintain close relations with the academic community, alumni, professionals, and the local community, and to be able to clearly describe the mission of the school to people both inside and outside of the university.

In addition, the Dean is usually expected to undertake fairly extensive financial responsibilities, including developing external sources of funding for the school and actively engaging in fund-raising and grant-seeking activities to support students, faculty, and programs. The Dean is also expected to maintain American Library Association accreditation.

Salaries

Salaries for this position vary a great deal depending on specific job responsibilities and the location of the university. Typically, the salary for a Dean of the library school may range from $94,824 to 176,101, with an average of $135,463.

Employment Prospects

Because the number of schools of library and information science is finite, jobs for Deans are not expected to grow significantly, but will maintain a steady number of openings as Deans retire or move into other fields.

Advancement Prospects

Because the Dean represents the most senior member of the library and information science school, a person may advance primarily by accepting a position in a larger, more prestigious university.

Education and Training

In addition to a doctorate in library and information science (or a closely related field), the Dean must have a record of academic achievement commensurate with a senior-level faculty appointment. The person must have experience in academic administration, including management of fiscal and human resources, and have a clear commitment to collaborative leadership and excellence in teaching, research, and professional service. In addition, most academic libraries require the Dean to be committed to cultural diversity and equal opportunity.

Experience, Skills, and Personality Traits

A dean should provide energetic and imaginative leadership, with a thorough understanding of national trends in information science. Significant administrative experience, a commitment to fund-raising, and experience in developing partnerships inside and outside the university is important.

Unions and Associations

A Dean of a school of library and information science may belong to a variety of trade associations that provide educational guidance, support, conferences, and information to members. These might include the American Library Association, the American Society for Information Science, or the Special Libraries Association.

Tips for Entry

1. Attend annual conferences of library associations, where job listings are often posted.
2. E-mail discussion groups are a good source for job postings. LIBJOBS (www.ifla.org/II/lists/libjobs.htm) is one of the more popular ones.
3. Look for jobs on the Internet, such as on www.Lisjobs.com, the daily job postings on "Hot Jobs Online" at the website of the American Library Association (www.ala.org), or www.libraryjobpostings.org.
4. Check out *Jobs for Librarians and Information Professionals,* a comprehensive guide to on-line job resources for librarians and information professionals.
5. Another place to check is the major library trade publications, such as *Library Journal* (www.libraryjournal.com). There are also related publications, such as the *Chronicle of Higher Education* (http://chronicle.com/jobs) for academic library postings.

PROFESSOR OF LIBRARY AND INFORMATION SCIENCE

CAREER PROFILE

Duties: Teach courses in this field, in addition to research and publication

Alternate Title(s): None

Salary Range: $34,431 to $141,921 (12-month faculty)

Employment Prospects: Fair

Advancement Prospects: Fair

Best Geographical Location(s): University schools of library and information science are found throughout the United States

Prerequisites:

Education or Training—A master's degree and doctorate in library or information science or another doctoral degree appropriate for information studies

Experience—Administrative experience, teaching experience; library experience is helpful

Special Skills and Personality Traits—A vision for the roles of information professions in a changing world; excellent people and teaching skills

CAREER LADDER

```
┌─────────────────────────────────────┐
│  Assistant or Associate Dean, School of │
│  Library and Information Science     │
└─────────────────────────────────────┘

┌─────────────────────────────────────┐
│  Professor of Library and            │
│  Information Science                 │
└─────────────────────────────────────┘

┌─────────────────────────────────────┐
│  Associate Professor of Library and  │
│  Information Science                 │
└─────────────────────────────────────┘
```

Position Description

The Professor of Library and Information Science is responsible for teaching courses in this field including library science, cataloging, technical services, children's literature, youth services, school librarianship, and more. Professors also may be responsible for advising master's and doctoral students, assisting with curriculum matters, helping to develop school policies, and conducting scholarly research ending in publication.

Salaries

Salaries for this position vary a great deal depending on the size and location of the university, but (for a 12-month position) range from $94,824 to $176,101. The average salary for a full Professor of Library and Information Science is $135,463.

Employment Prospects

Because the number of schools of library and information science are finite, jobs for Professors are not expected to grow significantly, but will maintain a steady number of openings as Professors retire or move into other fields.

Advancement Prospects

Professors are the most senior faculty member's in library and information science; a Professor may advance primarily by accepting a teaching position in a larger, more prestigious university or by moving into a more administrative position such as assistant or associate dean of the library and information science school.

Education and Training

The Professor should have an M.L.I.S. and a doctorate in library and information science, communication, or information systems (or a closely related field), and a record of academic achievement commensurate with a senior-level faculty appointment. The professor should be able to demonstrate the potential for research and publication and the ability to provide high-quality instruction to graduate students. The professor should have a clear commitment to collaborative leadership and excellence in teaching, research, and professional service.

Professors of Library and Information Science should be able to teach and conduct research in a variety of areas, including information architecture, information science, knowledge management, data mining, digital libraries, special librarianship, health science librarianship, and specialized literatures. Professors should have a systems perspective and a strong commitment to research as well as graduate and undergraduate education.

Experience, Skills, and Personality Traits

Professors should have willingness and ability to work well with both students and faculty, excellent research skills, and excellent written and oral communication. Successful college-level instruction is also important.

Unions and Associations

A Professor of Library and Information Science may belong to a variety of trade associations that provide educational guidance, support, conferences, and information to members. These might include the American Library Association, the American Society for Information Science, or the Special Libraries Association.

Tips for Entry

1. Attend annual conferences of library associations, where jobs listings are often posted.
2. E-mail discussion groups are a good source for job postings. LIBJOBS (www.ifla.org/II/lists/libjobs.htm) is one of the more popular ones.
3. Look for jobs on the Internet, such as on www.Lisjobs.com, the daily job postings on "Hot Jobs Online" at the website of the American Library Association (www.ala.org), or www.libraryjobpostings.org.
4. Check out *Jobs for Librarians and Information Professionals,* a comprehensive guide to on-line job resources for librarians and information professionals.
5. Another place to check is the major library trade publications, such as *Library Journal* (www.libraryjournal.com). There are also related publications, such as the *Chronicle of Higher Education* (http://chronicle.com/jobs) for academic library postings.

GOVERNMENT LIBRARIES

GOVERNMENT ARCHIVES TECHNICIAN

CAREER PROFILE

Duties: Provide reference services; detect missing items; prepare indexes and shelf lists; select, prepare, and verify records for repair; review records for declassification and public access; perform accession and disposal tasks

Alternate Title(s): Archives Assistant

Salary Range: $19,100 to $50,000+

Employment Prospects: Good

Advancement Prospects: Good

Best Geographical Location(s): Larger cities may offer more possibilities

Prerequisites:

Education or Training—Bachelor's degree, one year of graduate work, or master's degree

Experience—Several years of experience in archives

Special Skills and Personality Traits—Good organizational and people skills; computer capability; office skills; attention to detail

CAREER LADDER

```
┌─────────────────────────────┐
│        Archivist            │
└─────────────────────────────┘

┌─────────────────────────────┐
│     Archives Technician     │
└─────────────────────────────┘

┌─────────────────────────────┐
│        Entry Level          │
└─────────────────────────────┘
```

Position Description

The primary task of the Archives Technician is to help the archivist maintain physical and intellectual control over records of enduring value. The Archives Technician helps arrange, describe, and preserve such records.

The Archives Technician works with relatively small quantities of records important enough to be retained for an extended period, including paper, film, electronic records, photographs, video and sound recordings, computer tapes, and video and optical disks, as well as the more traditional unpublished letters, diaries, and other manuscripts. Archives are located in federal, state, and local governments and can range from large, well-funded operations providing a variety of archival services to limited activities dependent upon a part-time volunteer staff.

Archives Technicians provide reference service in response to oral or written inquiries; perform detailed arrangement work at the individual page, document, or filing unit level; verify correct arrangement; and detect missing or misfiled items. They also prepare detailed aids such as indexes and shelf lists; select, prepare, and verify records

for repair; review records for declassification and public access; and perform accession and disposal tasks.

Salaries

Salaries, benefits, and working conditions vary, depending on the size and nature of the government institution, but it is a civil service position. The federal government General Schedule (GS) salary scales range from 1 to 15; eligibility depends on education and work experience. Federal Government Archives Technician positions usually range from GS-5 ($27,287) through GS-9 ($46,206) (2004 rates). Salaries can range from a low of $19,100 to $50,000+.

Employment Prospects

Competition for jobs as an Archives Technician is expected to be keen as qualified applicants outnumber job openings. College graduates with experience in archives and extensive computer skills should have the best opportunities for jobs. Most Government Archives Technicians work in federal, state, and local government. All state governments have archival or historical records sections, and many federal Government Archives Technicians work for the National Archives and Records Administration or the U.S. Department of Defense.

Advancement Prospects

Eligibility for promotion in many civil service jobs is based on experience, and qualified workers take written and oral tests for advanced positions. Government Archives Technicians typically advance by transferring to a larger unit. With the exception of Technicians working in small government museums, an advanced degree in history, library science, or a related field may be needed to move into the position of archivist. Technician positions often serve as a stepping-stone for individuals interested in archival work.

Education and Training

Individuals can prepare for a career as an Archives Technician through a variety of educational programs, but most entry-level positions require an undergraduate degree or at least three years of experience. Although Archives Technicians have a variety of undergraduate majors, most receive degrees in library science, political science, or American history.

The number and content of archival education offerings, especially multicourse programs, has continued to expand in recent years. Graduate archival programs may offer a variety of courses that include basic archival theory, methods, and/or practice of appraisal, arrangement, description, preservation, reference services, outreach, legal concerns, and ethics. In addition, programs may offer such courses as records management, aspects of library and information science, and historical and research methods.

Experience, Skills, and Personality Traits

Archives Technicians must be able to organize large amounts of information and write clear instructions for its retrieval and use. In addition, good computer and office skills and the ability to work with electronic records and databases are increasingly important. Archives Technicians must be committed to customer service as well as heritage and information management.

Unions and Associations

Government Archives Technicians do not belong to unions, but they can belong to a variety of trade associations that provide educational guidance, support, conferences, and information to members, such as the Society of American Archivists.

Tips for Entry

1. Jobs in most federal libraries require that you establish civil service eligibility. Contact the Office of Personnel Management (OPM) at www.usajobs.opm.gov for help. Federal jobs that don't need to hire through OPM include the U.S. Foreign Service, the judicial and legislative branches of the government, the Library of Congress, the National Science Foundation, the United Nations Secretariat, the U.S. Postal Service, and others.

2. To locate federal job openings around the world, contact OPM's Career America Connection at (912) 757-3000 or (202) 606-2700, or check out the federal jobs website at www.fedworld.gov/jobs/jobsearch.html.

3. Visit your local governmental archives to check on available Technician positions.

4. Look for job ads in the Society of American Archivists' (SAA) on-line employment bulletin (www.archivists. org/employment/index.asp).

5. Check daily job postings on "Hot Jobs Online" at the website of the American Library Association (www. ala.org) or other Internet websites that list library job postings, such as http://www.libraryjobpostings.org.

6. Subscribe to archival journals and periodicals to keep current with latest classified ads and trends, such as the SAA *Employment Bulletin,* the *Archival Outlook,* the *American Archivist,* or the *American Libraries* magazine.

7. Attend the annual SAA convention in late summer, or check job boards at the placement service listing library-related jobs at annual ALA conventions.

8. Visit the ALISE website, which offers links to all library schools, each of which has state and national employment listings (www.alise.org).

GOVERNMENT ARCHIVIST

CAREER PROFILE

Duties: Buy, preserve, maintain, exhibit, and store valuable items that can be used in exhibitions, publications, and educational programs

Alternate Title(s): Archival Manager, Historical Editor

Salary Range: $20,010 to $69,706+

Employment Prospects: Good

Advancement Prospects: Good

Best Geographical Location(s): Washington, D.C.; state capitals and government centers throughout the country

Prerequisites:

Education or Training—Undergraduate and graduate degree in library science, political science, American history, or similar major

Experience—Many jobs request three to five years of professional experience with project management experience

Special Skills and Personality Traits—Good organizational and people skills; computer capability; communication skills; attention to detail

Licensure/Certification—Voluntary certification is available from the Academy of Certified Archivists

CAREER LADDER

```
┌─────────────────────────────────────┐
│   Archivist for Larger Government    │
│            Organization or           │
│   Director of Government Archives    │
└─────────────────────────────────────┘

┌─────────────────────────────────────┐
│        Government Archivist          │
└─────────────────────────────────────┘

┌─────────────────────────────────────┐
│   Government Archives Technician     │
└─────────────────────────────────────┘
```

Position Description

Federal, state, and local governments all maintain their own archives, which may be part of a library, museum, or historical society, or they may exist as a distinct unit. They can range from large, well-funded operations providing a variety of archival services to limited activities dependent upon a part-time volunteer staff.

A Government Archivist preserves the heritage of a people and a region, helps patrons, and plans exhibitions, as well as selecting, arranging, and cataloging government archives. In addition, the Archivist appraises and/or edits archival records and historically valuable materials, participates in research activities based on archival materials, and directly manages the acquisition, disposition, and safekeeping of archival materials. The primary task of the Government Archivist is to establish and maintain physical and intellectual control over records of enduring value.

Archives are kept permanently to preserve the past and to allow others to discover it. Materials can be in the form of files, papers, books, photographs, drawings, maps, films, and video and audio tapes. On a daily basis, Archivists are involved with methods of classification—indexing, cataloging, and listing this material so that staff and members of the public are able to find what they want without too much trouble.

Any medium containing recorded information can be part of the Archivist's responsibility, including letters, books, and other paper documents; photographs; blueprints; audiovisual materials; and computer records. These items also include historical documents, audiovisual materials, institutional records, works of art, coins, stamps, minerals, clothing, maps, living and preserved plants and animals, buildings, computer records, or historic sites. Any document that reflects transactions or procedures can be considered a record. Records may be saved on any medium, including paper, film, videotape, audiotape, electronic disk, or computer, or they may be copied onto some other format to protect the original, and to make them more accessible to researchers who use the records.

The archivist selects, arranges, describes, and ensures the long-term preservation of these records, and helps researchers who wish to use them. In addition, the Archivist prepares descriptions and reference aids for the archives, such as lists, indexes, guides, bibliographies, abstracts, microfilmed copies, and cross-indexes materials.

The Government Archivist also develops and implements procedures for the acquisition, processing, and preservation of archival materials, and tries to obtain materials available in libraries, private collections, or other sources. In addition, more senior Archivists also carry out traditional management tasks such as overseeing budgets, staff, and strategy. The Government Archivist is concerned with a few records important enough to be kept for a long time, including paper, film, electronic records, photographs, video and sound recordings, computer tapes, video disks, unpublished letters, diaries, and manuscripts. Archival records are the products of everyday activity, which are used for their administrative value and for purposes other than those for which they were created. (For example, Native Americans may use archival records to establish legal claims to land and privileges guaranteed by federal and state governments.)

Archivists may coordinate educational and public outreach programs, such as tours, workshops, lectures, and classes, and may work with government officials to administer plans and policies. They also may research topics or items relevant to their collections.

Archivists determine what portion of the vast amount of records maintained by the government agency for which they work should be made part of permanent historical holdings, and which of these records should be put on exhibit. They maintain records in their original arrangement according to the creator's organizational scheme, and describe records to facilitate retrieval.

At the same time, government archives must be protected against theft and damage, so they are kept in secure rooms under optimal storage conditions. This means that Archivists have to be familiar with modern techniques regarding preservation, pest control, and fire protection. Because paper's high acidity can trigger natural disintegration, the Archivist must continually restore these records. As modern Archivists incorporate technology into their work, more records can be stored and exhibited electronically.

Some Government Archivists are expected to inspect archives on site (in old buildings and churches, for example) or be involved in talks and exhibitions.

Salaries

Salaries, benefits, and working conditions vary to an incredible degree, from low-paying jobs with small, local archives,

to the federal National Archives in Washington, D.C. Average salaries in the federal government are usually higher than those in local and state organizations. The average annual salary for Government Archivists ranges from a low of $20,010 for local government positions to a high of more than $69,706 for federal government supervisory archival positions. Most Government Archivists have civil service status.

Employment Prospects

Nearly a third of all Archivists work in federal, state, and local government, and about half of those jobs are in the Washington, D.C., area. Most federal Archivists work for the National Archives and Records Administration; others manage military archives in the U.S. Department of Defense. All state governments have archival or historical records sections that also hire Archivists.

Archivists sometimes begin their careers on grant-funded projects; however, many eventually achieve long-term job stability. As qualified applicants outnumber job openings, experts expect competition for these positions to be aggressive. Those with the best chance of landing a good Government Archivist job are graduates with solid computer skills and master's degrees in both library science and history, with a concentration in archives or records management.

The job situation for Government Archivists is expected to improve as organizations emphasize establishing archives and organizing records and information on the local and state level, and as the public becomes more interested in science, art, history, and technology. While Archivists tend not to leave their jobs once they find one, the need to replace workers who leave the occupation or stop working will create some additional job openings.

Advancement Prospects

Eligibility for promotion in many civil service jobs is based on experience, and qualified workers must take written and oral tests for advanced positions. Many local and state government archives are very small, with limited promotion opportunities; federal archives, however, may offer more opportunities for Archivists interested in advancement.

Some advanced Archivist positions (such as director of a large state or federal archive) may require a doctorate in history, library science, or a related field.

Archivists can choose to continue their education by attending a variety of meetings, conferences, and workshops sponsored by archival, historical, and museum associations, or by attending in-house training sessions sponsored by the National Archives.

Education and Training

There are many ways to become an Archivist. Students with postgraduate work in history may combine that degree with practical training or course work offered by a professional archival association. Others who have a master's degree in library and information science can add an archives special-ization. Still others may obtain a master's degree in archival science/studies (M.A.S.). Training and experience in con-ducting research are also helpful.

Most entry-level Government Archivist positions require an undergraduate and a graduate degree, which includes completion of a practicum and in-depth archival coursework. Many Archivists work in archives or museums while com-pleting their formal education to gain experience that they'll need when they begin to look for a job after graduation.

A few institutions offer master's degrees in archival stud-ies, featuring courses in basic archival theory, methods, and practice. In addition, library programs may offer courses that include records management, aspects of library and information science, management, and historical and research methods. More and more Archivists are combining a double master's degree in history and library science. About 65 colleges and universities offer courses or practical training in archival science as part of history, library sci-ence, or another discipline.

Special Requirements

The Academy of Certified Archivists offers voluntary certi-fication for Archivists, who must have experience in the field and pass an examination offered by the Academy before being certified.

Experience, Skills, and Personality Traits

Federal archives require professional experience in archival science or a directly related field of work (such as history) that involved the collection, appraisal, analysis, or synthesis of information having historical or archival values.

Archivists should be committed to heritage, interested in new technology, and able to explain complex ideas in sim-ple terms. They should be comfortable in working with the public and good team players, able to manage budgets, and be logical thinkers (for sorting activities). It is also impor-tant that Archivists be sensitive to the confidential nature of some material.

Unions and Associations

Government Archivists can belong to a variety of trade asso-ciations that provide educational guidance, support, confer-ences and information to members, such as the Society of American Archivists.

Tips for Entry

1. Consider an internship while you're still in school, such as with the National Archives and Records Administration (NARA, 8601 Adelphi Road, Room 1200, College Park, MD 20740-6001).
2. Look for job ads in the Society of American Archivists' on-line employment bulletin (www.archivists.org/employment/index.asp).
3. Attend the annual convention of the Society of Amer-ican Archivists (SAA) in late summer, or check job boards at the placement service listing library-related jobs at annual ALA conventions.
4. Jobs in most federal libraries require that you establish civil service eligibility. Contact the Office of Personnel Management (OPM) at www.usajobs.opm.gov for help. Federal jobs that don't need to hire through OPM include the U.S. Foreign Service, the judicial and leg-islative branches of government, the Library of Con-gress, the National Science Foundation, the United Nations Secretariat, the U.S. Postal Service, and others.
5. To locate federal job openings around the world, con-tact OPM's Career America Connection at (912) 757-3000 or (202) 606-2700, or check out the federal jobs website at www.fedworld.gov/jobs/jobsearch.html.
6. Check daily job postings on "Hot Jobs Online" at the website of the American Library Association (www.ala.org) or other websites that list library job postings, such as: http://www.libraryjobpostings.org.
7. Subscribe to archival journals and periodicals to keep current with latest classified ads and trends, such as the SAA *Employment Bulletin,* the *Archival Outlook,* the *American Archivist,* or the *American Libraries* magazine.

GOVERNMENT DOCUMENTS LIBRARIAN

CAREER PROFILE

Duties: Locate, evaluate, and organize information published by government bodies

Alternate Title(s): Government Documents Information Specialist

Salary Range: $24,510 to $66,590+

Employment Prospects: Good

Advancement Prospects: Good

Best Geographical Location(s): Most positions are available in larger governmental institutions in cities, but job openings are available throughout the United States

Prerequisites:

Education or Training—Master's of library science is required

Experience—An internship in a government documents collection is excellent preparation for a position as Government Documents Librarian

Special Skills and Personality Traits—Flexibility; patience; the ability to work with details; statistical ability; computer knowledge

CAREER LADDER

```
┌─────────────────────────────────┐
│   Library Director or Government │
│   Documents Librarian in a       │
│   Larger Government Institution  │
└─────────────────────────────────┘

┌─────────────────────────────────┐
│   Government Documents           │
│   Librarian                      │
└─────────────────────────────────┘

┌─────────────────────────────────┐
│   Assistant Government Documents │
│   Librarian, or Entry Level      │
└─────────────────────────────────┘
```

Position Description

Government Documents Librarians work in federal and state libraries and archives, specializing in locating, evaluating and organizing information published by government bodies. They play a vital role in preserving the record of government action and decision making, and in the world of academic and institutional research. Both published and unpublished government information appears in print, CD-ROM, on-line, and multimedia formats. Libraries that collect and provide access to government documents do so through Internet access, by purchasing it through government printing offices or commercial book dealers that sell government publications, or through membership in depository library programs, acquiring information from governments without charge. Depositories agree to make this information available to the entire community for free. The Federal Depository Library Program is the depository program of the United States Government. Other programs are for documents of the different state governments and for those of foreign countries.

Government Documents Librarians manage the depository collections and make sure that library staff and users follow the rules for such programs. They evaluate and select documents, reference works, and Internet resources that are not provided as a part of the library's depository programs.

The government documents section of a library is also usually responsible for maps and geographic information systems. An important part of their work is the processing of documents, because they are classified according to unique schemes contained in the Superintendent of Documents Classification System (SUDOC). Librarians must be familiar with this system and work closely with the cataloging department to ensure that they follow the rules.

Most government documents are excluded from commercial reference works, so the Government Documents Librarian is responsible for providing an invaluable reference service including reference desk, telephone, and electronic mail services, as well as user and staff education classes. The Librarian must be willing to design and implement educational and outreach programs in order to inform users about the services and resources available.

Salaries

Salaries for this position vary a great deal depending on specific job responsibilities and the location of the library. Beginning full-time Government Documents Librarians with a master's degree in library and information studies accredited by the ALA but with no professional experience can expect a salary range of $30,126 to $37,580; with experience, the salary may surpass $66,590.

Employment Prospects

The U.S. Government Printing Office states that most U.S. federal information is now available electronically, but there are still more than 1,200 depository libraries helping to disseminate this information and ensure free access. More and more libraries are recognizing the need to provide information specialists to help patrons with statistical datasets, geographic information systems, and electronic access to government information. While there may be fewer positions specifically described as "government information librarians," positions are still readily available for people qualified in the area of government information, especially if the candidate is familiar with the use of statistical datasets.

Advancement Prospects

Eligibility for promotion in many civil service jobs is based on experience, and qualified workers take written and oral tests for advanced positions. Government Documents Librarians can move into administrative positions such as department head, library director, or chief information officer, with more experience and administrative skills, knowledge of automated systems, and additional training. Advancement opportunities are better in larger government operations.

Education and Training

Most Government Documents Librarian positions require a master of library science (M.L.S.) degree, preferably from a school accredited by the American Library Association (ALA). Undergraduate degrees in almost any subject area are appropriate.

Most M.L.S. programs take one to two years to complete and include courses in the foundations of library and information science, including the history of books and printing, intellectual freedom and censorship, and the role of libraries and information in society. Other basic courses cover material selection and processing, the organization of information, reference tools and strategies, and user services. Courses are adapted to educate Librarians to use new resources brought about by advancing technology such as on-line reference systems, Internet search methods, and automated circulation systems.

Computer-related coursework is an important part of an M.L.S. degree. Some programs offer interdisciplinary degrees combining technical coursework in information science with traditional training in library science. Librarians participate in continuing training once they are on the job to keep abreast of new information systems brought about by changing technology.

Experience, Skills, and Personality Traits

The ability to accept and work with change is one of the most important characteristics of a Government Documents Librarian. Other characteristics include patience, the ability to work with details, statistical ability, and computer knowledge.

Unions and Associations

Government Documents Librarians are civil service employees, and thus do not belong to unions. However, they can join a variety of trade associations that provide educational guidance, support, conferences, and information to members. These might include the National Association of Government Archives and Records Administrators, the American Library Association (ALA), the American Society for Information Science, or the Special Libraries Association.

Tips for Entry

1. Make contacts. Join professional organizations for Librarians to provide a network through which you may hear about job opportunities.
2. E-mail discussion groups such as LIBJOBS and LISJOBS are a good source for job postings. Topical groups are also a good place for finding advertisements in a particular field of librarianship. For example, Web4Lib often receives library webmaster-type job postings.
3. Check out the placement service that lists library-related jobs at annual ALA conventions.
4. Look for jobs on the Internet, such as on www.Lisjobs. com. Check daily job postings on "Hot Jobs Online" at the website of the American Library Association (www.ala.org), or other Internet websites that list library job postings, such as www.libraryjobpostings. org. Visit the Association for Library and Information Science Education website, which has links to all library schools, each of which has state and national employment listings (www.alise.org), or the American Society of Information Science website job line (www. asis.org/Jobline).
5. *Jobs for Librarians and Information Professionals* is a comprehensive guide to on-line job resources for librarians and information professionals.
6. Subscribe to major library trade publications, such as *Library Journal* and *American Libraries*.

7. To locate federal job openings around the world, contact OPM's Career America Connection at (912) 757-3000 or (202) 606-2700, or check out the federal jobs website at www.fedworld.gov/jobs/jobsearch.html.

8. Jobs in most federal libraries require that you establish civil service eligibility. Contact the Office of Personnel Management (OPM) at www.usajobs.opm.gov for help. Federal jobs that don't need to hire through OPM include the U.S. Foreign Service, the judicial and legislative branches of government, the Library of Congress, the National Science Foundation, the United Nations Secretariat, the U.S. Postal Service, and others.

GOVERNMENT LIBRARY TECHNICIAN

CAREER PROFILE

Duties: Help clients access library or information center materials, and help locate, buy, catalog, and circulate materials

Alternate Title(s): Library Assistant, Media Aide, Library Technical Assistant

Salary Range: $14,410 to $38,000+

Employment Prospects: Excellent

Advancement Prospects: Excellent

Best Geographical Location(s): Government libraries throughout the country use Library Technicians

Prerequisites:

Education or Training—High school diploma is required; an associate's degree in liberal arts or library technical services with one or more years of library experience is preferred; diploma from library technician course acceptable

Experience—Several years of experience working in a library is helpful; computer skills are needed for many jobs

Special Skills and Personality Traits—Good people skills; attention to detail; neatness; organizational skills; aptitude for computers; good English writing and speaking skills; willingness to attend conferences and workshops; willingness to learn new skills

CAREER LADDER

```
┌─────────────────────────────┐
│         Librarian           │
└─────────────────────────────┘

┌─────────────────────────────┐
│     Library Technician      │
└─────────────────────────────┘

┌─────────────────────────────┐
│        Entry Level          │
└─────────────────────────────┘
```

Position Description

Government Library Technicians help clients access information throughout the federal, state, and local government library system, primarily with the federal government (primarily the U.S. Department of Defense and the Library of Congress). Typically, a Library Technician in a government library spends most time coding, searching, shelving, shifting, shelf reading, and sorting library publications; carrying out circulation or registration duties or both; preparing a variety of library materials in processing new acquisitions; and performing a variety of other detailed, nonroutine, or clerical duties.

Technicians usually work with a librarian on a range of duties. Library Technicians at a government library must provide quick reference information, reshelve books, implement programs, design or maintain webpages, and provide technical support to library or information center clients.

Technicians also compile lists of government-related books, periodicals, articles, and audiovisual materials; analyze collections; and recommend materials.

Library Technicians are assuming greater responsibilities, in some cases taking on tasks previously performed by Librarians. Depending on the employer, Library Technicians can have other titles, such as library technical assistant or media aide. Library Technicians direct library users to standard references, organize and maintain periodicals, prepare volumes for binding, handle interlibrary loan requests, prepare invoices, perform routine cataloging and coding of library materials, retrieve information from computer databases, and supervise support staff.

Library Technicians in a government library perform circulation desk duties, including issuing library cards, checking collection materials in and out, collecting fines, and handling complaints. They also perform specialized and routine clerical tasks such as payroll preparation, data entry, preparing reports and payroll information, ordering materials and supplies, collecting money, cleaning and repairing damaged materials, and answering the telephone, providing advice, and directing calls.

Technicians who prepare library materials may sit at desks or computer terminals for long periods and can develop headaches or eyestrain from working with video display terminals. Some duties, like calculating circulation statistics, can be repetitive and boring. Others, such as performing computer searches using local and regional library networks and cooperatives, can be interesting and challenging. Library Technicians may lift and carry books and climb ladders to reach high stacks.

Salaries

Salaries of Library Technicians in the federal government averaged $36,788 in 2003. Median annual earnings of Library Technicians in local government were $23,310 in 2002. Salaries for this position vary a great deal depending on the responsibilities and location of the library.

Employment Prospects

Employment of Library Technicians in government libraries is expected to grow about as fast as the average for all occupations through 2012, as computerization of these libraries means that Technicians can now take over many tasks formerly performed only by librarians. However, tighter budgets and cutbacks in many government libraries may slow growth. Some job openings will occur when Library Technicians transfer to other fields or leave the labor force.

Advancement Prospects

Library Technicians in government libraries can be promoted to positions with extra responsibilities, or Technicians can assume more responsibility by moving from a local or state library into a federal library, where more opportunities exist.

Education and Training

Training requirements for Library Technicians vary, from a high school diploma to specialized postsecondary training. Library Technicians need at least a high school diploma and perhaps a diploma from a Library Technician course; some

Technicians also have an associate's or bachelor's degree. Some two-year colleges offer an associate of arts degree in library technology, with courses including both liberal arts and library-related study. Students learn about library and media organization and operation, and how to order, process, catalog, locate, and circulate library materials and work with library automation. Libraries and associations offer continuing education courses to keep Technicians abreast of new developments in the field.

Some government libraries hire individuals with work experience or other training, while others train inexperienced workers on the job; still others require that Technicians have an associate's or bachelor's degree.

Given the widespread use of technology in libraries, computer skills are of the utmost importance.

Experience, Skills, and Personality Traits

Library Technicians must be committed to working with people and have the ability to pay close attention to details; neatness; organizational skills, aptitude for computers; good English writing and speaking skills; willingness to attend conferences and workshops; and a willingness to learn new skills.

Unions and Associations

Librarian Technicians working in government libraries can join a variety of trade associations that provide support and information to members. These might include the Library Assistants and Technicians Group, the American Society for Information Science, the American Library Association, or the Special Libraries Association.

Tips for Entry

1. Information on getting a job as a Library Technician with the federal government may be obtained from the Office of Personnel Management at (912) 757-3000 or (800) 877-8339. Information is also available on the Internet at www.usajobs.opm.gov.

2. Information about requirements and applications for a job at the Library of Congress can be obtained from the Human Resources Office, Library of Congress, 101 Independence Avenue, SE, Washington, DC 20540.

3. State library agencies can furnish information on requirements for Technicians, and general information about career prospects in the state. Several of these agencies maintain job hotlines that report openings for Library Technicians.

GOVERNMENT LIBRARIAN

CAREER PROFILE

Duties: Assist patrons, manage staff, select and purchase materials, prepare new materials, supervise assistants, manage technology

Alternate Title(s): Information Specialist

Salary Range: $24,510 to $70,238+

Employment Prospects: Good

Advancement Prospects: Good

Best Geographical Location(s): Because government libraries are found throughout the country, all locations may hold employment possibilities

Prerequisites:

Education or Training—Master's degree in library or information science (M.L.S.)

Experience—Student internship in another library or volunteer experience is helpful

Special Skills and Personality Traits—Good people skills; detail-oriented; flexibility; good written and verbal communication skills

CAREER LADDER

```
┌─────────────────────────────────┐
│   Government Library Director    │
└─────────────────────────────────┘

┌─────────────────────────────────┐
│      Government Librarian        │
└─────────────────────────────────┘

┌─────────────────────────────────┐
│       Assistant Librarian        │
└─────────────────────────────────┘
```

Position Description

Librarianship is fundamentally a service profession. Most Government Librarians juggle many different duties and projects, including working at the reference desk, helping with research, conducting training sessions, and supervising staff. Most library work involves organizing, such as cataloging and classifying materials or organizing projects. In addition, Librarians must increasingly combine traditional duties with tasks involving quickly changing technology.

Librarians help government employees find information and use it effectively for personal and professional purposes, so they must know a great deal about scholarly and public information sources. They also must follow trends related to publishing, computers, and the media to effectively oversee the selection and organization of library materials. They manage staff and develop and direct information programs and systems for the public to ensure that information is organized to meet users' needs.

Most Government Librarian positions incorporate three aspects of library work: user services, technical services, and administrative services. Even Librarians specializing in one of these areas perform other responsibilities. Librarians in user services work with the public to help them find the information they need. Librarians in technical services acquire and prepare materials for use and often do not deal directly with the public. Librarians in administrative services oversee the management and planning of libraries, negotiate contracts for services, materials, and equipment, supervise library employees, perform public relations and fund-raising duties, prepare budgets, and direct activities to ensure that everything functions properly.

In small government libraries or information centers, Librarians usually handle all aspects of the work, including keeping up with current literature and other available resources, and selecting materials from publishers, wholesalers, and distributors. Librarians prepare new materials by classifying them by subject matter, and describe books and other library materials so they are easy to find. They supervise assistants who prepare cards, computer records, or other access tools that direct users to resources. In large libraries, Librarians often specialize in a single area, such as acquisitions, cataloging, bibliography, reference, special collections, or administration. Teamwork is increasingly important to ensure quality service to the public.

Librarians also compile lists of books, periodicals, articles, and audiovisual materials on particular subjects, analyze collections, and recommend materials. They collect and organize books, pamphlets, manuscripts, and other materials in a specific field, such as rare books, genealogy, or music.

Many libraries have access to remote databases and maintain their own computerized databases. The widespread use of automation in libraries makes database searching skills important to Librarians, who develop and index databases and help train users to develop searching skills for the information they need. The Internet also is expanding the amount of available reference information. Librarians must know how to use these resources in order to locate information.

Salaries

The average annual salary for Government Librarians ranges from a low (for local government libraries) of $24,510 to $70,238 for federal government nonsupervisory, supervisory, and managerial positions.

Employment Prospects

Employment of Government Librarians is expected to grow about as fast as the average for all occupations over the 2004–12 period. The increasing use of computerized information storage and retrieval systems continues to contribute to slow growth in the demand for Librarians. Computerized systems make cataloging easier, so that library technicians can now handle the job. In addition, many libraries are equipped for users to access library computers directly from their homes or offices. These systems allow users to bypass Librarians and conduct research on their own. However, Librarians are needed to manage staff, help users develop database searching techniques, address complicated reference requests, and define users' needs. The need to replace Librarians as they retire will result in numerous additional job openings.

Advancement Prospects

Eligibility for promotion in many civil service jobs is based on experience, and qualified workers take written and oral tests for advanced positions. Experienced Librarians can advance to administrative positions, such as department head, library director, or chief information officer.

Education and Training

The federal government requires a master's degree in library science (M.L.S.) for most Government Librarian positions. Although many colleges and universities offer M.L.S. programs, the government prefers graduates of schools accred-ited by the American Library Association. Most M.L.S. programs require a bachelor's degree; any liberal arts major is appropriate. Computer-related coursework is an increasingly important part of an M.L.S. degree. Some programs offer interdisciplinary degrees combining technical coursework in information science with traditional training in library science.

Some states require certification of public Librarians employed in municipal, county, or regional library systems. Librarians participate in continuing training once they are on the job to keep abreast of new information systems brought about by changing technology.

Experience, Skills, and Personality Traits

Librarians must be able to communicate effectively with patrons, as they answer questions and provide reference help. Being personable and able to work well with others is a plus. In addition, excellent organizational and computer skills are important, along with curiosity, attention to detail, and a love of books, research, and education.

Unions and Associations

Librarians working in government libraries do not belong to unions, but they can join a variety of trade associations that provide educational guidance, support, conferences, and information to members. These might include the American Library Association, the American Society for Information Science, or the Special Libraries Association.

Tips for Entry

1. Get experience. If you are attending library school, take every opportunity available to work as a student assistant in the university libraries, do a practicum or internship in another library, or volunteer in the type of library which interests you most. Library administrators are likely to select a candidate with some relevant experience over one with none.

2. Jobs in most federal libraries require that you establish civil service eligibility. Contact the Office of Personnel Management (OPM) at www.usajobs.opm.gov for help. Federal jobs that don't need to hire through OPM include the U.S. Foreign Service, the judicial and legislative branches of government, the Library of Congress, the National Science Foundation, the United Nations Secretariat, the U.S. Postal Service, and others.

3. To locate federal job openings around the world, contact OPM's Career America Connection at (912) 757-3000 or (202) 606-2700, or check out the federal jobs website at www.fedworld.gov/jobs/jobsearch.html.

4. Subscribe to library journals and periodicals, such as *American Libraries* magazine.

5. Check daily job postings on "Hot Jobs Online" at the website of the American Library Association (www.

ala.org) or other Internet websites that list library job postings, such as www.libraryjobpostings.org, the American Society of Information Science website job line (http://www.asis.org/Jobline), or the Association for Library and Information Science Education (ALISE) website, which has links to all library schools, each of which has state and national employment listings: www.alise.org.

6. Attend library conventions or conferences and check job boards, such as the placement service that lists library-related jobs at annual ALA conventions.

LAW LIBRARIAN
(GOVERNMENT LAW LIBRARY)

CAREER PROFILE

Duties: Develop and direct information programs and systems at the federal, state, court, or county law library to ensure information is organized to meet users' needs; provide reference help for attorneys and judges; prepare and shelve new materials; supervise technicians

Alternate Title(s): None

Salary Range: $38,215 to $100,000+

Employment Prospects: Good

Advancement Prospects: Good

Best Geographical Location(s): All locations may hold employment possibilities

Prerequisites:

Education or Training—Master's degree in library science; a law degree is also helpful (and sometimes required)

Experience—Experience working in a law library is helpful

Special Skills and Personality Traits—Good people skills and superior organizational skills; attention to detail; flexibility; good written and verbal communication skills

CAREER LADDER

```
┌─────────────────────────────┐
│     Law Library Director     │
└─────────────────────────────┘

┌─────────────────────────────┐
│        Law Librarian         │
└─────────────────────────────┘

┌─────────────────────────────┐
│   Law Librarian Technician   │
└─────────────────────────────┘
```

Position Description

Law Librarians in government libraries fill many of the same positions that can be found at other libraries, handling technical services, cataloging, public services, collection development, and reference services. The staff members of a law library serve the larger organization—the court or governmental unit.

Government law libraries are found in every imaginable setting, including state, federal, county, and court libraries. Other government law libraries include prisons and those serving the needs of government agencies. All are supported with tax dollars and are therefore open to the public. The primary users of the government libraries are lawyers, judges, and other government officials, although the general public is entitled to use the library's services as well.

The Law Librarian working at a government facility will typically do a bit of everything, such as gather legal information (such as case law or statutes) that a judge or lawyer needs for a particular case being tried at that court. Many of these court libraries have been in existence for some time and have a sizable print collection, but time and funding may dictate the increased usage of electronic resources.

Most Law Librarians juggle many different duties and projects. In a given week, a Librarian might do research for a clerk or partner, serve on a committee, edit a newsletter, or conduct a training session. Other duties might include cataloging some books (in smaller libraries), supervising paraprofessionals, checking in serials, or negotiating contracts.

An essential feature of library work is organizing. Librarians catalog and classify material, and organize information and projects. Librarians also tend to think institutionally about policies and procedures—for example, setting up a check-out system for a court library that is likely to be used by all the attorneys and judges. They build and arrange an organization's information resources, which usually are limited to subjects of special interest to the organization. These special Librarians can provide vital information services by preparing abstracts and indexes of current periodicals, organizing bibliographies, or analyzing background information and preparing reports on areas of particular interest. Most Law Librarians are involved in setting library policy and making decisions about personnel and resources.

Salaries

Salaries for this position vary a great deal depending on specific job responsibilities and the location of the library. The average starting salary for a Law Librarian in a one-person library is about $38,215. The median for a director/chief Law Librarian is $63,636, but can surpass $100,000.

Employment Prospects

Law Librarians can apply for—and may even be recruited for—jobs in other parts of the country. It is often true that a Law Librarian needs to move in order to get a desired position. However, in larger cities there are plenty of opportunities with county, state, and court libraries, which usually are advertised and filled locally.

Advancement Prospects

Eligibility for promotion in many civil service jobs is based on experience, and qualified workers take written and oral tests for advanced positions. Experienced Librarians can advance to administrative positions, such as department head, library director, or chief information officer.

Education and Training

To qualify for virtually any professional job in a government law library, the Librarian usually must have a graduate degree in library science. Some law libraries hire lawyers with good research skills to work as reference Librarians; they pick up on-the-job knowledge about other library operations. Most jobs require a master's degree from an American Library Association (ALA)–accredited institution. The names of the degrees vary (B.M.L.S., M.L.I.S., M.S.I.S., M.L., M.A. in L.S.B.), but all reflect an appropriate entry-level educational requirement for careers in law librarianship.

Court librarians may or may not have law degrees. Almost 30 percent of all Law Librarians also have a J.D. or L.L.B. degree. If such a degree is required, most positions stipulate that this degree be earned from a law school accredited by the American Bar Association (ABA). Some

jobs state a preference for the law degree in addition to the requisite graduate degree in library science.

A law degree is less important for other positions in law libraries—for example, in cataloging, acquisitions, circulation, government documents, and computer services—although some people in those positions do have law degrees.

Experience, Skills, and Personality Traits

Law Librarians must be able to communicate effectively with attorneys and judges as they answer questions and provide reference help and be able to juggle a variety of research topics. Being personable and able to work well with others is a plus. Experience working in a law library is helpful.

Unions and Associations

Law Librarians working in government law libraries do not belong to unions, but they can belong to a variety of trade associations that provide educational guidance, support, conferences, and information to members. These might include the American Association of Law Libraries (AALL), the Special Libraries Association: Legal Division, the American Library Association, or the American Society for Information Science.

Tips for Entry

1. There are many jobs posted each year for Law Librarians. Jobs in law libraries are almost always advertised nationally, but jobs in court and county law libraries and firms may only be advertised locally.
2. Contact the placement committee of the AALL, which coordinates personal interviews at the association's annual meeting each July.
3. Check the job database on the AALL webpage (www. aallnet.org), which is updated regularly and includes jobs in all kinds of law libraries; in addition, check AALL chapter listservs and websites.
4. Check the job lists as advertised on the websites of the Special Library Association (www.sla.org) and the ALA (www.ala.org).
5. Jobs in most federal libraries require that you establish civil service eligibility. Contact the Office of Personnel Management (OPM) at www.usajobs.opm.gov for help. Federal jobs that don't need to hire through OPM include the U.S. Foreign Service, the judicial and legislative branches of government, the Library of Congress, the National Science Foundation, the United Nations Secretariat, the U.S. Postal Service, and others.
6. To locate federal job openings around the world, contact OPM's Career America Connection at (912) 757-3000 or (202) 606-2700, or check out the federal jobs website at www.fedworld.gov/jobs/jobsearch.html.

MEDICAL LIBRARIAN (GOVERNMENT HEALTH AGENCY)

CAREER PROFILE

Duties: Provide health information about new medical treatments, clinical trials and standard trials procedures, tests, and equipment to government employees and the public

Alternate Title(s): None

Salary Range: $45,000 to $100,000+

Employment Prospects: Good

Advancement Prospects: Good

Best Geographical Location(s): Washington, D.C., and surrounding areas (the location of most federal health-related agencies)

Prerequisites:

Education or Training—Graduate degree in library or information science

Experience—A background in science, health sciences, or allied health is helpful

Special Skills and Personality Traits—Strong oral and written communication skills; good interpersonal skills; solid computer skills

CAREER LADDER

```
┌─────────────────────────────────┐
│          Director of            │
│  Health Agency Medical Library  │
└─────────────────────────────────┘

┌─────────────────────────────────┐
│       Medical Librarian         │
│   (Government Health Agency)     │
└─────────────────────────────────┘

┌─────────────────────────────────┐
│    Medical Librarian, Assistant │
└─────────────────────────────────┘
```

Position Description

A Medical Librarian at a government health agency is responsible for retrieving, selecting, organizing, and disseminating health information to government workers and the public. Medical Librarians may evaluate advanced information technologies, teach users how to find health care information, and design and manage digital access. Medical Librarians in a health agency also provide general and subject reference assistance, develop and manage the collection, and supervise support staff. In addition, they must provide government workers and the public with the latest information on diseases, procedures, treatments, and research. Medical Librarians also select and maintain medical books, journals, and audiovisual materials.

Medical Librarians also must be familiar with key databases that cover biomedical literature, such as MEDLINE, a huge index of some 7 million articles published since 1966 that is the standard searching tool for medical literature, and Dialog, a database vendor that allows a user to search through numerous databases such as Biosis (abstracts of scientific articles) and Science Citation Index (abstracts of articles in diverse magazines and journals).

Salaries

Salaries vary according to the size and location of the health agency, the level of responsibility, and the length of employment. Salaries range from $45,000 to more than $100,000.

Employment Prospects

Employment of Medical Librarians in health agencies is especially strong as the need grows for organization amidst the technological information explosion. While smaller health agencies with medical libraries can be found throughout the United States, these special libraries tend to be located in the nation's capital or in larger cities; competition for these positions is therefore more competitive.

Advancement Prospects

There are a variety of opportunities for Medical Librarians in health agencies, depending on the interests and expertise of the individual Librarians. The more time, experience, and additional education an individual has, the better the advancement prospects. Because Medical Librarians have a number of marketable skills, they can move on to a variety of positions such as health agency website manager, medical informatics expert, chief information officer, or move into work as a community outreach coordinator for a public health agency.

Education and Training

The federal government requires a master's degree in library or information science from an ALA-accredited school or the equivalent in education and experience for Librarians who work in government agencies. Many government medical libraries in health agencies also require a background in science, health sciences, or allied health, or graduate courses in medical informatics or medical librarianship. A Medical Librarian should learn everything possible related to the medical field (for example, understanding biomedical references, principles of organization of information in the biomedical sciences, and on-line computer databases such as MEDLINE, from the National Library of Medicine.)

In addition, the National Library of Medicine offers an associate fellowship—a one year program for post-M.L.S. candidates interested in training for a leadership role in health science libraries.

Experience, Skills, and Personality Traits

Because Medical Librarians spend most of their days working with government employees and the public, strong interpersonal and communication skills are required. In addition, excellent organizational and computer skills are important, along with a solid background and interest in medicine or health-related issues. Librarians working in medical libraries need to be well organized with strong attention to detail. Because the Medical Librarian is expected to work with people from all walks of life and employees from different areas of government, the ability to communicate effectively is vital.

Unions and Associations

Medical Librarians working in government health agencies may belong to a variety of trade associations that provide educational guidance, support, conferences, and information to members. These might include the Medical Library Association, the American Library Association, the American Society for Information Science, or the Special Libraries Association.

Tips for Entry

1. Check out the job listings on the Medical Library Association website (www.mlanet.org/jobs/index.html).
2. Attend the annual May convention of the Medical Library Association and the annual American Library Association conventions to check jobs listings.
3. Check daily job postings on "Hot Jobs Online" at the website of the American Library Association (www.ala.org).
4. Subscribe to library journals and periodicals such as *American Libraries* magazine.
5. Investigate other websites that list library job postings, such as: http://www.libraryjobpostings.org; the ALISE website, which has links to all library schools, each of which has state and national employment listings (www.alise.org); or the job line at the website of the American Society of Information Science (http://www.asis.org/Jobline).

PUBLIC RECORDS INFORMATION BROKER

CAREER PROFILE

Duties: Search local, county, state, or federal public records (and occasionally on-line) for information about individuals, corporations, and property

Alternate Title(s): Independent Researcher

Salary Range: $45 to $85 per hour ($86,400 to $163,210 per year)

Employment Prospects: Excellent

Advancement Prospects: Good

Best Geographical Location(s): Public Record Information Brokers can be found throughout the United States

Prerequisites:

Education or Training—Master's degree in library science

Experience—Experience working in a public records office or county courthouse is helpful

Special Skills and Personality Traits—Research skills; organizational skills; computer literacy; ability to work well with others; ability to work well under pressure

CAREER LADDER

```
┌─────────────────────────────┐
│         Director of         │
│ Information Brokerage Firm  │
└─────────────────────────────┘

┌─────────────────────────────┐
│ Public Records Information  │
│           Broker            │
└─────────────────────────────┘

┌─────────────────────────────┐
│      Information Broker      │
└─────────────────────────────┘
```

Position Description

Public Records Information Brokers provide their clients with information about specific corporations, individuals, and properties by searching for public documents such as bankruptcy filings, professional licenses, vital statistics records (for birth, death, marriage, divorce, and adoption information), civil and criminal court records, property ownership records, tax liens, Uniform Commercial Code (UCC) filings, and vehicle registrations.

Legislation such as the federal Freedom of Information Act and state Public Records Act enable public access to government records. Public Records Information Brokers are familiar with methods of access to this information and can locate specific records among the abundance of information available.

Public Records Information Brokers can provide manual, telephone, and on-line research through access to research libraries and thousands of on-line databases from the U.S. and abroad. Large and small studies provide clients with instant education, comprehensive reports, or answers to specific questions. Information Brokers collect resources, not answers. This ability to know where to find specific public records information distinguishes Information Brokers from many others who collect facts, rather than learning where to find them again when needed. This allows Brokers to be flexible and not get bogged down in building elaborate databases.

While many commercial on-line and Internet systems offer specialized access to public records, much of what clients need still can only be found buried in county courthouse files, which can best be located through an established network of local researchers.

For example, an Information Broker specializing in public records might be hired by a prospective corporate buyer to search local, state, and federal court documents to uncover a corporation's structure, outstanding company debts, and availability of appropriate licenses and permits. The broker could also determine if the corporation has ever been cited by any state or federal agencies for violations or enforcement actions, and if the company has been involved in significant litigation.

Alternatively, a Public Records Information Broker could be hired by a citizens' group formed to investigate a rash of residents' illnesses. The Broker might be asked to learn more about a new power plant in the neighborhood, checking with federal and state agencies such as the Environmental Protection Agency, the Department of Transportation, and the Occupational Safety and Health Administration for compliance issues.

Small business owners sometimes hire Public Records Information Brokers to conduct preemployment screening for employees responsible for handling goods and cash, making sure that they don't have a history of theft or unsafe driving. The Broker could check criminal and driving records, as well as verify previous positions the applicant has held.

Public Records Information Brokers may be hired by parents checking the safety record of a prospective day care facility, checking with local and state authorities to see if the facility is properly licensed and hires employees free from a history of child-related crimes, and that the drivers have a clean safety record if the children will be driven on field trips. Professional screening of court and driving records can help assure parents that the day care center is safe for their child.

Freelance Public Records Information Brokering typically involves handling a single project with a deadline and a specific budget, although some Information Brokers work on a continuing basis. An Information Broker can expect to spend a great deal of time researching questions on CD-ROM databases or the Internet, either in the Broker's office or in libraries, courthouses, or government records depositories.

Salaries
An independent Public Records Information Broker may charge between $45 and $85 per hour, depending on the specific type of information being sought. However, many of the services and databases used by Information Brokers incur separate hourly fees, which must be deducted from the Broker's fee.

Employment Prospects
The demand for information in the public record continues to rise, and the sheer amount of available information creates a demand for information professionals who are adept at finding the correct data and presenting it in the client's desired format.

Other trends demonstrate the market for information brokering: as corporations downsize, for example, many people who have lost jobs are the same people who will wind up being hired to provide consulting or other services such as information brokering to the very organization that let them go.

Advancement Prospects
Often, Public Records Information Brokers initially work for an information brokerage, eventually leaving to set up their own independent public records consulting business.

As Information Brokers slowly build a business, it usually reaches the point where they realize they must focus on their business full time, as their client load increases and their responsibilities multiply.

Education and Training
Many Information Brokers have an advanced degree in library and information science, as well as some experience working with public records. Increasingly, Public Records Information Brokers specialists may have advanced degrees in an area related to law or government. Extra classes in information brokering, marketing, and business planning are also helpful.

Experience, Skills, and Personality Traits
The most important attribute of the Public Records Information Broker is excellent research skills, along with organizational skills and computer literacy. Because searching for information requires the ability to explain a subject in terms that both a human and a computer can understand, excellent word skills are vital for Information Brokers: They must identify not just appropriate terms but also synonyms and the likelihood of any of those terms appearing with other terms.

Personal attributes include developing the ability to serve as a tactful intermediary between an information source and a client, knowing how to ask questions effectively, and knowing how to charm the information from a source without being threatening.

Because the Information Broker usually runs an independent business, the ability to work well with customers is extremely important. Running a business also requires a separate set of skills over and above those needed for the information profession, including bookkeeping and general office skills, marketing, advertising, and self-motivation.

Unions and Associations
Public Records Information Brokers may belong to a variety of trade associations that provide educational guidance, support, conferences, and information to members. These might include the Association for Information Professionals, the Society for Competitor Intelligence Professionals, the Public Record Retrievers Network, the American Society for Information Science and Technology, the Library and Information Technology Association, or the National Information Standards Organization.

Tips for Entry
1. Before going into business for yourself, consider first working for an information brokerage firm. Visit the *Burwell World Directory of Information Brokers* (www.burwellinc.com) to find out how to locate the directory, which lists more than 1,800 information brokerages.

2. After you have a few years of experience, consider striking out on your own; first, develop a comprehensive business and marketing plan; and design your company's logo.

3. Set up a website to advertise your services as an Information Broker.

4. Contact local businesses or law firms and present your résumé, discussing how your skills may benefit the company.

5. Consider a listing in the Burwell directory, which lists information brokers from around the world. It is considered the world's most comprehensive guide to independent information experts.

6. Sign up for classes on information brokering, marketing, and business planning.

7. Check the Information Professionals Institute seminar schedule and the seminar schedules at major on-line conferences, such as National Online Meeting (NOM) or Online World for additional classes, and check out continuing education seminars at local universities or community colleges.

8. Review *The Information Brokers Handbook,* available in bookstores.

PUBLIC POLICY INFORMATION BROKER

CAREER PROFILE

Duties: Search local, county, state, or federal public records (and occasionally on-line) for information related to public policy

Alternate Title(s): Independent Researcher, Information Professional

Salary Range: $45 to $85 per hour

Employment Prospects: Excellent

Advancement Prospects: Good

Best Geographical Location(s): Public Policy Information Brokers can be found throughout the United States

Prerequisites:

Education or Training—Master's in library science

Experience—Experience working in a public records office or county courthouse is helpful

Special Skills and Personality Traits—Research skills; organizational skills; computer literacy; ability to work well with others; ability to work well under pressure

CAREER LADDER

```
┌─────────────────────────────────┐
│         Director of             │
│  Information Brokerage Firm      │
└─────────────────────────────────┘

┌─────────────────────────────────┐
│  Public Policy Information Broker │
└─────────────────────────────────┘

┌─────────────────────────────────┐
│        Information Broker         │
└─────────────────────────────────┘
```

Position Description

Information Brokers can serve individual government agencies at a federal, state, or local level. These agencies frequently need examples of policies from other jurisdictions to help develop their own. Public Policy Information Brokers collect these examples through on-line research as well as primary interviews with similar agencies.

Government agencies often need technology trends and specific data to design their information technology systems and workplace situations. Public Policy Information Brokers can research and identify what works in similar agencies, research human resource policy and procedures, and collect benchmark examples. Public Policy Information Brokers specialize in collecting resources. This ability to know where to find specific public policy information distinguishes these Information Brokers from many others who collect facts, rather than learning where to find them again when needed. This allows Brokers to be flexible and not get bogged down in building elaborate databases. Then the Broker must be able to present information so that it is understandable and accessible to the client.

Although most government clients have access to on-line resources, many individuals discover that searching for information is a complicated and frustrating process. For this reason, many are only too glad to turn over the more complex parts of their information-seeking to professionals. For example, a state agency in the process of upgrading statewide data networks might hire a Public Policy Information Broker to conduct a literature search on the experience of other state agencies in the United States. The Information Broker would also search trade publications to identify technology trends and protocols, and locate vendors for equipment supply and planning, construction, and maintenance services.

Local governments considering new ordinances might hire a Broker to locate examples of similar ordinances in other jurisdictions, and identify resources in national organizations or regional governments.

Government human resource departments often require the help of Public Policy Information Brokers as they establish or revise their own policies relating to sexual or gender discrimination, disability access, acceptable Internet use, and so on. The Information Broker in this case would collect current legal writings and examples of successful policies in other governmental agencies, and contact public interest associations that offer pertinent background literature.

Public Policy Information Professionals often operate as temporary contractors or consultants, working through a public competitive bidding framework for jobs. Usually, freelance Public Policy Information Brokering involves a fixed project with a deadline and a specific budget, although some Information Brokers work on a continuing basis. An Information Broker can expect to spend a great deal of time researching questions on CD-ROM databases or the Internet, either in the Broker's office or in libraries, courthouses, or government records depositories.

Salaries

An independent Public Policy Information Broker may charge between $45 and $85 per hour, depending on the specific type of information being sought. However, many of the services and databases used by Information Brokers incur separate hourly fees, which must be deducted from the Broker's fee.

Employment Prospects

The demand for information to help determine public policy continues to rise, and the sheer amount of available information creates a demand for information professionals who are adept at finding the correct data, and presenting it in the client's desired format. An experienced librarian with research skills and computer know-how can turn those assets into a thriving business.

Advancement Prospects

While many Information Brokers start out working for a large firm, most eventually get to the point where they feel comfortable starting their own independent broker business.

Education and Training

Many Information Brokers have an advanced degree in library and information science, as well as some experience working with public records. Increasingly, these Information Brokers may have advanced degrees in some area related to law or government.

Experience, Skills, and Personality Traits

Information Brokers must be excellent problem solvers, talented at analyzing problems; when given questions or problems, the Broker must be able to identify not only the central piece of each problem, but the most likely way in which it can be solved by finding missing information. A Public Policy Information Broker must be able to assess information for quality, utility, and accuracy, and be able to organize information into patterns and relationships. Brokers must know how to read through scattered collections of information to sort it into related facts, and then use the related materials to discern trends and patterns.

Because the Information Broker is usually running an independent business, the ability to work well with customers is extremely important. Running a business also requires skills in bookkeeping, marketing, promotion, tax preparation, and office organization.

Unions and Associations

Public Policy Information Brokers may belong to a variety of trade associations that provide educational guidance, support, conferences, and information to members. These might include the Association for Information Professionals, the Society for Competitor Intelligence Professionals, the Public Record Retrievers Network, the American Society for Information Science and Technology, the Library and Information Technology Association, or the National Information Standards Organization.

Tips for Entry

1. Before going into business for yourself, consider first working for an information brokerage firm. Check out the *Burwell World Directory of Information Brokers* (www.burwellinc.com), which lists more than 1,800 information brokerage companies.
2. After you have a few years of experience, consider striking out on your own. Develop a comprehensive business and marketing plan; design your company's logo.
3. Set up a website to advertise your services as an Information Broker.
4. Contact government agencies and present your résumé, discussing how your skills may benefit the company.
5. Consider a listing in the Burwell directory, which lists information brokers from around the world. It is considered the world's most comprehensive guide to independent information experts.
6. Sign up for classes on information brokering, marketing, and business planning.
7. Check out the Information Professionals Institute seminar schedule and the seminar schedules at major on-line conferences, such as National Online Meeting (NOM) or Online World for additional classes, and check out continuing education seminars at local universities or community colleges.

K–12 LIBRARIES

LIBRARY CLERK (K–12 LIBRARY)

CAREER PROFILE

Duties: Register students and faculty patrons, work with students, sort and shelve books, issue and receive library materials

Alternate Title(s): Library Aide or Circulation Assistant

Salary Range: $14,800 to $18,000+

Employment Prospects: Excellent

Advancement Prospects: Good

Best Geographical Location(s): Elementary, middle, and high school public and private libraries throughout the country use Library Clerks

Prerequisites:

Education or Training—High school diploma; diploma from library clerk course

Experience—Secretarial experience helpful

Special Skills and Personality Traits—Interest in working with children; attention to detail; neatness; organizational skills; aptitude for computers; good English writing and speaking skills; willingness to learn new skills

CAREER LADDER

```
┌─────────────────────────────────────┐
│ Library Assistant or Library Technician │
│          (K–12 Library)              │
└─────────────────────────────────────┘

┌─────────────────────────────────────┐
│     Library Clerk (K–12 Library)     │
└─────────────────────────────────────┘

┌─────────────────────────────────────┐
│            Entry Level               │
└─────────────────────────────────────┘
```

Position Description

Library Clerks work with students and faculty, registering patrons to permit them to borrow books, periodicals, and other library materials. They may plan and conduct story hours; prepare presentations or after-school programs to school-age special interest groups; and set up displays related to children's programming. They may help select and answer questions about children's materials or recruit and coordinate schedules and duties of volunteers as needed.

In addition, the K–12 Library Clerk may open and close the library and assume responsibility for operating the library on evenings, Saturdays, or during the summer, as scheduled. They may work at the circulation desk and replace material in shelving areas, stacks, or files according to identification number and title.

Many Clerks use their typing and computer skills to process materials orders and to update library catalogs.

Salaries

Salaries for this position vary a great deal depending on the location and size of the K–12 library, but they range from a low of $14,800 to $18,000 and above.

Employment Prospects

Working as a Library Clerk in a K–12 setting is attractive to retirees and others who want a part-time schedule, and for this reason, there is a lot of movement into and out of the occupation, reflecting the limited investment in training and subsequent weak attachment to this occupation. Opportunities should be good for people interested in jobs as Library Clerks through 2012, according to the U.S. Bureau of Labor Statistics, since many openings will become available each year to replace workers who transfer to another occupation. Some positions become available as Library Clerks move upward within the library.

Efforts to contain costs may mean more hiring of support staff such as Library Clerks, which also means Clerks are taking on more responsibility. While school libraries are not usually directly affected by the ups and downs of the business cycle, some clerks may lose their jobs if there are cuts in the school budget.

Because school library support positions are advertised only locally, it is important to check the classified ad sections of newspapers. Many times, the on-line version will be more convenient than the print, because you can frequently search the classifieds by keyword. Ads are usually posted whenever a job comes open, and generally mention a title and brief description of the position.

Advancement Prospects

A Library Clerk can usually advance by transferring to a position with more responsibilities, either as a library assistant or technician. Advancement opportunities are better in larger school libraries and may be more limited in smaller ones. Most libraries fill office and administrative support vacancies by promoting individuals within their organization, so Library Clerks who acquire new skills, experience, and training improve their advancement opportunities.

Education and Training

A high school diploma is generally required for a position as a Library Clerk, and standard secretarial and computer skills are highly desirable. Library Clerks often learn the skills they need in high schools, business schools, and community colleges. Business education programs offered by these institutions typically include courses in typing, word processing, shorthand, business communications, records management, and office systems and procedures.

Additional training for Library Clerks usually takes place on the job under the guidance of a supervisor or an experienced library assistant or technician. Most Library Clerks continue to receive instruction on new procedures and library policies after their initial training ends.

Experience, Skills, and Personality Traits

Training or experience with children or early childhood education is helpful. It is very important for a Library Clerk in a K–12 setting to be able to capture and hold the attention of young children and to help children use computers. Experience with computers and good interpersonal skills are important. Because Library Clerks deal directly with students and faculty, a professional appearance and pleasant personality are important. A clear speaking voice and fluency in the English language also are essential, because these employees frequently use the telephone or public address systems.

Unions and Associations

Library Clerks working in school libraries may belong to a variety of trade associations that provide educational guidance, support, conferences, and information to members. These might include the Library Assistants and Technicians Group, the American Association of School Librarians (AASL), the American Library Association, the American Society for Information Science, or the Special Libraries Association.

Tips for Entry

1. Library Clerk jobs may be found in the classified section of your local newspaper, in either the print or on-line versions.
2. Visit local school libraries and speak with the principal or human resources director about possible jobs.
3. Take every opportunity available to get experience; volunteer in a college or university library (although any library experience is good). Library administrators are likely to prefer a candidate with some relevant experience.
4. Make contacts. Join various professional organizations for librarians and keep in touch with your library friends to provide a network through which you may hear about job opportunities.
5. Send out your résumé. Find out the name and address of every school library in your area where you might like to work (the telephone book is helpful; call to find out to whom to address your cover letter). When openings occur, administrators often pull out their collection of unsolicited résumés and contact the candidates.

LIBRARY ASSISTANT (K–12 LIBRARY)

CAREER PROFILE

Duties: Make library resources available to students and teachers, helping librarians and library technicians

Alternate Title(s): None

Salary Range: $14,410 to $38,000+

Employment Prospects: Excellent

Advancement Prospects: Good

Best Geographical Location(s): School libraries throughout the country use Library Assistants

Prerequisites:

Education or Training—High school diploma, with Library Technology Certificate or equivalent K–12 library experience; college degree helpful

Experience—Experience working in a library is helpful; computer skills are needed for many jobs

Special Skills and Personality Traits—Good people skills; attention to detail; neatness; organizational skills; aptitude for computers; good English writing and speaking skills; willingness to learn new skills

CAREER LADDER

```
┌─────────────────────────────────┐
│ Library Technician or Supervisor │
└─────────────────────────────────┘

┌─────────────────────────────────┐
│        Library Assistant         │
└─────────────────────────────────┘

┌─────────────────────────────────┐
│          Library Clerk           │
└─────────────────────────────────┘
```

Position Description

The role of the Library Assistant in a school library is to help the school librarian select and organize materials, as well as help students and teachers with research. Assistants also may coordinate and implement children's programming and services, such as story hours, and attend workshops and meetings to remain up-to-date in children's services issues, policies, and new techniques. They also need to keep current with children's library materials and services by reading catalogs, professional journals, and other literature. Assistants also may "pull" (remove from circulation) library materials that need to be mended, discarded, and/or replaced; process new library materials received for circulation; and maintain the school library's card catalog.

In addition, the Library Assistant helps the school library media specialist with class library schedules and scheduling, and helps train volunteers and new Library Assistants.

Salaries

Salaries for this position vary a great deal depending on the responsibilities and location of the school library, although workers with college degrees are likely to start at higher salaries and advance more easily than those without degrees. Average annual earnings of Library Assistants range from $14,410 to more than $38,000.

Employment Prospects

The job outlook is good, and there are many opportunities for flexible schedules; more than half of all Library Assistants have part-time schedules. Opportunities should be good for people interested in jobs as Library Assistants through 2012, since there is a lot of turnover in these positions. Many openings will become available each year to replace workers who transfer to another occupation or as Library Assistants are promoted within the library.

As school districts are forced to cut personnel to balance their budgets, this may mean more jobs for library support staff such as Library Assistants. School library support positions are almost always advertised only locally, so the best way to find these jobs is to check the classified ad sections of newspapers.

Advancement Prospects

A Library Assistant may be given more responsibilities or be promoted to the position of library technician after a certain period of time. Advancement opportunities are better in larger school libraries, and may be more limited in smaller ones. Library Assistants who acquire new skills, experience, and training improve their advancement opportunities. In some K–12 libraries, a college degree may be required for advancement to management positions.

Education and Training

Library Assistants in a K–12 library usually need only a high school diploma, since the school library personnel will provide any necessary training on the job.

Experience, Skills, and Personality Traits

Love of children, familiarity with computers, and good interpersonal skills are equally important. Because many Library Assistants deal directly with students and faculty, a professional appearance and pleasant personality are important. A clear speaking voice and fluency in the English language also are essential, because these employees frequently use the telephone or public address systems. Good spelling and computer literacy often are needed, particularly because most work involves considerable computer use.

Unions and Associations

Library Assistants working in academic libraries may belong to a variety of associations that provide educational guidance, support, conferences, and information to members. These might include the Library Assistants and Technicians Group, the American Association of School Librarians (AASL), the American Society for Information Science, the American Library Association, or the Special Libraries Association.

Tips for Entry

1. Jobs in this field may be found in the classified section of your local newspaper.
2. Take every opportunity available to get experience; volunteer in a library, since administrators are likely to select a candidate with some relevant experience over one with none.
3. Make contacts. Join various professional organizations for librarians and keep in touch with your library friends to provide a network through which you may hear about job opportunities.
4. Send out your résumé. Find out the name and address of every school library in your area where you might like to work (the telephone book is helpful; call to find out to whom to address your cover letter). When openings occur, administrators often pull out their collection of unsolicited résumés and contact the candidates.

CHILDREN'S LIBRARY TECHNICIAN

CAREER PROFILE

Duties: Help students and teachers access library or information center materials, and help locate, buy, catalog, and circulate materials

Alternate Title(s): Library Assistant, Media Aide, Library Technical Assistant

Salary Range: $14,410 to $38,000+

Employment Prospects: Excellent

Advancement Prospects: Excellent

Best Geographical Location(s): Larger cities may offer more possibilities, but children's school libraries throughout the country use Library Technicians

Prerequisites:

Education or Training—High school diploma is required; associate or bachelor's degree in liberal arts or library technical services with one or more years of library experience is preferred; diploma from library technician course acceptable

Experience—Experience working in a children's library is helpful

Special Skills and Personality Traits—Excellent computer skills; love of children and children's literature; attention to detail; neatness; organizational skills; aptitude for computers; good English writing and speaking skills; willingness to attend conferences and workshops; willingness to learn new skills

CAREER LADDER

```
┌─────────────────────────────┐
│     Children's Librarian     │
└─────────────────────────────┘

┌─────────────────────────────┐
│ Children's Library Technician │
└─────────────────────────────┘

┌─────────────────────────────┐
│         Entry Level          │
└─────────────────────────────┘
```

Position Description

Children's Library Technicians help their patrons access information and help find, buy, catalog, and circulate materials, and encourage and teach students to use the library and media center. Library Technicians also help teachers obtain instructional materials and assist students with special assignments.

Library Technicians usually work with a librarian, although in small libraries they may work on their own, juggling many different duties and projects, such as shelving books, providing reference help, organizing materials, and reading book reviews and publishers' catalogs to keep up with current literature and other available resources. Technicians in small libraries handle a range of duties, whereas those in larger K–12 school libraries usually specialize. They prepare computer records and other access tools that direct users to resources. In addition, Library Technicians may be involved in loaning books, films, pictures, maps, microforms, and videotapes. They must know where to locate specialized materials in the library, provide quick reference information, reshelve books, implement programs and library tours, and design or maintain the school library's web pages.

Technicians also compile lists of books, periodicals, articles, and audiovisual materials on particular subjects related to the areas in which students are studying; analyze collections; and recommend and organize books, pamphlets, manuscripts, and other materials.

As school libraries use more new technology, such as CD-ROM, the Internet, virtual libraries, and automated databases, the duties of school Library Technicians will continue to expand. Many Library Technicians are already beginning to assume greater responsibilities, taking on tasks previously performed by librarians. At the same time, increased automation has reduced the amount of clerical work Library Technicians perform.

In some school libraries, Library Technicians also are responsible for operating and maintaining audiovisual equipment such as projectors, tape recorders, and videocassette recorders. They are also called upon to design posters, bulletin boards, or displays.

Children's Library Technicians usually have the same workday schedule as classroom teachers, and similar vacation schedules.

Salaries

Salaries for this position vary a great deal depending on the size of the school library and whether it is located in an urban, suburban, or rural area. Median annual earnings of Children's Library Technicians were $21,770 in 2002; the lowest 10 percent earned less than $14,410, and the highest 10 percent earned more than $38,000.

Employment Prospects

Employment of school Library Technicians is expected to grow about as fast as the average for all occupations through 2012. Increasing use of computerized circulation and information systems should spur job growth; since computerized systems has made cataloging easier, Library Technicians can now handle these jobs. In addition, as school budgets tighten, some districts are hiring more Technicians and fewer librarians to staff their libraries.

Advancement Prospects

Library Technicians may begin their careers at the circulation desk of small school libraries, checking books in and out for students. After gaining experience, they may become responsible for storing and verifying information. As they advance, they may become involved in budget and personnel matters in their department. Some Library Technicians advance to supervisory positions and eventually are placed in charge of the day-to-day operation of their department.

Education and Training

For most school library positions, Technicians need at least a high school diploma; many also require a diploma from a library technician course; some technicians also have an associate or bachelor's degree. Some two-year colleges offer an associate of arts degree in library technology, in both liberal arts and library-related study. In these courses, students learn about library and media organization and operation, and how to order, process, catalog, locate, and circulate library materials and work with library automation. Libraries and associations offer continuing education courses to keep technicians abreast of new developments in the field.

Some school districts hire individuals with work experience or other training, while others train inexperienced workers on the job. Some libraries require that Technicians have an associate or bachelor's degree.

Experience, Skills, and Personality Traits

Library Technicians in a K–12 library need to feel a commitment to working with children and a love for children's literature. A thorough understanding of childhood development at different ages is also helpful.

Given the widespread use of technology in school libraries, computer experience is required for many jobs. An understanding of databases, library automation systems, online library systems, on-line public access systems, and circulation systems is valuable.

In addition, Library Technicians need the ability to pay close attention to details; neatness; organizational skills, good English writing and speaking skills; willingness to attend conferences and workshops, and willingness to learn new skills.

Unions and Associations

Librarian Technicians working in school libraries may belong to a variety of trade associations that provide educational guidance, support, conferences, and information to members. These might include the American Association for School Librarians, the Association for Library Service to Children, the Young Adult Library Services Association, and the American Library Association.

Tips for Entry

1. Jobs in this field may be found in the job listings for all related trade associations, such as the American Library Association, or in magazines such as *American Libraries.*
2. Check your local newspaper classified ads for job listings for Library Technicians in local school district libraries.
3. Check daily job postings on "Hot Jobs Online" at the website of the American Library Association (www.ala.org).
4. Attend library conventions or conferences and check job boards.
5. Check out the placement service that lists library-related jobs at annual ALA conventions.
6. Investigate other websites that list library job postings, such as: http://www.libraryjobpostings.org.
7. Visit the ALISE website, which has links to all library schools, each of which has state and national employment listings (www.alise.org).
8. Visit the American Society of Information Science website job line (http://www.asis.org/Jobline).

CHILDREN'S LIBRARIAN

CAREER PROFILE

Duties: Provide reference and reading guidance to children; develop and maintain the children's collection; write book reviews; establish and maintain working relationships with schools; develop and implement programs

Alternate Title(s): Children's Services Manager

Salary Range: $24,510 to $66,590

Employment Prospects: Good

Advancement Prospects: Good

Best Geographical Location(s): School districts and public libraries throughout the country have openings for Children's Librarians

Prerequisites:

Education or Training—Master's of library science or a master's degree with a specialty in children's literature or children's libraries

Experience—Teaching, experience with children, and computer experience can be very helpful

Special Skills and Personality Traits—People-oriented; good storyteller; comfortable with technology; knowledgeable about childhood developmental stages; strong management and public relations skills

CAREER LADDER

```
┌─────────────────────────────┐
│  Children's Library Director │
└─────────────────────────────┘

┌─────────────────────────────┐
│     Children's Librarian     │
└─────────────────────────────┘

┌─────────────────────────────┐
│ Assistant Children's Librarian │
└─────────────────────────────┘
```

Position Description

A Children's Librarian has total responsibility for the libraries in elementary, middle, or high schools, and in public libraries. Experts in children's literature, they assist young patrons, manage staff, read book reviews and vendor catalogs, arrange attractive library displays, select and buy materials, prepare new materials, and manage technology.

In public children's libraries, Librarians often plan special events such as story hours, summer reading programs, reading or writing contests. In school libraries, many Children's Librarians also teach library and research skills, read or tell stories, and provide computer technology assistance.

Just like public libraries for adults, children's libraries have changed radically over the past 10 to 15 years from an institution housing paper records and books to a center offering a full range of special media including CD-ROMs, computers, films, videotapes, and recordings. Children's Librarians may serve as information specialist, teacher, instructional partner, and program administrator to develop strategies and teaching methods promoting the integration of technology into the curriculum.

Depending on the size of the library and the number of support staff, a Children's Librarian may juggle a wide range of duties, such as supervising staff, serving as budget director, purchaser, cataloger, repairer, and archivist. Children's Librarians in schools also work with the teaching staff to improve lessons, thus enabling the school to reach the learning standards required by the state. They are expected to be good teachers as well as library experts. In fact, in many school libraries, Children's Librarians help teachers develop curricula, acquire materials for classroom instruction, and sometimes team-teach. They work closely with individual teachers in designing learning tasks and integrating the information and communication abilities required to meet subject matter standards.

Children's Librarians are also familiar with the latest technology, including databases, Internet skills, and word processing (such as the ability to teach Word or PowerPoint), and usually help instruct staff and students in these areas.

The Children's Librarian works with students in grades K through 12, teaching staff, teaching aides and assistants, administrative staff, clerical staff, school board members, fellow librarians, and the community. At public libraries and in all grade levels of school libraries, children's libraries are typically staffed by one full-time Librarian with a half-time clerk at the elementary and K–8 levels, or a full-time clerk in a middle school or high school. Many schools use student assistants and adult volunteers. As a program administrator, the Children's Librarian works with the school community to define policies and direct all related activities, and plans, executes, and evaluates the program to ensure its quality both at a general level and on a day-to-day basis.

School Librarians usually have the same workday schedule as classroom teachers and similar vacation schedules.

Salaries

Salaries differ among schools according to district, number of graduate or in-service credits, and experience. Children's Librarians are hired on the same salary schedule as classroom teachers, including full benefits. Starting salary range is from $24,510 to $50,000 for a nine-month contract, and may reach $66,590 based on an advanced degree and several years of teaching experience.

Employment Prospects

Employment prospects for Children's Librarians are very good, providing the individual is willing to relocate. The demand for Children's Librarians with an M.L.S. degree is growing and will continue to increase, and the number of school districts seeking full-time professionals has more than doubled since 1990.

Advancement Prospects

Children's Librarians can move into larger public or school libraries or become library director or chief information officer, with more experience, administrative skills, knowledge of automated systems, and additional training.

Education and Training

A master's degree in librarianship from a program accredited by the American Library Association or a master's degree with a specialty in school library media from an educational unit accredited by the National Council for the Accreditation of Teacher Education (NCATE) is the appropriate first degree for a Children's Librarian.

Special Requirements

Certification may be required for all Children's Librarians who teach in the school system, and to be certified as both a librarian and a teacher. Requirements are different from one state to the next, but there are general patterns. Children's Librarians who work in schools are usually expected to have some coursework in education, teaching methods, and psychology, and to have performed some type of internship. Many states now have reciprocity agreements so that they can accept each other's certificates. This means that a Children's Librarian who is certified in one state may be eligible for certification in another just by providing proof of certification.

Experience, Skills, and Personality Traits

Children's Librarians should love children's literature and enjoy working with youths, parents, teachers, and community leaders. They should be comfortable with computers, good with people, well organized, and understand childhood developmental stages. Strong management and public relations skills also come in handy.

Unions and Associations

Librarians working in K–12 libraries may or may not belong to a union, but they also can belong to a variety of trade associations that provide educational guidance, support, conferences, and information to members. These might include the Association for Library Service to Children (a division of ALA), the Young Adult Library Services Association (a division of ALA), the American Library Association, the American Society for Information Science, or the Special Libraries Association.

Tips for Entry

1. Take every opportunity available to work as a student assistant in the university libraries, do a practicum or internship in another library, or volunteer in the type of library which interests you most. Children's library administrators are likely to select a candidate with some relevant experience over one with none.
2. For a position in a school library, contact school superintendents in areas where you'd like to work to discover positions in K–12 school libraries.
3. Check out classified ads for "school librarian" or "children's librarian" listings.
4. Check out university placement offices that maintain job lists for children's library positions.
5. Join professional organizations to provide a network through which you may hear about job opportunities.
6. Find out the name and address of every library with a children's department where you might like to work (the telephone book is helpful; call to find out to

whom to address your cover letter). When openings occur, administrators often pull out their collection of unsolicited résumés and contact the candidates.

7. E-mail discussion groups such as LIBJOBS and LIS-JOBS are a good source for job postings. Topical groups are also a good place for finding advertisements in a particular field of librarianship.

8. Look for jobs on the Internet, such as on www. Lisjobs.com. Check daily job postings on "Hot Jobs Online" at the website of the American Library Association (www.ala.org), and investigate other Internet websites that list library job postings, such as: http://www.libraryjobpostings.org or the Ameri-

can Society of Information Science website job line (http://www.asis.org/Jobline). Or visit the ALISE website, which has links to all library schools, each of which has state and national employment listings (www.alise.org).

9. *Jobs for Librarians and Information Professionals* is a comprehensive guide to on-line job resources for librarians and information professionals.

10. Subscribe to major library trade publications, such as *Library Journal* and *American Libraries.*

11. Attend library conventions or conferences and check job boards, such as the placement service that lists library-related jobs at annual ALA conventions.

MEDIA SPECIALIST

CAREER PROFILE

Duties: Handles the full range of instructional technology, including CD-ROMs, films, videotapes, recordings, and graphic materials

Alternate Title(s): Media Center Specialist

Salary Range: $26,000 to $50,000 (nine-month contract)

Employment Prospects: Good

Advancement Prospects: Good

Best Geographical Location(s): Larger school districts throughout the country have openings for media specialists

Prerequisites:

Education or Training—Master's of library science or a master's degree with a specialty in school library media

Experience—Teaching experience and experience with children

Special Skills and Personality Traits—Patience; superior communication skills; creativity; time management skills

Licensure/Certification—State certification as school library media specialist (where required) and/or teaching certificate

CAREER LADDER

```
┌─────────────────────────────────┐
│    Director of Media Center     │
└─────────────────────────────────┘

┌─────────────────────────────────┐
│       Media Specialist          │
└─────────────────────────────────┘

┌─────────────────────────────────┐
│   Assistant Media Specialist    │
└─────────────────────────────────┘
```

Position Description

A school Media Specialist is the manager of an elementary, middle, or high school media center, which is a recent development in school libraries and now includes a full range of special media, including CD-ROMs, computers, films, videotapes, recordings, and art materials. Media Specialists work in library media centers within the public school system in the role of information specialist, teacher, instructional partner, and program administrator to develop strategies and teaching methods promoting the integration of technology into the curriculum.

A Media Specialist might wear many library hats, from supervising staff to being a budget director, purchaser, cataloger, repairer, and archivist. School Media Specialists are teachers of library and research skills, and work with the teaching staff to improve lessons, thus enabling the school to reach the learning standards required by the state. Media Specialists are expected to be good teachers, and often come to the school library from a regular teaching position. In fact, in many school library media centers, Media Specialists help teachers develop curricula, acquire materials for classroom instruction, and sometimes team-teach.

Most importantly, a school Media Specialist is familiar with the latest technology, including database knowledge, Internet skills, and word processing (such as the ability to teach Word or PowerPoint) as well as instructing staff and students in their uses. A school Media Specialist promotes the school media center as a necessary part of the school.

The school Media Specialist works with students in grades K through 12, teaching staff, teaching aides and assistants, administrative and clerical staff, school board members, fellow librarians, and the community. At all grade levels, media centers are typically staffed by one full-time librarian who has a half-time clerk at the elementary or K–8 levels or a full-time clerk in a middle school or high school.

While many schools report using student assistants, the median number working in the library is one, and adult volunteers still play a small role.

The library Media Specialist analyzes learning and information needs and locates resources that will meet those needs. He or she constantly updates personal skills and knowledge in order to work effectively with teachers, administrators, and other staff.

The library Media Specialist develops policies, practices, and curricula that allow students to develop the full range of information and communication abilities. He or she works closely with individual teachers in designing learning tasks and integrating the information and communication abilities required to meet subject matter standards.

The library Media Specialist also evaluates information resources in all formats. Working in an environment that has been profoundly affected by technology, the library Media Specialist both masters sophisticated electronic resources and maintains a constant focus on the nature, quality, and ethical use of information available in these and in more traditional tools.

As a program administrator, the library Media Specialist works with the school community to define the policies of the library media program and direct all related activities. Proficient in managing staff, budgets, equipment, and facilities, the library Media Specialist plans, administers, and evaluates the program to ensure its quality.

Media Specialists usually have the same workday and vacation schedules as classroom teachers.

Salaries

Salaries differ among schools according to district, number of graduate or in-service credits, and experience. Library Media Specialists are hired on the same salary schedule as classroom teachers, including full benefits. Starting salaries range from $26,000 to $32,000 for a nine-month contract, and may reach $50,000 with an advanced degree and several years of teaching experience.

Employment Prospects

The demand for people with the M.L.S. degree is growing and will continue to increase. The number of school districts seeking full-time Media Specialists has more than doubled since 1990, according to the Indiana University School of Library and Information Science.

Advancement Prospects

Because technology has become such a vital part of all types of libraries throughout the country, the Media Specialist is in an extremely strong position relative to advancement. With a solid background in modern technology and a strong educational background, the Media Specialist could most likely advance into an administrative position in many different types of libraries.

Education and Training

The specific requirements to become a school Media Specialist differ from state to state, but all school library Media Specialists are required to meet certification requirements established by individual states. In addition, a school Media Specialist usually must have a master's degree in librarianship from a program accredited by the American Library Association, or a master's degree with a specialty in school library media from an educational unit accredited by the National Council for the Accreditation of Teacher Education (NCATE). Academic work in education with courses in teaching methods, psychology, and related subjects is usually required. An internship or student teacher experience is generally required.

Special Requirements

In most states the position of school library Media Specialist requires a valid teaching license.

Experience, Skills, and Personality Traits

Because of the nature of the Media Specialist's job, a solid foundation and passion for technology in all its forms is important for this position, including computer literacy. In addition, Media Specialists in the K–12 library should enjoy being with children, have an above-average academic background, and be enthusiastic, warm, and positive. Attention to detail and good organizational skills are also important.

Unions and Associations

Media Specialists working in libraries do not usually belong to unions, but they can belong to a variety of trade associations that provide educational guidance, support, conferences, and information to members. These might include the American Library Association, the Association for Library Service to Children (a division of ALA), or the Young Adult Library Services Association (also a division of ALA).

Tips for Entry

1. Consult www.k-12jobs.com for positions available at public, private, vocational, and technical schools.
2. Subscribe to library journals and periodicals, such as *American Libraries* magazine.
3. Check daily job postings on "Hot Jobs Online" at the website of the American Library Association (www.ala.org).
4. Attend library conventions or conferences and check job boards.
5. Check out the placement service that lists library-related jobs at annual ALA conventions.
6. Investigate other websites that list library job postings, such as http://www.libraryjobpostings.org, or visit the ALISE website, which has links to all library schools, each of which has state and national employment listings (www.alise.org). The American Society of Information Science website job line (http://www.asis.org/Jobline) may also be helpful.

OUTSIDE THE LIBRARY

MAP LIBRARIAN

CAREER PROFILE

Duties: Organize, catalog, and interpret map collections; answer reference inquiries; select map collections for purchase

Alternate Title(s): Map Information Specialist

Salary Range: $32,891 to $50,000+

Employment Prospects: Good

Advancement Prospects: Good

Best Geographical Location(s): Larger cities may offer more possibilities, but map libraries are found in academic, public, federal, and special libraries

Prerequisites:

Education or Training—Master's degree in library science and undergraduate degree in geography

Experience—Appropriate background in academic areas related to geography, including geographic information systems (GIS)

Special Skills and Personality Traits—Attention to detail; love of books and maps; love of learning; ability to work independently; good organizational skills; willingness to work hard

CAREER LADDER

```
┌─────────────────────────────────────┐
│   Map Librarian at Larger Library or │
│        Director of Map Library       │
└─────────────────────────────────────┘

┌─────────────────────────────────────┐
│            Map Librarian             │
└─────────────────────────────────────┘

┌─────────────────────────────────────┐
│        Assistant Map Librarian       │
└─────────────────────────────────────┘
```

Position Description

A map library collection consists of government- and commercially produced paper maps, atlases, reference materials, microfilm, and digital spatial data. Much of the digital data are for use in a geographic information system (GIS), a computerized mapping system that can capture, store, manipulate, analyze, and display all forms of geographic and spatial information. Data can be in the form of themes such as population, zoning, topology, or aerial photos and can range in scale. Data produced for use in a GIS are created by local, state, federal, international, and commercial agencies; some are distributed freely but most are for sale.

Most libraries do not have funds to buy these resources, given that it might take several hundred CDs of data to cover just one state at an adequate scale. If data are not detailed enough, the map probably will be useless. Map Librarians must find alternative ways to obtain these resources. They must also inform the GIS professionals about the funding issues facing libraries and how such issues affect the public.

A Map Librarian is a librarian who has specialized in maintaining map collections. A broad academic background in geography and/or cartography is helpful. Map Librarians work in federal libraries, academic libraries, special libraries, and public libraries.

The traditional responsibilities of librarians make up the day-to-day work of a Map Librarian's activities, including organizing, cataloging, and maintaining collections, teaching patrons how to use the library, answering reference questions, and selecting maps for acquisition. Map Librarians also recommend ways of preserving and housing materials in their care.

Beyond these typical responsibilities, the activities of Map Librarians reflect their own interests and the nature of the institution where they work. They may organize exhibits and work with other institutions to coordinate lectures, classes, or other public programs. Those employed by map dealers gather materials from many publishers for sale to customers in a store or by mail order.

In addition, Map Librarians may compile bibliographies, pursue research, or write reviews of new publications. They may teach cartography or other classroom subjects within their area of specialization.

Map Librarians may have to organize training programs for library staff, researchers, or interns. Librarians may be members of professional organizations, serving on regional, national, or international committees concerned with such topics such as librarianship education, cataloging standards, library management, and information storage and retrieval.

Most Map Librarians work with the public, whether in full-time public service positions or as a part-time responsibility in addition to their other duties. Map Librarians who work in cataloging or acquisitions may have no contact with the public.

Salaries

Salaries for this position vary a great deal depending on the responsibilities and location of the library. Although beginning Map Librarians may start at $32,891, the average salary of a Map Librarian without supervisory responsibilities ranges between $42,704 and $50,000 and above.

Employment Prospects

Employment prospects for Map Librarians are good, as more positions are expected to open than there will be Librarians to fill them through 2012.

Advancement Prospects

Map Librarians may move into any number of supervisory and administrative positions. While smaller collections are administered by a single Librarian with a small support staff, Map Librarians in large academic and public libraries may head their department and direct budget, personnel, facilities, and collection management.

Education and Training

Few library schools offer classes in map librarianship, or may include only a section on the specialty in a survey course. Some may offer a course every few years. Therefore, on-the-job training is often required in the field. Training should include an education in geography, cartography, and the liberal arts, and must be the equivalent of at least substantial undergraduate work. In addition to an undergraduate degree, most employers require a master's degree in library or information science.

Experience, Skills, and Personality Traits

Fascination with history and maps draws individuals interested in librarianship to this field of specialization. Successful Map Librarians share intellectual curiosity, attention to detail, and the ability to organize ideas as well as things. Experience with current cataloging practices and with geographic information systems (GIS) helpful; good people skills are vital.

Unions and Associations

Map Librarians do not usually belong to unions, but they may belong to a variety of trade associations that provide educational guidance, support, conferences, and information to members. These include the Association of Canadian Map Libraries and Archives, The North American Cartographic Information Society, the American Library Association, the American Society for Information Science, or the Special Libraries Association.

Tips for Entry

1. To learn about the profession's current activities and to make useful contacts, join the North American Cartographic Information Society as a student member.
2. Visit the on-line job site for the North American Cartographic Information Society (http://www.nacis.org).
3. E-mail discussion groups such as LIBJOBS and LIS-JOBS are a good source for job postings. Topical groups are also a good place for finding advertisements in a particular field of librarianship.
4. Check out job sites on the Internet, including www.Lisjobs.com, the daily job postings on "Hot Jobs Online" at the website of the American Library Association (www.ala.org), the American Society of Information Science website job line (www.asis.org/Jobline), or www.libraryjobpostings.org. Or visit the ALISE website, which has links to all library schools, each of which has state and national employment listings (www.alise.org).
5. Check out *Jobs for Librarians and Information Professionals,* a comprehensive guide to on-line job resources for librarians and information professionals.
6. Subscribe to major library trade publications, such as *Library Journal* and *American Libraries.*

FILM/VIDEO LIBRARIAN

CAREER PROFILE

Duties: Organize, catalog, and interpret film and video collections; answer reference inquiries; select video or film collection for acquisition

Alternate Title(s): Film Information Specialist

Salary Range: $32,891 to $50,000+

Employment Prospects: Good

Advancement Prospects: Good

Best Geographical Location(s): Larger cities may offer more possibilities, but film and video libraries are found in many academic, public, federal, and special libraries across the country

Prerequisites:

Education or Training—Master's degree in library science

Experience—Appropriate background in film can be helpful

Special Skills and Personality Traits—Attention to detail; love of films; love of learning; ability to work independently; good organizational skills; willingness to work hard

CAREER LADDER

```
┌─────────────────────────────────────┐
│  Film/Video Librarian at Larger     │
│  Library or Director of Film/Video  │
│  Library                            │
└─────────────────────────────────────┘

┌─────────────────────────────────────┐
│        Film/Video Librarian         │
└─────────────────────────────────────┘

┌─────────────────────────────────────┐
│    Assistant Film/Video Librarian   │
└─────────────────────────────────────┘
```

Position Description

One of the most common types of special librarians is the Film or Video Librarian, who advises libraries on which materials to acquire, plans film programs for the public or with other libraries, and advises library personnel on the best use of the institution's collection. Film/Video Librarians work in all types of institutions: federal libraries, academic libraries, special libraries, and public libraries.

The traditional responsibilities of librarians make up the day-to-day work of a Film/Video Librarian's activities, including organizing, cataloging, and maintaining collections, teaching users how to search the collection, answering reference questions, and selecting videos and films for acquisition. Film/Video Librarians also recommend ways of preserving and housing materials in their care.

Video and film collections involve far more than popular movies and DVDs. Film/Video Librarians also must be knowledgeable about the full range of educational videos, including consumer health and fitness videos, documentaries on such topics as Romanian orphans, the Confederate flag, the sinking city of Venice, and 20th-century wars. An important part of a library's video collection includes biographies of famous people, such as Benjamin Franklin, Donald Rumsfeld, Ronald Reagan, Sigmund Freud, or Venus and Serena Williams.

Beyond these typical responsibilities, the activities of Film/Video Librarians reflect their own interests and the nature of the institution where they work. For example, they may plan film exhibits or retrospectives, and collaborate with other institutions in organizing film lectures, classes, or other public programs. In addition, Film/Video Librarians may compile bibliographies, pursue research, or write reviews of new publications, and they may teach film or other classroom subjects within their areas of specialization.

Librarians may be required to organize training programs for library staff, researchers, or interns. Librarians may be members of professional organizations, serving on regional, national, or international committees concerned with topics such as education for librarianship, cataloging standards, library management, and information storage and retrieval.

Salaries

Salaries for this position vary a great deal depending on the responsibilities and location of the library. Although beginning Film/Video Librarians may start at $32,891, the average salary of a Video Librarian without supervisory responsibilities ranges between $42,704 and $50,000 and above.

Employment Prospects

Most Film/Video Librarians work with the public, whether they hold full-time public service positions or interact with the public part time in addition to their other job duties. As Film/Video Librarians leave the work force, new positions open up. To have the widest choice of positions, an applicant should be prepared to relocate, especially to urban areas with large libraries where the chances of jobs are higher.

Advancement Prospects

Film/Video Librarians may move into any number of supervisory and administrative positions. While smaller collections are administered by a single Librarian with a small support staff, Film/Video Librarians in large academic and public libraries may head their department and oversee budgets, personnel, facilities, and collection management.

Education and Training

Training for Film/Video Librarians should include as broad an education as possible in both film and the liberal arts. In addition, a master's degree in library or information science is required.

Experience, Skills, and Personality Traits

Fascination with films is the basis for most Film/Video Librarians' interest in this specialization. Intellectual curiosity, a concern for detail, and the ability to organize ideas as well as things are essential.

Unions and Associations

Film/Video Librarians do not usually belong to unions, but they can belong to a variety of trade associations that provide educational guidance, support, conferences, and information to members. These include the American Institute for Conservation of Historic and Artistic Works, the American Film Institute, the American Library Association, Art Libraries Society of North America, the National Association of Media and Technology Centers, or the Association for Information Media and Equipment.

Tips for Entry

1. Join professional associations to network for new positions, such as the National Association of Media and Technology Centers or the Association for Information Media and Equipment (AIME).
2. Participate in e-mail discussion groups. LIBJOBS and LIS-JOBS are a good source for job postings. Topical e-mail discussion groups are also a good place for finding advertisements in video librarianship.
3. Look for jobs on the Internet. Check out www.Lisjobs.com, the daily job postings on "Hot Jobs Online" at the website of the American Library Association (www.ala.org), the American Society of Information Science website jobline (www.asis.org/Jobline), and www.libraryjobpostings.org. Or visit the ALISE website, which has links to all library schools, each of which has state and national employment listings: www.alise.org.
4. Check out *Jobs for Librarians and Information Professionals,* a comprehensive guide to on-line job resources for librarians and information professionals.
5. Subscribe to major library trade publications, such as the *Video Librarian* (www.videolibrarian.com), *Library Journal,* or *American Libraries.*

MUSIC LIBRARIAN

CAREER PROFILE

Duties: Organize, catalog, and maintain collections; answer reference inquiries; select music, books, journals, recordings, microforms, and sometimes manuscripts and other rare materials for acquisition

Alternate Title(s): Director of Music Library

Salary Range: $32,891 to $50,000+

Employment Prospects: Good

Advancement Prospects: Good

Best Geographical Location(s): Larger cities may offer more possibilities for Music Librarians in nontraditional positions, such as with music publishers, dealers, societies, and foundations

Prerequisites:

Education or Training—Master's degrees in both library science and music are required

Experience—The best introduction to music librarianship as a career is to work in a music library as a volunteer; full-time, part-time, and hourly positions are available in public and academic libraries and with music publishers and performance ensembles

Special Skills and Personality Traits—Aptitude and training in both music and librarianship are necessary, together with attention to detail, love of books and music, love of learning, and willingness to work hard

CAREER LADDER

```
┌─────────────────────────────────────┐
│  Music Librarian at Larger Library or │
│       Director of Music Library       │
└─────────────────────────────────────┘

┌─────────────────────────────────────┐
│           Music Librarian             │
└─────────────────────────────────────┘

┌─────────────────────────────────────┐
│       Assistant Music Librarian       │
└─────────────────────────────────────┘
```

Position Description

Music Librarians may be found in a variety of specialized libraries, including radio and television station libraries, music publishers and dealers, musical societies and foundations, or even bands and orchestras. A Music Librarian is basically a librarian who is further qualified to specialize in music. A broad musical background is essential, since the Music Librarian may be called upon to work with music of any style, medium, or era.

Music Librarians' responsibilities include organizing, cataloging, and maintaining collections, answering reference questions, and selecting music, books, journals, recordings, and sometimes rare materials for acquisition. Music Librarians also must know how to preserve and house music-related materials in their care.

Beyond these typical responsibilities, the activities of Music Librarians reflect their own interests and the nature of the place where they work. Music Librarians who work for symphony orchestras and broadcasting stations organize and maintain libraries of performance materials or recordings for use only by those particular organizations. Librarians employed by music publishers may have editorial duties or manage the inventory of rental music. Those employed by music dealers gather materials from many publishers for retail sale to over-the-counter and mail-order customers.

Music Librarians may be responsible for organizing training programs for library staff, researchers, or interns. Librarians may choose to join professional organizations, where they can serve on regional, national, or international committees concerned with topics such as librarianship education, cataloging standards, library management, and information storage and retrieval.

Salaries

Salaries for this position vary a great deal depending on the Music Librarians' responsibilities and the place where they work. Although beginning Music Librarians may start at $32,891, the average salary of a Music Librarian ranges between $42,704 and $50,000 and above.

Employment Prospects

Many Music Librarians who are also musicians find that they can combine their library job with a part-time second career as a performer.

Advancement Prospects

Music Librarians may move into any number of supervisory and administrative positions. While smaller collections are administered by a single Librarian with a small support staff, Music Librarians in larger libraries may head their department and oversee budgets, personnel, facilities, and collection management.

Education and Training

Some library schools offer special courses or internships in music librarianship. Training for music librarianship should include as broad an education as possible in both music and the liberal arts, with music training the equivalent of at least substantial undergraduate work. Undergraduates who intend to go on to train to become Music Librarians need a broad background in the humanities, since they will need to be familiar with the relationship of music to other disciplines. Further, knowledge of a foreign language is very important. Because music and music-related literature are published in many countries and languages, basic cataloging and bibliographic research require a working knowledge of German and at least one Romance language.

Most employers require a master's degree in library or information science. A second master's degree in music may be required or highly desired for some positions.

Experience, Skills, and Personality Traits

Individuals drawn to this type of librarianship feel a commitment to music. Intellectual curiosity, a concern for detail, and the ability to organize ideas as well as things are essential.

Unions and Associations

Music Librarians in alternative settings can belong to a variety of trade associations, such as the Music Library Association, the American Library Association, the American Society for Information Science, or the Special Libraries Association.

Tips for Entry

1. To learn about the profession's current activities and to make useful contacts, join the Music Library Association as a student member.
2. Visit the placement service job list on the Music Library Association (MLA) website (www.musiclibraryassoc.org).
3. Attend the annual MLA meeting in the late winter or early spring, or visit the nearest regional chapter (there are 12) that meet regularly.
4. E-mail discussion groups such as MLA-L, LIBJOBS, and LIS-JOBS are a good source for job postings. Topical groups are also a good place for finding advertisements in a particular field of librarianship.
5. Check out job lists on the Internet, such as www.Lisjobs.com, the daily job postings on "Hot Jobs Online" at the website of the American Library Association (www.ala.org); or the American Society of Information Science website job line (www.asis.org/Jobline) or www.libraryjobpostings.org. Visit the ALISE website, which has links to all library schools, each of which has state and national employment listings (www.alise.org).
6. Check out *Jobs for Librarians and Information Professionals,* a comprehensive guide to on-line job resources for librarians and information professionals.
7. Subscribe to major library trade publications, such as *Library Journal* and *American Libraries.*

HOSPITAL MEDICAL LIBRARIAN

CAREER PROFILE

Duties: Provide health information about new medical treatments, clinical trials and standard trials procedures, tests, and equipment to patients, their families, and health care workers

Alternate Title(s): None

Salary Range: $45,000 to $100,000+

Employment Prospects: Good

Advancement Prospects: Good

Best Geographical Location(s): Major cities with larger hospitals and medical centers are usually the best location for the largest medical libraries

Prerequisites:

Education or Training—Graduate degree in library or information science

Experience—A background in science, health sciences, or allied health is helpful

Special Skills and Personality Traits—Strong oral and written communication skills; good interpersonal skills; solid computer skills

CAREER LADDER

```
┌─────────────────────────────────────┐
│  Director of Hospital Medical Library │
└─────────────────────────────────────┘

┌─────────────────────────────────────┐
│      Hospital Medical Librarian       │
└─────────────────────────────────────┘

┌─────────────────────────────────────┐
│      Medical Librarian, Assistant     │
└─────────────────────────────────────┘
```

Position Description

A Medical Librarian at a hospital or medical center is responsible for retrieving, selecting, organizing, and disseminating health information to patients, their families, and health care workers. Medical Librarians may evaluate advanced information technologies, teach users how to find health care information, and design and manage digital access.

A Hospital Medical Librarian also provides general and subject reference assistance, develops and manages the collection, and supervises support staff. In addition, the Hospital Medical Librarian must provide patients and health care workers with the latest information on diseases, procedures, treatments, and research. Hospital Medical Librarians also select and maintain medical books, journals, and audiovisual materials.

Medical Librarians also must be familiar with key databases that cover biomedical literature, such as MEDLINE, a huge index of some 7 million articles published since 1966 that is the standard searching tool for medical literature, and Dialog, a database vendor that allows a user to search through numerous databases such as Biosis (abstracts of scientific articles) and Science Citation Index (abstracts of articles in diverse magazines and journals).

Working as a Hospital Medical Librarian can provide an active, mobile career that enables the Librarian to forge exciting partnerships with clinicians and researchers.

Salaries

Salaries vary according to the size and location of the hospital, the level of responsibility, and the length of employment. Salaries range from $45,000 to more than $100,000.

Employment Prospects

Employment of Hospital Medical Librarians is especially strong as the need grows for organization amidst the technological information explosion. While hospitals and medical centers housing medical libraries can be found throughout the country, they tend to be located in or near larger cities; competition for these positions is therefore more intense.

Often, part-time jobs open up unexpectedly and need to be filled quickly; there may not even be time to advertise the job. Joining various professional organizations and keeping in touch with library friends will provide a network through which you may hear about part-time opportunities when they arise.

Advancement Prospects

There are a variety of opportunities for Hospital Medical Librarians depending on the interests and expertise of the individual librarian. The more time, experience, and additional education an individual has, the better the advancement prospects. Because Medical Librarians have a number of marketable skills, they can move on to a variety of positions such as Web manager for a medical center, medical informatics expert, chief information officer, or director of a nursing school library.

Education and Training

A master's in library and information science from an ALA-accredited school is required for any position as a Medical Librarian (although many colleges and universities offer M.L.S. programs, employers often prefer graduates of the approximately 56 schools accredited by the American Library Association). In addition, many medical libraries also require a background in science, health sciences, or allied health, or graduate courses in medical informatics or medical librarianship. The Medical Librarian should learn everything possible related to the medical field (for example, understanding biomedical references, principles of organization of information in the biomedical sciences, and on-line computer databases such as MEDLINE, from the National Library of Medicine.)

In addition, the National Library of Medicine offers an associate fellowship—a one-year program for post-M.L.S. candidates interested in training for a leadership role in health science libraries.

Experience, Skills, and Personality Traits

Because Medical Librarians spend most of their days working with the public and with health care workers, strong interpersonal and communication skills are required. In addition, excellent organizational and computer skills are important, along with a solid basis and interest in medicine or health-related issues. Librarians working in medical libraries need to be flexible and well organized, with strong attention to detail. The Medical Librarian should have an ability to work well under pressure in a fast-paced environment, and be familiar with medical terminology.

Because the Medical Librarian is expected to work with people from all walks of life and hospital employees from different areas of the hospital, the ability to communicate effectively is vital.

Unions and Associations

Medical Librarians working in hospitals may belong to a variety of trade associations that provide educational guidance, support, conferences, and information to members. These might include the Medical Library Association, the American Library Association, the American Society for Information Science, the Medical Librarian Association, or the Special Libraries Association.

Tips for Entry

1. Get experience. If you're attending library school, take every opportunity available to work as a student assistant in the university libraries, do a practicum or internship in a medical library, or volunteer in a medical library. Library administrators may not expect an applicant for part-time employment to have as much experience as a candidate for a full-time position, but they are likely to select a candidate with some relevant experience over one with none.
2. Check out the job listings on the Medical Library Association website (www.mlanet.org/jobs/index.html), and attend the annual May convention of the MLA, where you can check out the jobs listing.
3. Jobs in this field also may be found in the job listings for all related trade associations, beginning with the American Library Association (ALA). Check out the placement service that lists library-related jobs at annual ALA conventions.
4. Look for job ads in *American Libraries* magazine.
5. Check daily Internet job postings on websites such as "Hot Jobs Online" of the American Library Association (www.ala.org); the American Society of Information Science website job line (http://www.asis.org/Jobline); or www.libraryjobpostings.org. Or visit the ALISE website, which has links to all library schools, each of which has state and national employment listings (www.alise.org).

LIBRARY WEB DEVELOPMENT MANAGER

CAREER PROFILE

Duties: Coordinates the design, development, and maintenance of the library's webpages and helps develop the library's website using new services, interactive applications, and improvements to the site's usability

Alternate Title(s): Webmaster

Salary Range: $29,664 to $45,677

Employment Prospects: Excellent

Advancement Prospects: Excellent

Best Geographical Location(s): Public libraries can be found throughout the country, but in general large public and academic libraries in large cities have more opportunities for Library Web Development Managers

Prerequisites:

Education or Training—B.A. or B.S. in computer science together with a master's degree in library and information science from an accredited institution

Experience—Experience in an academic library performing Web development

Special Skills and Personality Traits—Experience in training staff and users; excellent communication and computer skills; ability to work under pressure and meet project deadlines and goals

CAREER LADDER

```
┌─────────────────────────────────┐
│ Library Web Development Manager  │
│        for Larger Library        │
└─────────────────────────────────┘

┌─────────────────────────────────┐
│ Library Web Development Manager  │
└─────────────────────────────────┘

┌─────────────────────────────────┐
│      Library Web Assistant       │
└─────────────────────────────────┘
```

Position Description

As the gateway to both information and library services, the library's website is of growing importance in today's technological age. The Library Web Development Manager is often responsible for concept design, developing design and navigation guidelines for the site, developing new applications for users and staff, setting standards of web excellence for library staff who build and maintain webpages, and training staff as needed. Library Web Development Managers typically work with the various groups responsible for library web content and with fellow systems analysts and administrators. The Manager typically develops style sheets and standards, and ensures the currency and accuracy of Web links and information. The Manager also designs and supports customized WWW extensions such as enhanced indexing, electronic forms, and future applications, and works closely with library staff to monitor and evaluate new Web development tools, such as graphics software, HTML editors, and search applications.

The Library Web Development Manager is responsible for writing and maintaining code, as well as creating databases and interfaces, automated tools, and custom graphics. Active participation in library Web development groups and standards organizations is usually expected. In addition, the Manager develops and promotes standards and style guides for use by library Web developers, and tracks new Web development tools and provides training and guidance in their use.

Salaries

Salaries for this position vary a great deal depending on the responsibilities and location of the library. The average salary of a Library Web Development Manager ranges between $29,664 and $45,677.

Employment Prospects

Because worldwide use of the Internet will only increase and become more complex, the employment outlook for Web management and development among librarians is expected to continue to increase.

Advancement Prospects

Web Development Managers may move into a broad range of administrative and supervisory positions. While the technical aspects of smaller public libraries are often administered and operated by a single professional Web Development Manager plus a small support staff, in large public or academic libraries Web Development Managers may hold management positions as assistant heads or department heads, with budget, personnel, facilities, and hardware management responsibilities.

Education and Training

For most Web Development Manager positions, a library will require an undergraduate degree in computer science together with an M.S.L. from an accredited institution (although many colleges and universities offer M.S.L. programs, employers often prefer graduates of the approximately 56 schools accredited by the American Library Association). In addition, most libraries will look for programming experience and knowledge of Web development tools, especially PHP, Perl, Java, JavaScript, XML, ASP, JSP, and HTML. Library Web Managers also should have experience with Web editing and development software tools such as Dreamweaver and Cold Fusion, as well as graphics creation programs such as Adobe Photoshop. Experience in building interactive applications and applied knowledge of relational databases is also helpful.

Experience, Skills, and Personality Traits

Experience in an academic library performing Web development is usually required, as is experience with MySQL or Microsoft SQL. Library Web Managers should be able to collaborate with a variety of colleagues on various kinds of team and project groups, and should have experience in training staff and users, excellent communication and computer skills, ability to work under pressure and be able to meet project deadlines and goals. Knowledge of academic libraries and their mission is essential.

Unions and Associations

Library Web Development Managers may belong to a variety of trade associations that provide educational guidance, support, conferences, and information to members. These might include the American Society for Information Science and Technology, the American Library Association, the Association for Library Collections and Technical Services (ALCTS), the Library and Information Technology Association (LITA), the Council on Library and Media Technology, the Council on Library and Information Resources, or the Association of College and Research Libraries.

Tips for Entry

1. To learn about the profession's current activities and to make useful contacts, consider joining a professional association, such as the American Society for Information Science and Technology (www.asis.org).
2. Visit the placement service on the website of the American Society for Information Science and Technology (www.asis.org/Jobline).
3. Attend annual conferences of library associations, where job listings are often posted.
4. Look for jobs on the Internet, such as on www.Lisjobs.com, the daily job postings on "Hot Jobs Online" at the website of the American Library Association (www.ala.org), or www.libraryjobpostings.org. Or check out *Jobs for Librarians and Information Professionals,* a comprehensive guide to on-line job resources for librarians and information professionals. Visit the ALISE website, which has links to all library schools, each of which has state and national employment listings (www.alise.org). Libweb (http://sunsite.berkeley.edu/Libweb) can help you locate library homepages.
5. E-mail discussion groups are a good source for job postings. LIBJOBS (www.ifla.org/II/lists/libjobs.htm) is one of the more popular ones. Topical groups are also a good place for finding advertisements in Systems Librarianship.
6. Also check major library trade publications, such as *Library Journal* (www.libraryjournal.com). There are related publications, such as the *Chronicle of Higher Education* (http://chronicle.com/jobs) for academic library postings.

SCIENCE LIBRARIAN

CAREER PROFILE

Duties: Search scientific databases, structures, and patents; perform scientific reference work; abstract and index a variety of scientific publications for scientific industries, groups, or associations

Alternate Title(s): None

Salary Range: $42,000 to $100,000+

Employment Prospects: Good

Advancement Prospects: Good

Best Geographical Location(s): Major cities with large science-related industry, groups, and associations are usually the best location for the largest science libraries

Prerequisites:

Education or Training—Master's in information or library science accredited by the American Library Association, plus a certificate of specialization in a particular area of science, such as chemistry or biology

Experience—Several years of experience in a science library is helpful, as is a background in science or health sciences

Special Skills and Personality Traits—Strong oral and written communication skills; good interpersonal skills; solid computer skills

CAREER LADDER

```
┌─────────────────────────────────┐
│   Director of Science Library   │
└─────────────────────────────────┘

┌─────────────────────────────────┐
│        Science Librarian        │
└─────────────────────────────────┘

┌─────────────────────────────────┐
│   Assistant Science Librarian   │
└─────────────────────────────────┘
```

Position Description

A Science Librarian specializes in searching of scientific databases, structure searching, patent searching, scientific reference work, and abstracting and indexing a variety of scientific publications for scientific associations or corporations.

The Science Librarian has expert knowledge of information resources, including the ability to critically evaluate and filter them; evaluates on-line versions of databases; and knows the best textbooks, journals, and electronic resources in specific areas of science.

The Science Librarian controls the supply of information by selecting what is relevant and usable for the customer, and selects and analyzes information that meets specific organizational goals. The Science Librarian has specialized scientific knowledge, and monitors an organization's interests in a specific branch of science by reading core journals

and other key sources, enabling the development of in-depth science information services.

The Science Librarian also manages convenient, accessible, and cost-effective information services. For example, the Librarian might develop a strategic plan linked to the business goals of the scientific organization, setting up effective management, supervision, and budget processes. The Science Librarian may build an effective information services staff team, conduct complex searches, obtain documents in print or electronic form, build a core in-house library collection, analyze and synthesize information, and develop specialized thesauri and lists of indexing terms for scientific databases.

The Science Librarian provides excellent instruction and support for library and information service users, including teaching Internet courses for employees or developing specialized user searching courses on information resources related to the business goals. The Science Librarian keeps up to date with the latest training and instructional techniques and provides troubleshooting service, on-line reference, and assistance for employees accessing information services from the desktop.

The Science Librarian also assesses information needs and designs and markets value-added information services and products to meet identified needs. For example, the Librarian might conduct regular needs assessments using research tools such as questionnaires, focus groups, and key informant interviews. The Science Librarian could identify information needs by becoming a member of project teams, contributing unique or unusual needs assessment findings to the professional literature.

The Science Librarian also uses appropriate information technology to acquire, organize, and disseminate information, such as creating an on-line catalog of the library collection and linking catalog searching to a document delivery service. The Librarian works with the information management team to select appropriate software and hardware for desktop access to the library catalog and other databases, and provides a support service for electronic information service users. The Science Librarian also keeps up to date with new electronic information products and methods of information delivery. The Librarian uses appropriate business and management approaches to communicate the importance of information services to senior management. This might involve developing a business plan for the library, calculating a return on investment for the library and its services, or developing a marketing plan for the library. The Science Librarian might report to management on continuous quality improvement efforts, demonstrating how library and information services add value to the organization.

The Science Librarian also develops specialized information products for use inside or outside the organization or by individual clients. This might include creating a database of in-house documents such as reports, technical manuals or resource materials used for special projects, or creating searchable full-text document files. The Science Librarian can provide on-line technical manuals, and create a homepage on the Internet for the organization, linking it to other websites.

The Science Librarian also monitors scientific industry trends and disseminates information to key people in the organization or to individual clients, refocusing information services on new business needs. The Science Librarian is often an effective member of the senior management team and a consultant to the organization on information issues, and monitors compliance with copyright law.

The Science Librarian might negotiate contracts with database vendors, obtain patent information, and develop information policies for the organization, monitor major business trends and world events, and anticipate science trends so that the library and information services can be realigned to take advantage of them.

Salaries

Salaries for this position vary a great deal depending on the responsibilities of the position and the size of the industry or group supporting the library. Salaries may range from $42,000 to more than $100,000.

Employment Prospects

Employment of Science Librarians in industry or associations is increasing as the need grows for organization amidst the explosion of technological information. While private industry and nonprofit associations housing science libraries can be found throughout the country, the larger institutions tend to be located in or near larger cities; competition for these positions is therefore more intense.

Often, part-time jobs open up unexpectedly and need to be filled quickly; there may not even be time to advertise the job. Joining various professional organizations and keeping in touch with library friends will provide a network through which you may hear about part-time opportunities when they arise.

Advancement Prospects

A variety of advancement opportunities exist for Science Librarians, depending on the interests and expertise of the individual. The more time, experience, and additional education a person has, the better the advancement prospects. Because Science Librarians have a number of marketable skills, they can move on to a variety of positions such as Web manager for a medical center or company, science information expert, chief information officer, or director of a science library.

Education and Training

An M.L.S. is required. Although many colleges and universities offer M.L.S. programs, employers often prefer graduates of the approximately 56 schools accredited by the American Library Association. In addition to a master's degree in library science, many science libraries require a certificate of specialization in a particular area of science, such as chemistry or biology. Some library schools offer a special program combining the M.L.S. with a science information specialist program.

Experience, Skills, and Personality Traits

Science Librarians should have a solid foundation in science, Web development skills, database skills, and the ability to handle a service-oriented position. They should seek out challenges and see new opportunities both inside and outside the library, recognizing that information-seeking is part of the creative process. Science Librarians should have effective communications skills and good business skills, be flexible and positive, and be willing to take on different responsibilities and respond to changing needs.

Union and Associations

Science Librarians may belong to a variety of associations that provide educational guidance, support, conferences, and information to members. These might include the American Library Association, the American Society for Information Science, the Special Libraries Association, the American Chemical Society Division of Chemical Information, the Drug Information Association, the Medical Library Association, the Association of Vision Science Librarians, the Association of Academic Health Sciences Libraries, the Research Libraries Group, or the Association of Research Libraries.

Tips for Entry

1. Get experience. If you're attending library school, take every opportunity available to work as a student assistant in the university libraries; do a practicum or internship in a science library. Library administrators may not expect an applicant for part-time employment to have as much experience as a candidate for a full-time position, but they are likely to select a candidate with some relevant experience over one with none.

2. Jobs in this field may be found in the job listings for all related trade associations, beginning with the American Library Association (ALA). Check out the placement service that lists library-related jobs at annual ALA conventions.

3. Look for job ads in *American Libraries* magazine.

4. Check daily Internet job postings, such as on "Hot Jobs Online" at the website of the American Library Association (www.ala.org); the American Society of Information Science website job line (www.asis.org/Jobline); or visit the ALISE website, which has links to all library schools, each of which has state and national employment listings (www.alise.org).

DOCUMENT DELIVERY SPECIALIST

CAREER PROFILE

Duties: Track down materials such as photocopies of journal articles, patents, dissertations, government documents, industrial, federal and military standards, market research studies, and annual reports for clients or library patrons

Alternate Title(s): Document Delivery Expert

Salary Range: $45 to $100 an hour

Employment Prospects: Excellent

Advancement Prospects: Good

Best Geographical Location(s): Because Document Delivery Specialists generally use computerized networks, location is relatively unimportant; however, proximity to a variety of clients is likely better near urban areas

Prerequisites:

Education or Training—Master's degree in library or information science from ALA-accredited university; additional graduate degree helpful

Experience—Familiarity with an integrated library system; supervisory experience

Special Skills and Personality Traits—Strong organizational skills; effective oral and written communication skills; ability to work independently

CAREER LADDER

```
┌─────────────────────────────────────┐
│  Owner, Document Delivery Company    │
└─────────────────────────────────────┘

┌─────────────────────────────────────┐
│    Document Delivery Specialist      │
└─────────────────────────────────────┘

┌─────────────────────────────────────┐
│            Entry Level               │
└─────────────────────────────────────┘
```

Position Description

Document delivery companies complement the services of on-line researchers by locating and obtaining various kinds of literature, from market research reports and conference proceedings to journal articles and government documents.

Usually, document delivery involves a fixed project with a deadline and a specific budget, although some Document Delivery Specialists work on a continuing basis. Typical clients include the smaller company without a staff researcher; it is far more cost-effective for such a business to hire an information professional on an as-needed basis. During a typical research project, there will usually be a number of specific research citations, but the actual article or report may not be available on-line, either on the Internet or in fee-based databases. That's where the Document Delivery Specialist comes in.

The Document Delivery Specialist provides documents to clients within a company, such as other librarians, human resource professionals, scientists, marketing and management supervisors, legal consultants, accounting experts, intellectual property advisers, and manufacturing department heads.

For example, if a European pharmaceutical company wants to receive U.S. approval for its new drug, the Document Delivery Specialist can provide copies of the necessary government submission forms, the Code of Federal Regulations Title 21, the U.S. Pharmacopeia, and information on good manufacturing practices. Or, if an attorney involved in patent litigation needs documentation to support a client's case, including a paper presented at a scientific conference more than 50 years ago, the Document Delivery Specialist could locate the paper and provide a copy of the complete historical file from the U.S. patent office.

Busy librarians may struggle to answer reference questions, manage corporate Intranets, train users on new databases and CD-ROM products, and handle complicated and diminishing budgets. Document Delivery Specialists can provide assistance by offering customized support services to these special libraries, including document delivery, book and journal acquisition services, and specialized searches.

The Document Delivery Specialists augments the power of the librarian in a corporate or nonprofit information center by being an invisible partner, so that the librarian is free to be visible to patrons and better positioned to contribute to the mission of the organization.

Information access is no longer a hit-or-miss exercise. Instead, using sophisticated tools such as OPACS (on-line public access catalogs) and the Internet, Document Delivery Specialists can locate and order a wide range of materials.

Successful Document Delivery Specialists offer information solutions to fit their clients' needs, providing quality work while adhering to high ethical standards.

Salaries

An independent Document Delivery Specialist may charge between $45 and $100 per hour, depending on the specific type of information being sought (many choose to specialize in one or two fields, in order to hone their skills). However, many of the services and databases used by Document Delivery Specialists incur separate hourly fees, which come out of the Specialist's fee.

Employment Prospects

As the 21st century begins, the value of the Document Delivery Specialist becomes more important as an ever-growing amount of information is moving faster through countless media. Although computers and the Internet are part of almost everyone's lives, serious research remains a specialty that is most efficiently performed by a professional. As the idea of outsourcing some library services such as document delivery became more acceptable, Document Delivery Specialists began more and more often to offer specialized database searching, automated systems development, and market research.

Advancement Prospects

Document Delivery Specialists usually begin by working for a document delivery company. After several years of experience, many professionals set up their own businesses.

Education and Training

Many Document Delivery Specialists have an advanced degree in library and information science, as well as some experience working in a library setting. Increasingly, Specialists have advanced degrees in such diverse areas as law, medicine, or business. Additional education in business subjects can be helpful to those specialists who own their own businesses.

Experience, Skills, and Personality Traits

The most important attribute of the Document Delivery Specialist is excellent research skills, along with good computer and organizational skills. Because the specialist usually runs an independent business, the ability to work well with customers is extremely important. In addition, running a business requires a separate set of skills, including marketing, advertising, public relations, financial planning, and organizational and time management skills.

Unions and Associations

Document Delivery Specialists can belong to a variety of trade associations that provide educational guidance, support, conferences, and information to members. These might include the American Library Association, the International Federation of Library Associations and Institutions Section on Document Delivery and Interlending, American Society for Information Science, or the Special Libraries Association.

Tips for Entry

1. Before going into business for yourself, consider first working for a document delivery firm. After you have a few years of experience, consider striking out on your own. First, set up a website to advertise your services as a Document Delivery Specialist.
2. E-mail discussion groups such as LIBJOBS and LIS-JOBS are a good source for job postings.
3. Look for jobs on the Internet, such as on www.Lisjobs.com, the daily job postings on "Hot Jobs Online" at the website of the American Library Association (www.ala.org), the American Society of Information Science website job line (www.asis.org/Jobline), www.libraryjobpostings.org, or the ALISE website, which has links to all library schools, each of which has state and national employment listings (www.alise.org).
4. Check out *Jobs for Librarians and Information Professionals,* a comprehensive guide to on-line job resources for librarians and information professionals.
5. Subscribe to major library trade publications, such as *Library Journal* and *American Libraries,* and join associations that might help you land a job, such as the International Federation of Library Associations and Institutions Section on Document Delivery.

PUBLIC LIBRARIES

PUBLIC LIBRARY CLERK

CAREER PROFILE

Duties: Compile records, register patrons, sort and shelve books, and issue and receive library materials

Alternate Title(s): Library Aide or Circulation Assistant

Salary Range: $14,800 to $20,000+

Employment Prospects: Excellent

Advancement Prospects: Good

Best Geographical Location(s): Large cities may offer more possibilities, but public libraries throughout the country use Library Clerks

Prerequisites:

Education or Training—High school diploma

Experience—Secretarial experience helpful

Special Skills and Personality Traits—Good people skills; attention to detail; neatness; organizational skills; aptitude for computers; good English writing and speaking skills; willingness to learn new skills

CAREER LADDER

```
┌─────────────────────────────┐
│   Library Assistant or      │
│   Library Technician        │
└─────────────────────────────┘

┌─────────────────────────────┐
│   Library Clerk             │
└─────────────────────────────┘

┌─────────────────────────────┐
│   Entry Level               │
└─────────────────────────────┘
```

Position Description

Library Clerks perform routine tasks such as shelving books and periodicals, signing out material, or maintaining books and equipment. Many Clerks use their typing and computer skills to process materials orders and to update library catalogs. They work under the direction of staff trained in the library and information profession. Library Clerks compile records, sort and shelve books, and issue and receive library materials such as pictures, cards, slides, and microfilm. They locate library materials for loan and replace material in shelving area, stacks, or files according to identification number and title. Library Clerks also work with the public, registering patrons to permit them to borrow books, periodicals, and other library materials. They record the borrower's name and address from an application and then issue a library card. Most Library Clerks enter and update patrons' records using computer databases.

Salaries

Salaries for this position vary a great deal depending on specific job responsibilities and location of the library, but they range from a low of $14,800 to $20,000 and above.

Employment Prospects

This work is attractive to retirees and others who want a part-time schedule, and for this reason, there is a lot of movement into and out of the occupation, reflecting the limited investment in training and subsequent weak attachment to this occupation. Opportunities should be good for people interested in jobs as Library Clerks through 2012, according to the U.S. Bureau of Labor Statistics, since many openings will become available each year to replace workers who transfer to another occupation. Some positions become available as Library Clerks move upward within the library.

Efforts to contain costs in public libraries may mean more hiring of support staff such as Library Clerks than librarians. Also, due to changing roles within libraries, Library Clerks are taking on more responsibility. While public libraries are not usually directly affected by the ups and downs of the business cycle, some of these workers may lose their jobs if there are cuts in government budgets.

Because many public library positions are advertised only locally, it's worth checking the classified ad sections of newspapers. Many times, the on-line version will be more convenient than the print, because you can frequently search the classifieds by keyword. Ads are usually posted whenever a job comes open, and will mention a title and brief description of the position. In most cases, public library positions are filled at the local level, and Library Clerks working for public libraries are usually considered employees of the city or town where the library is located.

Advancement Prospects

A Library Clerk can usually advance by transferring to a position with more responsibilities. Library Clerks can be promoted to library assistants or library technicians. Advancement opportunities are better in larger public libraries and may be more limited in smaller ones. Most libraries fill office and administrative support positions by promoting individuals within their organization, so Library Clerks who acquire new skills, experience, and training improve their advancement opportunities.

Education and Training

A high school diploma is generally required for a position as a Library Clerk, and standard secretarial and computer skills are highly desirable. Library Clerks often learn the skills they need in high schools, business schools, and community colleges. Business education programs offered by these institutions typically include courses in typing, word processing, shorthand, business communications, records management, and office systems and procedures.

Additional training for Library Clerks usually takes place on the job under the guidance of a supervisor or an experienced library assistant or technician. Most Library Clerks continue to receive instruction on new procedures and library policies after their initial training ends.

Experience, Skills, and Personality Traits

Experience with computers and good interpersonal skills are equally important to employers. Many Library Clerks deal directly with the public, so a professional appearance and pleasant personality are important. A clear speaking voice and fluency in the English language also are essential, because these employees frequently use the telephone or public address systems. Library Clerks work in areas that are clean, well lit, and relatively quiet, although their work may be repetitive and stressful.

Unions and Associations

Library Clerks can belong to a variety of trade associations that provide educational guidance, support, conferences, and information to members. These might include the American Library Association, the Library Assistants and Technicians Group, the Association of Part-Time Librarians, the American Society for Information Science, or the Special Libraries Association.

Tips for Entry

1. Library Clerk jobs may be found in the classified section of your local newspaper, in either the print or online versions. Often administrators who have time to advertise choose this method.
2. Visit your local library and speak with the director about possible jobs.
3. Take every opportunity available to get experience; volunteer in the type of library that interests you. Library administrators are likely to prefer a candidate with some relevant experience.
4. Make contacts. Join various professional organizations for librarians and keep in touch with your library friends to provide a network through which you may hear about job opportunities.
5. Send out your résumé. Find out the name and address of every library in your area where you might like to work (the telephone book is helpful; call to find out to whom to address your cover letter). When openings occur, administrators often pull out their collection of unsolicited résumés and contact the candidates.

PUBLIC LIBRARY ASSISTANT

CAREER PROFILE

Duties: Organize library resources and make them available to users; help librarians and, in some cases, library technicians

Alternate Title(s): None

Salary Range: $20,800 to $35,000+

Employment Prospects: Excellent

Advancement Prospects: Good

Best Geographical Location(s): Larger cities may offer more possibilities, but public libraries throughout the country use Library Assistants

Prerequisites:

Education or Training—High school diploma, with Library Technology Certificate or equivalent public library experience; college degree helpful

Experience—Experience working in a library is helpful; computer skills are needed for many jobs

Special Skills and Personality Traits—Good people skills; attention to detail; neatness; organizational skills; aptitude for computers; good English writing and speaking skills; willingness to attend conferences and workshops; willingness to learn new skills

CAREER LADDER

```
┌─────────────────────────────────────┐
│   Library Technician or Supervisor   │
└─────────────────────────────────────┘

┌─────────────────────────────────────┐
│          Library Assistant           │
└─────────────────────────────────────┘

┌─────────────────────────────────────┐
│            Library Clerk             │
└─────────────────────────────────────┘
```

Position Description

Library Assistants assist the professional librarian or information specialist, in tasks such as selection and organization of materials in their subject specialty, as well as helping library customers with research. Their education gives them subject expertise, familiarity with research techniques and a broad base of knowledge. They build on this academic foundation as they gain library experience. They may also participate in acquisitions and technical services—ordering, processing, and cataloging materials—or provide services to patrons, such as charging out or receiving materials.

At the circulation desk, Assistants lend and collect books, periodicals, videotapes, DVDs, and other materials. When an item is borrowed, Assistants stamp the due date on the material and record the patron's identification from his or her library card. They inspect returned materials for damage, check due dates, and compute fines for overdue

material. Library Assistants review records to compile a list of overdue materials and send out notices. They also answer patrons' questions and refer those they cannot answer to a librarian.

Throughout the library, Assistants sort returned books, periodicals, and other items and return them to their designated shelves, files, or storage areas. They locate materials to be loaned, either for a patron or another library. Many card catalogs are computerized, so Library Assistants must be familiar with the computer system. If any materials have been damaged, these workers try to repair them. For example, they use tape or paste to repair torn pages or book covers and other specialized processes to repair more valuable materials.

Some Library Assistants specialize in helping patrons who have vision problems. Sometimes referred to as library clerks, talking-books clerks, or Braille-and-talking-books clerks, they review the borrower's list of desired material. They locate those materials or closely related substitutes from the library collection of large type or braille volumes, tape cassettes, and open-reel talking books. They complete the paperwork and give or mail them to the borrower.

Salaries

Salaries for this position vary a great deal depending on specific job responsibilities and the location of the library. Workers with college degrees are likely to start at higher salaries and advance more easily than those without degrees. Salaries range from $20,800 to more than $35,000.

Employment Prospects

The job outlook is good, and there are many opportunities for flexible schedules; more than half of all Library Assistants have part-time schedules. Opportunities should be good for people interested in jobs as Library Assistants through 2012. Turnover of these workers is quite high, reflecting the limited investment in training and subsequent weak attachment to this occupation. Many openings will become available each year to replace workers who transfer to another occupation or as Library Assistants move within the organization.

Employment is expected to grow about as fast as the average for all occupations through 2012. Efforts to contain costs in local governments may result in more hiring of library support staff than librarians. Also, due to changing roles within libraries, Library Assistants are taking on more responsibility. Because most are employed by public institutions, Library Assistants are not directly affected by the ups and downs of the business cycle. Some of these workers may lose their jobs, however, if there are cuts in government budgets.

Because many public library positions are advertised only locally, it's worth checking the classified ad sections of newspapers. Many times, the on-line version will be more convenient than the print, because you can frequently search the classifieds by keyword. Ads are usually posted whenever a job comes open, and will mention a title and brief description of the position. In most cases, public library positions are filled at the local level, and Library Assistants working for public libraries are usually considered employees of the city or town where the library is located.

Advancement Prospects

Advancement usually comes by transfer to a position with more responsibilities or by promotion to a supervisory position. Library Assistants can be promoted to library technicians, and eventually reach supervisory positions in public service or technical service areas. Advancement opportunities are better in larger libraries and may be more limited in smaller ones. Most libraries fill administrative support positions by promoting individuals within their organization, so Library Assistants who acquire new skills, experience, and training improve their advancement opportunities. In a number of libraries, a college degree may be required for advancement to management ranks.

Education and Training

Although many employers prefer to hire Library Assistants with a higher level of education, it is only required in a few positions. Orientation and training for Library Assistants usually takes place on the job, and new employees often learn job tasks through on-the-job training under the guidance of a supervisor or an experienced library technician. Most Library Assistants continue to receive instruction on new procedures and library policies after their initial training ends. Some formal classroom training also may be necessary, such as training in specific computer software.

Experience, Skills, and Personality Traits

Familiarity or experience with computers and good interpersonal skills often are equally important to employers. Many Library Assistants deal directly with the public, so a professional appearance and pleasant personality are important. A clear speaking voice and fluency in the English language also are essential, because these employees frequently use the telephone or public address systems. Good spelling and computer literacy often are needed, particularly because most work involves considerable computer use. Library Assistants work in areas that are clean, well lit, and relatively quiet, although their work may be repetitious and stressful.

Unions and Associations

Library Assistants can belong to a variety of trade associations that provide educational guidance, support, conferences and information to members. These might include the American Library Association, the Library Assistants and Technicians Group, the Association of Part-Time Librarians, the American Society for Information Science, or the Special Libraries Association.

Tips for Entry

1. Jobs in this field may be found in the classified section of your local newspaper. Often administrators who have time to advertise choose this method.
2. Take every opportunity available to get experience; volunteer in the type of library that interests you. Library administrators are likely to select a candidate with some relevant experience over one with none.
3. Make contacts. Join various professional organizations for librarians and keep in touch with your library

friends to provide a network through which you may hear about job opportunities.

4. Send out your résumé. Find out the name and address of every library in your area where you might like to work (the telephone book is helpful; call to find out to whom to address your cover let-

ter). When openings occur, administrators often pull out their collection of unsolicited résumés and contact the candidates.

5. If you're targeting a specific institution or geographic area, take a look at individual library websites for postings.

PUBLIC LIBRARY TECHNICIAN

CAREER PROFILE

Duties: Help clients access library or information center materials, and help locate, buy, catalog, and circulate materials

Alternate Title(s): Library Assistant, Media Aide, Library Technical Assistant

Salary Range: $14,410 to $38,000+

Employment Prospects: Excellent

Advancement Prospects: Excellent

Best Geographical Location(s): Large cities may offer more possibilities, but public libraries throughout the country use Library Technicians

Prerequisites:

Education or Training—High school diploma, associate or bachelor's degree, or diploma/certificate from library technician course

Experience—Experience working in a library is helpful; computer skills are needed for many jobs

Special Skills and Personality Traits—Good people skills; attention to detail; neatness; organizational skills; aptitude for computers; good English writing and speaking skills; willingness to attend conferences and workshops; willingness to learn new skills

CAREER LADDER

```
┌─────────────────────────────┐
│         Librarian           │
└─────────────────────────────┘

┌─────────────────────────────┐
│     Library Technician      │
└─────────────────────────────┘

┌─────────────────────────────┐
│        Entry Level          │
└─────────────────────────────┘
```

Position Description

Library Technicians help clients access information and help find, buy, catalog, and circulate materials. They usually work with a librarian, although in small libraries they may work on their own, juggling many different duties and projects such as shelving books, providing reference help, organizing materials, reading book reviews and publishers' catalogs to keep up with current literature and other available resources.

Library Technicians prepare cards, computer records, or other access tools for patrons, and may be involved in loaning books, films, pictures, maps, microforms, and DVDs and videotapes. They may spend the day performing a wide variety of tasks, from locating specialized materials in the library, providing quick reference information, reshelving books, implementing programs and library tours for children and adults, and designing or maintaining webpages, to providing technical support to library or information center clients.

Library Technicians direct library users to standard references, organize and maintain periodicals, prepare volumes for binding, handle interlibrary loan requests, prepare invoices, perform routine cataloging and coding of library materials, retrieve information from computer databases, and supervise support staff.

They also may provide research from commercial databases, provide research from Internet searches or on-line databases, and much more. Technicians also compile lists of books, periodicals, articles, and audiovisual materials on particular subjects; analyze collections; recommend materials; and collect and organize books, pamphlets, manuscripts, and other materials.

The widespread use of computerized information storage and retrieval systems has meant that Library Technicians now handle more technical jobs, such as entering catalog information into the library's computer, that were once performed by librarians. As libraries use more and more new technologies, such as CD-ROMs, the Internet, virtual libraries, and automated databases, the duties of Library Technicians will continue to expand and evolve.

At the same time, the increased automation of record-keeping has reduced the amount of clerical work performed by Library Technicians. Many libraries now offer self-service registration and circulation with computers, decreasing the time Library Technicians spend manually recording and inputting records.

Some Library Technicians operate and maintain audiovisual equipment, such as projectors, tape recorders, and videocassette recorders, and assist users with microfilm or microfiche readers. They also design posters, bulletin boards, or displays.

Salaries

Salaries for this position vary a great deal depending on specific job responsibilities and the location of the library. Median annual earnings of Library Technicians in 2002 were $24,090. The middle 50 percent earned between $18,150 and $31,140. The lowest 10 percent earned less than $14,410, and the highest 10 percent earned more than $38,000.

Employment Prospects

The outlook is extremely strong for Library Technicians, and increasing use of computerized circulation and information systems should spur job growth. Since computerized systems have made cataloging easier, Library Technicians can now handle these jobs. While budget constraints of many libraries may moderate growth, the need to replace Library Technicians as they advance or leave the profession means there will still be many additional job openings.

While many individuals have completed special programs in library technical assistance, the need for Technicians is so strong that many libraries have hired individuals who have not completed postsecondary educational courses, offering on-the-job training. Eventually, specialized postsecondary school training may become required for Technician jobs, but at the moment this is not the case.

Because many public library positions are advertised only locally, it's worth checking the classified ad sections of newspapers. Many times, the on-line version will be more convenient than the print, because you can frequently search the classifieds by keyword. Ads are usually posted whenever a job opening occurs, and will mention a title and brief description of the position. In most cases, public library positions are filled at the local level, and Library Technicians working for public libraries are usually considered employees of the city or town where the library is located.

Advancement Prospects

Library Technicians usually advance by assuming added responsibilities. For example, Technicians may begin at the circulation desk, checking books in and out for customers. After gaining experience, they may become responsible for storing and verifying information. As they advance, they may become involved in budget and personnel matters in their department. Some Library Technicians advance to supervisory positions and are in charge of the day-to-day operation of their department. Other Technicians may move into circulation service directorships, supervisors of clerical personnel, or supervisors of support staff.

Education and Training

Training requirements for Library Technicians vary, from a high school diploma to specialized postsecondary training. Library Technicians need at least a high school diploma and perhaps a diploma from a Library Technician course; some Technicians also have an associate or bachelor's degree. Some employers hire individuals with work experience or other training, while others train inexperienced workers on the job. Some libraries require that Technicians have an associate or bachelor's degree. Given widespread use of technology in libraries, computer skills are needed for many jobs. An understanding of databases, library automation systems, on-line library systems, on-line public access systems, and circulation systems is valuable.

Some two-year colleges offer an associate of arts degree in library technology, in both liberal arts and library-related study. In these courses, students learn about library and media organization and operation, and how to order, process, catalog, locate, and circulate library materials and work with library automation. Libraries and associations offer continuing education courses to keep Technicians abreast of new developments in the field.

Experience, Skills, and Personality Traits

Library Technicians need to feel a commitment to working with people; the ability to pay close attention to details; neatness; organizational skills; aptitude for computers; good English writing and speaking skills; willingness to attend conferences and workshops; and a willingness to learn new skills.

Unions and Associations

Librarian Technicians working in libraries could belong to a variety of trade associations that provide educational guidance, support, conferences, and information to members. These include the American Library Association, the

Library Assistants and Technicians Group, and the Public Library Association.

Tips for Entry

1. Jobs in this field may be found in the classified section of your local newspaper. For more targeted ads, check out the job listings for all related trade associations, beginning with the American Library Association.

2. Take every opportunity available to get experience; volunteer in the type of library that interests you. Library administrators are likely to select a candidate with some relevant experience over one with none.

3. Make contacts. Join various professional organizations for librarians and keep in touch with your library friends to provide a network through which you may hear about job opportunities.

4. Send out your résumé. Find out the name and address of every library in your area where you might like to work (the telephone book is helpful; call to find out to whom to address your cover letter). When openings occur, administrators often pull out their collection of unsolicited résumés and contact the candidates.

5. E-mail discussion groups such as LIBJOBS and LIS-JOBS are a good source for job postings. Topical groups are also a good place for finding advertisements in a particular field of librarianship. For example, Web4Lib often receives library Webmaster-type job postings.

6. Look for jobs on the Internet, such as on www.Lisjobs.com. *Jobs for Librarians and Information Professionals* is a comprehensive guide to on-line job resources for librarians and information professionals.

7. Check daily job postings on "Hot Jobs Online" at the website of the American Library Association (www.ala.org). Investigate other Internet websites that list library job postings, such as www.libraryjobpostings.org, or the American Society of Information Science website jobline (www.asis.org/Jobline).

8. Other helpful on-line sites include Newspapers.com or Newspaperlinks.com.

9. Visit the ALISE website, which has links to all library schools, each of which has state and national employment listings (www.alise.org).

10. Subscribe to major library trade publications, such as *Library Journal* and *American Libraries.*

11. If you're targeting a specific institution or geographic area, take a look at individual library websites for postings.

12. Attend library conventions or conferences and check job boards, and be sure not to miss the placement service which lists library-related jobs at annual ALA conventions.

PUBLIC LIBRARIAN

CAREER PROFILE

Duties: Assist patrons; manage staff; select and purchase materials; prepare new materials; supervise assistants; manage technology

Alternate Title(s): Information Specialist

Salary Range: $24,510 to $66,590+

Employment Prospects: Good

Advancement Prospects: Good

Best Geographical Location(s): Positions in rural areas may be more plentiful, since competition is stiff for jobs in large metropolitan areas

Prerequisites:

Education or Training—Master's degree in library or information science (M.L.S.)

Experience—Student internship or volunteer experience in a library is helpful

Special Skills and Personality Traits—Good people skills; communications skills; organizational ability; excellent computer skills; attention to detail; willingness to work independently; organizational ability

Licensure/Certification—Most States require that Public Librarians employed in municipal, county, or regional library systems be certified

CAREER LADDER

```
┌────────────────────────────────────┐
│ Library Director or Department Head │
│      or Chief Information Officer   │
└────────────────────────────────────┘

┌────────────────────────────────────┐
│          Public Librarian          │
└────────────────────────────────────┘

┌────────────────────────────────────┐
│         Library Technician         │
└────────────────────────────────────┘
```

Position Description

Service is the cornerstone of public librarianship. The size and character of the library determine whether Librarians perform all types of jobs in the library, or specialize in just one area, such as acquisitions or reference. Most Librarian positions incorporate three aspects of library work: user services, technical services, and administrative services.

The traditional concept of a library is being redefined from a place to access paper records or books to one that also houses the most advanced media, including CD-ROMs, the Internet, virtual libraries, and remote access to a wide range of resources. Consequently, more and more Librarians are combining traditional duties with tasks involving quickly changing technology.

In small libraries or information centers, Librarians usually handle all aspects of the work. They read book reviews, publishers' announcements, and catalogs to keep up with current literature and other available resources, and buy materials from publishers, wholesalers, and distributors. Librarians prepare new materials by classifying them by subject matter, and describe books and other library materials so they are easy to find. They supervise assistants who prepare cards, computer records, and other access tools that direct users to resources.

In large libraries, Librarians often specialize in a single area, such as acquisitions, cataloging, bibliography, reference, special collections, or administration. Teamwork is increasingly important to ensure quality service to the public. Librarians help people find information and use it effectively for personal and professional purposes, so they must be familiar with a wide variety of scholarly and public information sources. They also must follow trends in publishing, computers, and the media to effectively oversee the selection and organization of library materials. Therefore, this commitment to continuing education involves a knowledge of current local, state, and federal events, and contemporary themes.

Librarians also manage staff and develop and direct information programs and systems for the public. They organize collections of books, publications, documents, audiovisual aids, and other reference materials for convenient access. They may research, retrieve, and disseminate information from books, periodicals, reference materials, or commercial databases in response to requests and acquire and manage materials in various formats to add to the library collection.

Working with patrons on a daily basis is an important part of a Librarian's job, helping them select books and informational material. They demonstrate library equipment, explain how to use library facilities and procedures, and assemble and arrange display materials. In addition, Librarians may review or publish a list of library materials, including bibliographies and book reviews, and manage library resources stored in files, on film, or in computer databases. They may create databases and instruct staff and customers on database use in information retrieval.

Public Librarians need to understand and work with both the Dewey Decimal system and computer databases, while keeping abreast of current technological trends. Modern technology has transformed the Librarian's job. Automated registration of borrowers, circulation of materials, ordering, and cataloging are now common in all types of public libraries. Many libraries have access to remote databases and maintain their own computerized databases. The widespread use of automation in libraries makes database searching skills important to Librarians. Librarians develop and index databases and help train users to develop searching skills for the information they need. Some libraries are forming consortiums with other libraries through electronic mail, allowing patrons to simultaneously submit information requests to several libraries.

The Internet is expanding the amount of available reference information, giving research Librarians a powerful new tool in their work. Librarians must be aware of how to use these resources in order to locate information.

Librarians also compile lists of books, periodicals, articles, and audiovisual materials on particular subjects, analyze collections, and recommend materials. They collect and organize books, pamphlets, manuscripts, and other materials in a specific field, such as rare books, genealogy, or music. In addition, they coordinate programs such as storytelling for children and literacy skills and book talks for adults, conduct classes, publicize services, provide reference help, write grants, and oversee other administrative matters.

Public Librarians also need to create and follow budgets, and they must work with public officials, trustees, and community leaders to seek the funding required for a robust community library.

Work schedules for Librarians who serve the public directly may be busy, demanding, and even stressful, since answering questions and teaching patrons to use library resources can be taxing. Librarians typically work a five-day, 35-to-40-hour workweek, although many Librarians work part time or on call. Public Librarians may work evenings and weekends. In addition, the job may require a great deal of standing, stooping, bending, and reaching.

Salaries

Salaries for this position vary a great deal depending on the specific job responsibilities and location of the library. Beginning full-time Librarians with a master's degree in library and information studies accredited by the ALA, but with no professional experience, can expect a salary range of $30,126 to $37,580. Librarians with primarily administrative duties often earn more than other Librarians. Median annual earnings of Librarians are $43,090. The middle 50 percent earn between $33,560 and $54,250, the lowest 10 percent earn less than $24,510, and the highest 10 percent earn more than $66,590.

Employment Prospects

Employment of Librarians is expected to grow about as fast as the average for all occupations through 2012, but the number of librarian jobs is still projected to grow about 5 percent through 2008. Retiring Librarians and those leaving the profession for other reasons will create about 39,000 job openings through 2008.

The increasing use of computerized information storage and retrieval systems continues to contribute to slow growth in the demand for Librarians. Computerized systems make cataloging easier, so that library technicians can now handle the task. In addition, many libraries are equipped for users to access library computers directly from their homes or offices. These systems allow users to bypass Librarians and conduct research on their own.

However, Librarians will still be needed to manage staff, help users develop database searching techniques, address complicated reference requests, and define users' needs. Despite expectations of slower-than-average employment growth, the need to replace Librarians as they retire will result in numerous additional job openings. Moreover, the continuing demand for accurate and computer-delivered information has increased the need for Librarians with information management skills. This improves the job prospects for Librarians.

Applicants for librarian jobs in large metropolitan areas, where most graduates prefer to work, usually face competition; those willing to work in rural areas should have better job prospects.

Advancement Prospects

Librarians can advance to administrative positions such as department head, library director, or chief information officer, with more experience and administrative skills, knowledge of automated systems, and additional training. Advancement opportunities are better in larger library systems.

Education and Training

Most public library positions require a master of library science (M.L.S.) degree, preferably from a school accredited by the American Library Association (ALA). Undergraduate degrees in almost any subject area are appropriate.

Most M.L.S. programs take one to two years to complete. A typical graduate program includes courses in the foundations of library and information science, including the history of books and printing, intellectual freedom and censorship, and the role of libraries and information in society. Other basic courses cover material selection and processing, the organization of information, reference tools and strategies, and user services. Courses are adapted to educate Librarians to use new resources brought about by advancing technology such as on-line reference systems, Internet search methods, and automated circulation systems. Course options can include resources for children or young adults; classification, cataloging, indexing, and abstracting; library administration; and library automation.

Computer-related coursework is an increasingly important part of an M.L.S. degree. Some programs offer interdisciplinary degrees combining technical coursework in information science with traditional training in library science. Librarians participate in continuing training once they are on the job to keep abreast of new information systems brought about by changing technology.

Special Requirements

Most states require that Public Librarians employed in municipal, county, or regional library systems be certified. Specific requirements vary from state to state, but in general a graduate of an ALA-accredited program submits an application to the state librarian.

Experience, Skills, and Personality Traits

Librarians spend more than 60 percent of their day working with people, so strong interpersonal and communication skills are required. In addition, excellent organizational and computer skills are important, along with curiosity, attention to detail, a love of books, research, and education.

Working in a public library is a career for those who can wear many hats and work as a team player. The public library brings together all the various aspects of librarianship, working with all age groups and all types of requests for information.

Unions and Associations

Librarians can belong to public employee unions; they also can belong to a variety of trade associations that provide educational guidance, support, conferences, and information to members. These might include the American Library Association, the American Society for Information Science, or the Special Libraries Association.

Tips for Entry

1. Get experience. If you are attending library school, take every opportunity available to work as a student assistant in the university libraries, do a practicum or internship in another library, or volunteer in the type of library which interests you most. Library administrators are likely to select a candidate with some relevant experience over one with none.
2. Make contacts. Join various professional organizations for Librarians and keep in touch with your library friends to provide a network through which you may hear about job opportunities.
3. Send out your résumé. Find out the name and address of every library in your area where you might like to work (the telephone book is helpful; call to find out to whom to address your cover letter). When openings occur, administrators often pull out their collection of unsolicited résumés and contact the candidates.
4. E-mail discussion groups such as LIBJOBS and LIS-JOBS are a good source for job postings. Topical groups are also a good place for finding advertisements in a particular field of librarianship. For example, Web4Lib often receives library Webmaster-type job postings.
5. Check the classified ads in your local newspapers. Often, administrators who have time to advertise choose this method.
6. Look for jobs on the Internet, such as on www.Lisjobs. com. *Jobs for Librarians and Information Professionals* is a comprehensive guide to on-line job resources for Librarians and information professionals.
7. Check daily job postings on "Hot Jobs Online" at the website of the American Library Association (www.ala.org).
8. Investigate other websites that list library job postings, such as http://www.libraryjobpostings.org.
9. Visit the ALISE website, which has links to all library schools, each of which has state and national employment listings (www.alise.org).
10. Visit the American Society of Information Science website job line (http://www.asis.org/Jobline).
11. Subscribe to major library trade publications, such as *Library Journal* and *American Libraries*.

12. If you're targeting a specific institution or geographic area, take a look at individual websites for postings. The Folger Shakespeare Library, for example, has a separate employment opportunities page.

13. Attend library conventions (local, state, and national); check out the placement service that lists library-related jobs at annual ALA conventions.

PUBLIC LIBRARY CATALOGER

CAREER PROFILE

Duties: List library materials (usually in computerized catalogs) by author, title, subject, or keyword

Alternate Title(s): Librarian

Salary Range: $42,730 to $62,900

Employment Prospects: Good

Advancement Prospects: Good

Best Geographical Location(s): More positions are available in larger libraries in cities, although job openings are available throughout the United States

Prerequisites:

Education or Training—Master's degree in library or information science; a second master's in another subject is desirable

Experience—Experience as a volunteer with a library, archive, or museum is helpful

Special Skills and Personality Traits—Able to formulate and communicate complex verbal and written procedures; ability to work independently; good skills in foreign language, communication, and organization

CAREER LADDER

```
┌─────────────────────────────────┐
│   Cataloger in Larger Library    │
└─────────────────────────────────┘

┌─────────────────────────────────┐
│     Public Library Cataloger     │
└─────────────────────────────────┘

┌─────────────────────────────────┐
│     Assistant Cataloger or       │
│      Entry Level Position        │
└─────────────────────────────────┘
```

Position Description

Catalogers classify library materials, describing materials by subject, date published, format, author, title, and other characteristics, completing a record for each item. Catalogers spend their time acquiring and preparing materials and do not deal directly with the public. While this may seem straightforward, in fact the day to day job of a Cataloger requires constant decisions: Will a patron look for a book under an author's real name, or a pseudonym? Is acupressure common enough so that it warrants its own subject heading? In a set of three videos, should users know each title, or is the name of the set sufficient?

As each new item arrives at the library, the Cataloger records the title, author's name, publication information, and a short summary of the item (nonfiction reference, biography, jazz music recording, and so on). Cataloging is not always straightforward, however; Catalogers must make constant distinctions and decisions about materials, such as whether to drop a dated or misleading term, whether to group maps in a separate location under "travel" instead of being listed in the card catalog, and so on.

Certain items that are valuable or important may be photographed and assigned a code. Catalogers used to record all information on cards kept in files accessible to the public, but today data are keyed into database retrieval systems. Because many public libraries are now accessible on-line, making catalogs easy to use is even more important than before.

Modern Catalogers create different catalogs for different kinds of readers; a catalog for young children might use more graphics or might not emphasize alphabetical order; one for casual readers might include brief summaries of each book.

Catalogers search bibliographic databases to determine the relationship of materials in the library to existing bibliographic records. They apply cataloging rules to describe the item, determine subject content, and to establish or modify personal names, corporate names, uniform title(s), series and subject headings, access points, classification, and content designation. They review new and modified authority records submitted from participating libraries for formulation of headings and cross-references.

Cataloging information may be obtained from a variety of sources, such as the Library of Congress, the Online Computer Library Center (OCLC) or the Research Libraries Information Network (RLIN).

Catalogers also work with other Catalogers and technicians in planning and implementing priorities and strategies, and recommend changes and additions in descriptive and subject cataloging rules.

Public Library Catalogers maintain regular business hours unless a large number of books are acquired that need to be stored or displayed immediately, which may require overtime and weekend work. The sheer volume of their tasks can be overwhelming, as materials often come into a public library faster than they can be cataloged; this type of library job can be highly stressful.

Salaries

Salaries for this position vary a great deal depending on the responsibilities and location of the library, but the average is about $42,730. Catalogers in large public libraries in metropolitan areas, or those required to have specific knowledge in specialty areas, can expect to earn more than those employed in smaller institutions.

Employment Prospects

Although this availability of cataloging information from elsewhere makes it possible for many cataloging tasks to be done by assistants, there is always some need for original cataloging. Most libraries now are using computerized catalogs that allow patrons to search by author, title, subject or keyword, all of which needs to be entered by Catalogers. As patrons are now able to log on to on-line public library catalogs from home, the task of the Cataloger has become even more important. The number of jobs is projected to grow about 5 percent through 2012.

Advancement Prospects

Catalogers can become archivists or reference librarians, or take on administrative positions in public, private, or university libraries, or become Catalogers in museums. They can apply their methodical and analytical skills to other fields, such as history, bibliography, and data entry. Promotions usually come with experience and administrative skills, knowledge of automated systems, and additional training. Advancement opportunities are greater in larger library systems.

Education and Training

Catalogers generally need a master's degree in library or information studies, along with a bachelor's degree in general arts. Prospective Catalogers should supplement this education with courses in computers and business studies. It is also a

good idea to volunteer with a library, archive, or museum, as any experience in the field will be beneficial in the long run.

Experience, Skills, and Personality Traits

Catalogers need to understand integrated library systems, library applications, and other information technologies, and be familiar with cataloging rules, procedures, and practices. In addition to a thorough knowledge of the subject area, they should have excellent computer, communication, and organizational skills. Catalogers need to have professional cataloging experience in a public library and knowledge of AACR2, Library of Congress classification schedules. LCSH, and MARC formats.

Catalogers should enjoy research and be able to work independently with a thorough, methodical approach; they must have a reading knowledge of at least one foreign language, and skills in special knowledge areas. An interest in sorting and classification is important in a successful Cataloger.

Unions and Associations

Catalogers working in public libraries may belong to a variety of trade associations that provide educational guidance, support, conferences, and information to members. These might include the American Library Association, the American Society for Information Science, or the Special Libraries Association.

Tips for Entry

1. Get experience. If you are attending library school, take every opportunity available to work as a student assistant or volunteer in the cataloging department of the library. When you're ready to find a permanent job after graduation, you'll find that administrators are likely to select a candidate with some relevant experience over one with none.
2. Make contacts. Join professional organizations for librarians and keep in touch with your library friends to provide a network through which you may hear about job opportunities.
3. Send out your résumé. Find out the name and address of every library in your area where you might like to work (the telephone book is helpful; call to find out to whom to address your cover letter). When openings occur, administrators often pull out their collection of unsolicited résumés and contact the candidates.
4. E-mail discussion groups LIBJOBS and LIS-JOBS are a good source for job postings. Topical groups are also a good place for finding advertisements in a particular field of librarianship. For example, Web4Lib often receives library Webmaster-type job postings.
5. Look for jobs on the Internet, such as on www. Lisjobs.com. *Jobs for Librarians and Information Professionals* is a comprehensive guide to on-line job resources for librarians and information professionals.

Check daily job postings on "Hot Jobs Online" at the website of the American Library Association (www.ala.org). Investigate other websites that list library job postings, such as: www.libraryjobpostings.org

6. Visit the ALISE website, which has links to all library schools, each of which has state and national employment listings (www.alise.org), or the American Society of Information Science website job line (www.asis.org/Jobline).

7. Subscribe to major library trade publications, such as *Library Journal* and *American Libraries*.

8. If you're targeting a specific institution or geographic area, take a look at individual websites for postings. The Folger Shakespeare Library, in Washington, D.C., for example, has an employment opportunities page.

9. Check out the placement service that lists library-related jobs at annual ALA conventions.

ASSISTANT PUBLIC LIBRARY DIRECTOR

CAREER PROFILE

Duties: Assist the library director with hiring and training staff, attending meetings, scheduling, and handling public relations

Alternate Title(s): Associate Library Director

Salary Range: $42,629 to $100,000+

Employment Prospects: Good

Advancement Prospects: Good

Best Geographical Location(s): Large and small public libraries are located in every state; larger urban areas may have more opportunities

Prerequisites:

    Education or Training—Master's degree in library or information science (M.L.S.)

    Experience—At least three years' professional library experience usually required

    Special Skills and Personality Traits—Good people skills; communications skills; organizational ability; computer skills; managerial skills

CAREER LADDER

```
┌─────────────────────────────────────┐
│      Public Library Director         │
└─────────────────────────────────────┘

┌─────────────────────────────────────┐
│  Assistant Public Library Director   │
└─────────────────────────────────────┘

┌─────────────────────────────────────┐
│             Librarian                │
└─────────────────────────────────────┘
```

Position Description

Depending on the size of the library, the Assistant Public Library Director spends most hours on administrative tasks, although at smaller libraries he or she may also fill in on the reference desk or assisting patrons. The Assistant Director helps oversee the management of the library; performs public relations and fund-raising duties; and helps direct activities to make sure the library functions properly.

In addition to helping to run the library, an important part of the Assistant Director's day is to manage library employees, help evaluate new employees, and attend meetings, workshops, seminars, and conferences. The Assistant Director may be required from time to time to represent the director at state, regional, and national professional organizations.

Assistant Library Directors may need to work more than a standard 40-hour week, including some weekend and evening hours. They also must be able to use library equipment, including computers, printers, copiers, typewriters, microfilm readers, and fax machines. Assistant Library Directors also need to create and follow budgets, and they must work with public officials, trustees, and community leaders to seek the funding required for a robust community library.

Salaries

Salaries for this position vary a great deal depending on the responsibilities and location of the library. The starting salary for Assistant Library Directors and those who supervise support staff is about $43,000; with experience, annual income can top $100,000 at a large public library.

Employment Prospects

Employment prospects for Assistant Library Directors continue to be good as technological advancement opens up new opportunities in public libraries. Librarians' technological skills have improved their employment prospects and should continue to make this a strong career choice through 2012.

Advancement Prospects

After a few years working as a librarian and then Assistant Library Director, the logical next step on the library career ladder is to move into a directorship. Assistant Library Directors who pursue continuing education and technological advancement will find plenty of opportunities to move into more responsible administrative positions in larger public libraries. Promotions usually come with the acquisition of experience and administrative skills, knowledge of automated systems, and additional training. Advancement opportunities are greater in the larger library systems.

Education and Training

Most public library positions require a master of library science (M.L.S.) degree, preferably from a school accredited by the American Library Association (ALA). Undergraduate degrees in almost any subject area are appropriate. Several years of experience as a librarian in a public library is usually required.

Experience, Skills, and Personality Traits

Assistant Library Directors should possess strong interpersonal and communication skills, excellent organizational and computer skills, managerial skills, and be capable of dealing with employees, supervisors, patrons, trustees, and the public. In addition, Assistant Library Directors often are required to have at least three years of professional library experience.

Unions and Associations

Assistant or associate Library Directors do not usually belong to unions, but they can belong to a variety of trade associations that provide educational guidance, support, conferences, and information to members. These might include the American Library Association, the American Society for Information Science, the Association for Library Collections and Technical Services, Association for Records Managers and Administrators, or the Library Administration and Management Association.

Tips for Entry

1. Join various professional organizations to have a network through which you may hear about job opportunities.
2. Visit e-mail discussion groups such as LIBJOBS and LIS-JOBS, which are a good source for job postings. Topical groups are also a good place for finding advertisements in a particular field of librarianship.
3. Look for jobs on the Internet, on such sites as www.Lisjobs.com; the daily job postings on "Hot Jobs Online" at the website of the American Library Association (www.ala.org); the American Society of Information Science website job line (www.asis.org/Jobline); or www.libraryjobpostings.org.
4. Check out *Jobs for Librarians and Information Professionals,* a comprehensive guide to on-line job resources for librarians and information professionals.
5. Visit the ALISE website, which has links to all library schools, each of which has state and national employment listings (www.alise.org).
6. Subscribe to major library trade publications, such as *Library Journal* and *American Libraries.*
7. If you're targeting a specific institution or geographic area, take a look at individual websites for postings.
8. Attend library conventions or conferences and check job boards, and check out the placement service that lists library-related jobs at annual ALA conventions.
9. Check out the *American Library Directory,* which lists a wide variety of libraries in its two-volume directory, or the *Guide to Employment Sources in the Library and Information Professions,* which is available online at the American Library Association website.

PUBLIC LIBRARY DIRECTOR

CAREER PROFILE

Duties: Significant management responsibilities, including hiring and training staff, maintaining the facility, attending meetings, scheduling, budgeting, and handling public relations

Alternate Title(s): Library Administrator or Head Librarian

Salary Range: $72,384 to $274,519+

Employment Prospects: Good

Advancement Prospects: Good

Best Geographical Location(s): Larger cities may offer more possibilities, but libraries throughout the country have positions for director

Prerequisites:

Education or Training—Master's degree in library or information science (M.L.S.); a Ph.D. or D.L.S. (doctor of library science) may be necessary to obtain a director position in a top public library

Experience—Professional library experience, preferably in an administrative or managerial capacity in a public library

Special Skills and Personality Traits—Good people skills; administrative skills; communications skills and organizational ability; good computer and technology skills; intellectual curiosity; above-average academic ability; a desire for continuing education; ability to make decisions

CAREER LADDER

```
┌─────────────────────────────────────┐
│   Library Director of Larger Library │
└─────────────────────────────────────┘

┌─────────────────────────────────────┐
│       Public Library Director        │
└─────────────────────────────────────┘

┌─────────────────────────────────────┐
│   Assistant Public Library Director  │
└─────────────────────────────────────┘
```

Position Description

The Public Library Director plans, coordinates, and supervises all aspects of the library, and is usually responsible to the library board of trustees for implementing policies and services. A large part of the Director's job is administrative, and involves working with public officials, trustees, and community leaders to obtain the funding required for a robust community library. The Director must oversee the management and planning of the library; negotiate contracts for services, materials, and equipment; perform public relations and fund-raising duties; prepare budgets; and direct activities to make sure the library functions properly. There is virtually no time to read or interact with patrons, because the higher you climb on the library career ladder, the less free time you have for books.

In addition to running the library, an important part of the Director's day is to manage library employees and administer the library personnel policy, including evaluation of current employees. The Director must replace and add new personnel as needed, and keep the staff well-trained, including scheduling employees for either refreshment training or training for new responsibilities.

The increased use of automated information systems means that Library Directors can focus on administrative and budgeting responsibilities, grant writing, and specialized research requests, while delegating more technical and user services responsibilities to technicians.

Library Directors are also involved in planning public relations activities, maintaining a close relationship with county and local officials, community leaders, and civic groups to keep them informed of library needs. Planning new buildings or alterations and improvements in existing buildings throughout the system is another important part of the job.

The duties of a Library Director may require working beyond the standard 40-hour week and involve some weekend and evening work. The Director also attends workshops, seminars, and conferences, and is active in state, regional, and national professional organizations. The Director formulates draft proposals for federal and other library grants. He or she also must be able to use library equipment, including computers, printers, copiers, typewriters, microfilm readers, and fax machines.

In addition, the Library Director is responsible for the overall maintenance of the collection, keeping it current, attractive, and useful by setting up a schedule of replacement for encyclopedias; placing standing orders for annuals and irregular publications needed in reference; and systematically checking bibliographies and selection aids for new editions, replacement titles, and subject area expansion. The Director also must evaluate the current collection, maintain a continuous program of weeding to remove obsolete and worn-out materials, and conduct periodic inventory checks.

Salaries

Salaries for this position vary a great deal depending on the responsibilities and location of the library; $72,384 is the average salary for a Public Library Director in a suburban setting; rural Public Library Directors average less. The highest salaries for Library Directors of very large libraries, who supervise an extensive support staff, may top $274,519.

Employment Prospects

Employment prospects for Library Directors in public libraries are good; almost every village, town, and city in the United States has its own public library, and each of these libraries needs a Director.

Advancement Prospects

As the explosion of technology continues, opportunities continue to improve for Library Directors educated in ever-increasing technological areas. If the individual continues to keep up with his or her education, it should be possible to move into larger and more responsible administrative positions in larger public libraries. Library Directors often are required to have between three and five years of professional library experience as some type of librarian.

Education and Training

Most public library positions require a master of library science (M.L.S.) degree, preferably from a school accredited by the American Library Association (ALA). Undergraduate degrees in almost any subject area are appropriate.However, individuals interested in obtaining some of the top Director

positions in the country may find it helpful to have a Ph.D. or L.L.S. in library science or an advanced business degree.

Experience, Skills, and Personality Traits

Library Directors should be skilled in analyzing and resolving complex problems in a wide variety of areas, and be capable of dealing with employees, supervisors, patrons, trustees, news media, and the public. Directors should have good people skills and be able to maintain effective working relationships with the library board, staff, the general public, county officials, and private agencies and organizations. They should be flexible, adaptable, and be comfortable with both the public and technical aspects of the library.

In addition, a Library Director should be able to evaluate financial data and understand budgets; analyze the needs of the library; and maintain a collection of books, periodicals, and other documents in a variety of formats, including electronic, to meet those needs.

Unions and Associations

Library Directors working in public libraries do not usually belong to unions, but they can belong to a variety of trade associations that provide educational guidance, support, conferences, and information to members. These might include the American Library Association, the American Society for Information Science, the Association for Library Collections and Technical Services, Association for Records Managers and Administrators, the Association for Library Trustees and Advocates, or the Library Administration and Management Association.

Tips for Entry

1. Join various professional organizations for Library Directors to provide a network through which you may hear about job opportunities.
2. E-mail discussion groups LIBJOBS and LIS-JOBS are a good source for job postings. Topical groups are also a good place for finding advertisements in a particular field of librarianship.
3. Look for jobs on the Internet, such as on www. Lisjobs.com, the daily job postings on "Hot Jobs Online" at the website of the American Library Association (www.ala.org), the American Society of Information Science website job line (www.asis.org/ Jobline), or www.libraryjobpostings.org.
4. Check out *Jobs for Librarians and Information Professionals,* a comprehensive guide to on-line job resources for librarians and information professionals.
5. Visit the ALISE website, which has links to all library schools, each of which has state and national employment listings (www.alise.org).
6. Subscribe to major library trade publications, such as *Library Journal* and *American Libraries.*

7. If you're targeting a specific institution or geographic area, take a look at individual library websites for postings.
8. Attend library conventions or conferences and check job boards, and check out the placement service that lists library-related jobs at annual ALA conventions.

9. Check out the *American Library Directory,* which lists a wide variety of libraries in its two-volume directory, or the *Guide to Employment Sources in the Library and Information Professions,* which is available on-line at the American Library Association website.

GOVERNMENT DOCUMENTS LIBRARIAN (PUBLIC LIBRARY)

CAREER PROFILE

Duties: Work with the public in locating, evaluating, and organizing information published by government bodies

Alternate Title(s): Government Documents Information Specialist

Salary Range: $24,510 to $66,590+

Employment Prospects: Good

Advancement Prospects: Good

Best Geographical Location(s): Urban areas with large public libraries offer the best chance for positions, but job openings are available in most large cities in the United States

Prerequisites:

Education or Training—Master of library science is required

Experience—An internship experience in a government documents collection is excellent preparation for a position as government documents librarian

Special Skills and Personality Traits—Willingness to work with the public, flexibility, patience, attention to detail, statistical ability, and computer skills

CAREER LADDER

```
┌─────────────────────────────────┐
│      Library Director           │
└─────────────────────────────────┘

┌─────────────────────────────────┐
│  Government Documents Librarian │
└─────────────────────────────────┘

┌─────────────────────────────────┐
│  Assistant Government Documents │
│   Librarian or Entry Level      │
└─────────────────────────────────┘
```

Position Description

Government Documents Librarians who work in public libraries specialize in helping library patrons locate and evaluate information published by the government. This may include both published and unpublished government information that appears in print, CD-ROM, on-line, and multimedia formats.

Government Documents Librarians evaluate and select documents, reference works, maps, geographic information systems, and resources that are not provided as a part of the library's depository programs. Government Documents Librarians also must process documents classified according to unique schemes contained in the Superintendent of Documents Classification System (SUDOC). Librarians must be familiar with this system and work closely with the cataloging department to ensure that they follow the rules.

They may conduct instructional sessions in the use of documents, administer the federal and state government document depository programs, do some cataloging, help patrons access documents in various electronic formats, and participate in general reference service, bibliographic instruction, outreach, and collection development.

Government Documents Librarians are also responsible for providing reference desk, telephone, and electronic mail services, and spend time designing and implementing educational and outreach programs in order to inform users about the services and resources available. They give direct reference assistance to users seeking documents and other information, instruct patrons in the use of library resources, and help facilitate access to information in a variety of formats. They may also staff the reference desk on evenings and weekends.

The Government Documents Librarian also oversees the acquisition and processing of federal documents in multiple formats.

Salaries

Salaries for this position vary a great deal depending on specific job responsibilities and the location of the library. Beginning full-time Government Documents Librarians with a master's degree in library and information studies accredited by the ALA but with no professional experience can expect a salary range of $30,126 to $37,580; with experience, the salary may surpass $66,590.

Employment Prospects

According to the U.S. Government Printing Office, most U.S. federal information is now available electronically, but there are still more than 1,200 depository libraries that disseminate this information to ensure free access. More and more public libraries realize that Government Documents Librarians can help their patrons, who need help to understand and discover statistical sets of data, geographic information systems, and electronic access to government information.

Advancement Prospects

Government Documents Librarians can move into administrative positions such as department head, library director, or chief information officer, with more experience and administrative skills, knowledge of automated systems, and additional training. Advancement opportunities are better in large public library systems in urban areas, although this is also where competition is strongest.

Education and Training

Most Government Documents Librarian positions require a master of library science (M.L.S.) degree, preferably from a school accredited by the American Library Association (ALA). Undergraduate degrees in almost any subject area are appropriate.

Most M.L.S. programs take one to two years to complete, and include courses in the foundations of library and information science, including the history of books and printing, intellectual freedom and censorship, and the role of libraries and information in society. Other basic courses cover material selection and processing, the organization of information, reference tools and strategies, and user services. Courses are adapted to educate Librarians to use new resources brought about by advancing technology such as on-line reference systems, Internet search methods, and automated circulation systems.

Computer-related coursework is an important part of an M.L.S. degree. Some programs offer interdisciplinary degrees combining technical coursework in information science with traditional training in library science. Librarians

participate in continuing training once they are on the job to keep abreast of new information systems brought about by changing technology.

Experience, Skills, and Personality Traits

Government Documents Librarians must understand current issues and practices in processing and cataloging federal government publications, as well as being familiar with the U.S. Federal Depository Library Program and depository library standards. Characteristics of a good Government Documents Librarian include flexibility, patience, the ability to work with details and statistics, and computer knowledge.

Unions and Associations

Government Documents Librarians may belong to a variety of trade associations that provide educational guidance, support, conferences, and information to members. These might include the National Association of Government Archives and Records Administrators, the American Library Association, the American Society for Information Science, or the Special Libraries Association.

Tips for Entry

1. Get experience. If you are attending library school, take every opportunity available to work as a student assistant in the university library or do a practicum or internship in another library. Library administrators are likely to select a candidate with some relevant experience.

2. Make contacts. Join professional organizations for Librarians and keep in touch with your library friends to provide a network through which you may hear about job opportunities.

3. Send out your résumé. Find out the name and address of every library in your area where you might like to work (the telephone book is helpful; call to find out to whom to address your cover letter). When openings occur, administrators often pull out their collection of unsolicited résumés and contact the candidates.

4. E-mail discussion groups such as LIBJOBS and LIS-JOBS are a good source for job postings. Topical groups are also a good place for finding advertisements in a particular field of librarianship. For example, Web4Lib often receives library Webmaster-type job postings.

5. Check the classified ads in your local newspapers. Often, administrators who have time to advertise choose this method.

6. Look for jobs on the Internet, such as on www.Lisjobs. com. *Jobs for Librarians and Information Professionals* is a comprehensive guide to on-line job resources for Librarians and information professionals. Check

daily job postings on "Hot Jobs Online" at the website of the American Library Association (www.ala.org). Investigate other websites that list library job postings, such as: www.libraryjobpostings.org.

7. Visit the ALISE website, which has links to all library schools, each of which has state and national employment listings (www.alise.org), or the American Society of Information Science website job line (www.asis.org/Jobline).

8. Subscribe to major library trade publications, such as *Library Journal* and *American Libraries.*

9. If you're targeting a specific institution or geographic area, take a look at individual websites for postings. The Folger Shakespeare Library in Washington, D.C., for example, has a separate employment opportunities page.

10. Check out the placement service that lists library-related jobs at annual ALA conventions.

MUSIC LIBRARIAN (PUBLIC LIBRARY)

CAREER PROFILE

Duties: Teach users how to use the music materials; answer public reference inquiries; catalog and organize music

Alternate Title(s): None

Salary Range: $30,000 to $50,000+

Employment Prospects: Good

Advancement Prospects: Good

Best Geographical Location(s): Urban centers with large research libraries (such as the New York Public Library) offer more possibilities, but many public libraries throughout the country maintain music collections

Prerequisites:

Education or Training—Master's degrees in both library science and music

Experience—The best introduction to music librarianship as a career is to work in a music library as a volunteer; several years of experience in some capacity in music libraries is often required

Special Skills and Personality Traits—Patience, interest in working with the public, and love of books and music

Licensure/Certification—Most states require that public librarians employed in municipal, county, or regional library systems be certified

CAREER LADDER

```
┌─────────────────────────────────────┐
│         Music Librarian at           │
│     Larger Public Library or         │
│  Director of Music at Public Library │
└─────────────────────────────────────┘

┌─────────────────────────────────────┐
│     Music Librarian, Public Library  │
└─────────────────────────────────────┘

┌─────────────────────────────────────┐
│     Assistant Music Librarian,       │
│          Public Library              │
└─────────────────────────────────────┘
```

Position Description

Music Librarians can be found working in large research libraries such as the New York Public Library or in larger public libraries throughout the country. A Music Librarian who wants to work in a public library must be qualified in two disciplines: librarianship and musicology. A broad musical background also is essential, since music of any style, medium, or era can be found in a public library.

Music Librarians provide analytic entries to their collections that take into account both composers and performers. The day-to-day responsibilities of a Music Librarian in a public library are much the same as those of a traditional librarian: interacting with patrons, organizing and maintaining music collections, teaching patrons how to use the library, answering reference questions, and selecting music, books, journals, recordings, microforms, manuscripts, and other rare materials for acquisition.

In addition, Music Librarians may plan music-related exhibits and concerts at their own public library, or collaborate with other institutions to organize lectures, classes, or other public programs.

Salaries

Salaries for this position vary a great deal depending on the responsibilities and location of the library. Salaries for Music Librarians in a small public library may start below $30,000. The average salary of a Music Librarian ranges from $42,704 to $50,000 and above.

Employment Prospects

Most Music Librarians work with the public, whether they hold full-time public service positions or interact with the public part time in addition to their other job duties. Technical services librarians, such as those in cataloging or acquisitions, may not have any contact with the public. Many Music Librarians who are also musicians (and many are) find that they can combine their work as a performer with a part-time job as a Music Librarian.

While attending library school, students should take every opportunity available to work as student assistants in the university libraries, do a practicum or internship in a music library, or volunteer in the type of music library that interests them most. Library administrators may not expect an applicant for part-time employment to have as much experience as a candidate for a full-time position, but they are likely to select a candidate with some relevant experience over one with none.

Advancement Prospects

Music Librarians in public or research libraries typically advance by promotion into supervisory positions, including director of the music library. While music collections in smaller libraries often may be administered by a single Music Librarian, in large public and research libraries Music Librarians may hold management positions as assistant heads or department heads and have budget, personnel, facilities, and collection management responsibilities.

Education and Training

Dual master's degrees in musicology and library science are usually required for a job as a Music Librarian in a public library. Some schools offer a dual degree program for a master of library science–master of arts in music, and others offer at least some special courses or internships in music librarianship. Beyond this type of specialization, education for music librarianship should include a broad education in both music and the liberal arts.

Music Librarians also need a solid background in the humanities to better understand the relationship of music to other disciplines. Because music and information about music are published in many languages throughout the world, Music Librarians need a working knowledge of German and at least one Romance language.

Special Requirements

Most states require that public Librarians employed in municipal, county, or regional library systems be certified. In most states, graduates of ALA-accredited library schools submit an application to the state librarian (specific requirements differ from state to state).

Experience, Skills, and Personality Traits

Music Librarians in public libraries must enjoy working with patrons on all levels. Valuable personality traits for this career include patience, intellectual curiosity, attention to detail, computer skills, musical ability or in-depth understanding, and superior organizational skills. In addition, Music Librarians should have a broad musical background and training in music history.

Unions and Associations

Music Librarians may belong to a variety of trade associations that provide educational guidance, support, conferences, and information to members, including the Music Library Association, the American Library Association, the American Society for Information Science, or the Special Libraries Association.

Tips for Entry

1. Make contacts. Often, part-time jobs in music libraries open up unexpectedly and need to be filled quickly. There may not even be time to advertise the job. If you have joined various professional organizations for librarians and if you have kept in touch with your library friends, you will have a network through which you may hear about part-time opportunities when they arise.
2. To learn about the profession's current activities and to make useful contacts, join the Music Library Association (MLA) as a student member.
3. Visit the placement service joblist on the MLA website (www.musiclibraryassoc.org).
4. Attend the annual MLA meeting in the late winter or early spring, or visit the nearest regional chapter (there are 12) that meet regularly. Job postings are often listed here.
5. E-mail discussion groups such as MLA-L, LIBJOBS, and LIS-JOBS are a good source for job postings. Topical groups are also a good place for finding advertisements in a particular field of librarianship. Check out job lists on the Internet, such as www.Lisjobs.com, the daily job postings on "Hot Jobs Online" at the website of the American Library Association (www.ala.org); or the American Society of Information Science website job line (www.asis.org/Jobline) or www.libraryjobpostings.org. Visit the ALISE website, which has links to all library schools, each of which has state and national employment listings (www.alise.org).
6. Check out *Jobs for Librarians and Information Professionals,* a comprehensive guide to on-line job resources for librarians and information professionals.
7. Subscribe to major library trade publications, such as *Library Journal* and *American Libraries.*

REFERENCE LIBRARIAN

CAREER PROFILE

Duties: Work with the public to help them find the reference information they need; explain how to use the library's resources.

Alternate Title(s): None

Salary Range: $24,510 to $66,590+

Employment Prospects: Excellent

Advancement Prospects: Excellent

Best Geographical Location(s): Libraries throughout the country hire Reference Librarians; positions in rural areas may be more plentiful, since competition is stiff for jobs in large metropolitan areas

Prerequisites:

Education or Training—Master's degree in library or information science (M.L.S.)

Experience—Student internships or volunteer experience in another library is helpful

Special Skills and Personality Traits—Good people skills, communications skills; organizational ability; excellent computer skills; attention to detail; willingness to work independently; organizational ability

Licensure/Certification—Most states require that public librarians employed in municipal, county, or regional library systems be certified

CAREER LADDER

```
┌─────────────────────────────┐
│  Reference Librarian at Larger │
│  Library or Library Director   │
└─────────────────────────────┘

┌─────────────────────────────┐
│     Reference Librarian       │
└─────────────────────────────┘

┌─────────────────────────────┐
│  Assistant Reference Librarian │
└─────────────────────────────┘
```

Position Description

Reference Librarians refine and anticipate the information needs of the general public, researchers, students, clients, and other professionals, and then provide access to millions of resources. Reference Librarians direct patrons to reference sources, help them research information, explain how to use the library's equipment (such as microfilm readers, computers, and copiers), and obtain requested information from data retrieval systems. They also have been at the forefront of providing public access to technology and the Internet in order to reduce the digital divide.

Reference Librarians work with the public to help them find the information they need, analyzing users' needs to determine what information is appropriate, and searching for, acquiring, and providing information. The job also includes an instructional role, such as showing users how to access information. For example, Librarians commonly help users navigate the Internet, showing them how to most efficiently search for relevant information.

Reference Librarians create access to information and describe monographs, rare books, electronic resources, audiovisual materials, maps, and periodicals. They digitize, develop, and organize collections, and acquire educational materials.

On a typical day, a Reference Librarian might provide reference help; select and buy materials and prepare those materials by classifying them according to subject matter; supervise assistants who prepare cards, computer records, or other access tools that direct users to resources; and compile lists of books, periodicals, articles, and audiovisual materials on particular subjects. The Reference Librarian also might analyze collections and recommend materials, and collect and organize books, pamphlets, manuscripts, and other materials in a specific field.

Reference Librarians spend a significant portion of time at their desks or in front of computer terminals; extended work at video display terminals can cause eyestrain and headaches. Helping users obtain information for their jobs, recreational purposes, and other tasks can be challenging and satisfying; at the same time, working with users under deadlines can be demanding and stressful.

Salaries

Salaries for this position vary a great deal depending on the responsibilities and location of the library. Beginning full-time Reference Librarians with a master's degree in library and information studies accredited by the American Library Association (ALA) but with no professional experience can expect a beginning salary range of $30,126 to $37,580. Librarians with primarily administrative duties often earn more than other Librarians. Median annual earnings of Reference Librarians are $43,090. The middle 50 percent earn between $33,560 and $54,250, the lowest 10 percent earn less than $24,510, and the highest 10 percent earn more than $66,590.

Employment Prospects

It is expected that there will be a greater need for Reference Librarians because of the increasing diversity and growing population of library users, and because more Reference Librarians will reach retirement age in the next 10 years. Applicants for librarian jobs in large metropolitan areas, where most graduates prefer to work, usually face competition; those willing to work in rural areas should have better job prospects.

Advancement Prospects

Reference Librarians can advance to administrative positions such as department head, library director, or chief information officer, with more experience and administrative skills, knowledge of automated systems, and additional training. Advancement opportunities are better in larger library systems.

Education and Training

Although many colleges and universities offer M.L.S. programs, employers often prefer graduates of the approximately 56 schools accredited by the American Library Association (ALA). A Reference Librarian should have a master's degree in the library or information sciences (either an M.S.I. or M.L.S.) from an ALA-accredited school, and a B.A. in any field. Reference Librarians also can combine an M.L.S. with an M.B.A., J.D., M.A., M.S., or Ph.D. to serve as a Reference Librarian in a specialized field.

Experience, Skills, and Personality Traits

Reference Librarians are usually expected to have some experience with library reference and public services, as well as experience in bibliographic instruction. In addition, a Reference Librarian should have outstanding computer skills and Web skills, including experience with electronic resources, Internet use, and content evaluation. Reference Librarians also should be able to combine teaching and reference librarianship and the ability to work well independently and as a member of a collaborative team. Reference Librarians should have good analytical skills, including subject analysis, the ability to organize and describe resources, and the ability to write well. They should have a knowledge of languages, a strong desire to increase access to information, an eagerness to work in a cutting-edge environment, and excellent teaching, interpersonal, and communication skills.

Special Requirements

Most states require that Public Librarians employed in municipal, county, or regional library systems be certified by submitting an application to the state librarian. Specific requirements may vary from state to state.

Unions and Associations

Reference Librarians may belong to a variety of trade associations that provide educational guidance, support, conferences, and information to members. These might include the American Library Association, the Reference and User Services Association, the American Society for Information Science, or the Special Libraries Association.

Tips for Entry

1. Make contacts. Often, part-time jobs open up unexpectedly and need to be filled quickly. There may not even be time to advertise the job. If you have joined various professional organizations for librarians and if you have kept in touch with your library friends, you will have a network through which you may hear about part-time opportunities when they arise.

2. To learn about current job openings and to make useful contacts, consider joining a professional association such as the American Society for Information Science and Technology (www.asis.org).

3. Because positions in public libraries are often advertised locally, read classified ads in the cities where you are interested in working or monitor the on-line classifieds in these areas.

4. Attend annual conferences of library associations, where job listings are often posted.

5. E-mail discussion groups are a good source for job postings. Many local jobs are advertised on the internet. Find out what lists advertise jobs, and join them. Try LIBJOBS (www.ifla.org/II/lists/libjobs.htm), one of the more popular discussion groups. Topical groups

are also a good place for finding advertisements for Reference Librarians.

6. Use job websites such as www.Lisjobs.com; the daily job postings on "Hot Jobs Online" at the website of the American Library Association (www.ala.org), or www.libraryjobpostings.org. Or check out *Jobs for Librarians and Information Professionals,* a comprehensive guide to on-line job resources for Librarians and information professionals.

7. Another place to check is the major library trade publications, such as *Library Journal* (http://libraryjournal. reviewsnews.com/index.asp?layout=classifieds&category=Library+Jobs&publication=libraryjournal). There are also related publications, such as the *Chronicle of Higher Education* (http://chronicle.com/jobs) for academic library postings.

8. Visit the ALISE website, which has links to all library schools, each of which has state and national employment listings (www.alise.org). Libweb (http://sunsite. berkeley.edu/Libweb) can help you locate library homepages.

SYSTEMS LIBRARIAN (PUBLIC LIBRARY)

CAREER PROFILE

Duties: Manage and repair library computers, printers, and copiers, serve as library webmaster, manage online databases, answer technical questions, and assist patrons with computer problems

Alternate Title(s): Technology Librarian

Salary Range: $35,704 to $50,000+

Employment Prospects: Excellent

Advancement Prospects: Excellent

Best Geographical Location(s): Public libraries can be found throughout the country but, in general, larger public libraries in larger cities have more opportunities for Systems Librarians

Prerequisites:

Education or Training—Master's in library and information science; undergraduate degree in computer science helpful

Experience—Computer experience (both hardware and software) is very helpful

Special Skills and Personality Traits—Attention to detail; good communication, computer and people skills; ability to handle pressure

Licensure/Certification—Most states require that public librarians employed in municipal, county, or regional library systems be certified

CAREER LADDER

```
┌─────────────────────────────────┐
│   Director, Library Technology  │
└─────────────────────────────────┘

┌─────────────────────────────────┐
│       Systems Librarian         │
└─────────────────────────────────┘

┌─────────────────────────────────┐
│   Assistant Systems Librarian   │
└─────────────────────────────────┘
```

Position Description

A Systems Librarian differs from the traditional concept of a reference librarian or cataloger. Depending on the library, Systems Librarianship may involve a stimulating addition to conventional library tasks, or it may be defined as a unique position focusing almost entirely on library technology. Although job descriptions differ a great deal among libraries, in general a Systems Librarian serves as the library Webmaster, manages on-line databases, and manages and repairs computers, printers, and copy machines. Systems Librarians may oversee a few computer terminals with access limited only to the library catalog, or supervise multiple computer labs with an array of equipment and applications.

Because library workstations receive a lot of use and abuse, problems frequently occur, and most library print management systems have many points at which the process can break down: the printers, the network, the card reader, and the computer that controls the system. As a result, many Systems Librarians spend a great deal of time diagnosing and repairing malfunctions (of both hardware and software), investigating network faults, answering complex technology questions, and averting printing disasters. At the same time, the Systems Librarian is usually expected to work at the reference desk.

In addition to computers and their peripheral components, Systems Librarians often have responsibility for a host of software applications, e-mail functions, Web browsers, statistical and mathematical applications, programming languages, and sophisticated graphic design software. They also oversee a digital printing network and public photocopiers. Finally, Systems Librarians are often called upon to supervise staff, including library clerks, technicians, and assistants.

Salaries

Salaries for this position vary a great deal depending on the size and location of the public library, but typically range from $35,704 to more than $50,000.

Employment Prospects

Systems Librarianship is a financially stable career that will only become more important to public libraries as new technology continues to alter the way libraries do business. As more and more public libraries obtain newer and better computers, their need for a Systems Librarian to monitor and manage these systems will only increase.

Students attending library school should take every opportunity to work as a student assistant in the university libraries, do a practicum or internship in another library, or volunteer as a Systems Librarian. Library administrators may not expect an applicant for part-time employment to have as much experience as a candidate for a full-time position, but they are likely to select a candidate with some relevant experience over one with none.

Advancement Prospects

Systems Librarians may move into a broad range of administrative and supervisory positions. While the technical aspects of smaller public libraries are often administered and operated by a single professional Systems Librarian plus a small support staff, in large public libraries Systems Librarians may hold management positions as assistant heads or department heads, with budget, personnel, facilities, and hardware management responsibilities.

Education and Training

Systems Librarianship is an ideal way to combine librarianship with a technical background. These librarians generally need a master's degree in library or information studies, along with a bachelor's degree in computer science. Although many colleges and universities offer M.L.S. programs, employers often prefer graduates of the approximately 56 schools accredited by the American Library Association.

Alternatively, prospective Systems Librarians may supplement their M.L.S. degree with courses in computers, technology, and business studies. It is also a good idea to volunteer with a library, archive, or museum, as any experience in the field will be beneficial in the long run.

Experience, Skills, and Personality Traits

Systems Librarians should have experience with both software and hardware, in addition to common sense, excellent communication and computer skills, an interest in working with the public, a basic understanding of human nature, a desire to learn, and a sense of adventure.

Special Requirements

Most states require that Librarians employed in municipal, county, or regional public library systems be certified by submitting an application to the state librarian.

Unions and Associations

Systems Librarians may belong to a variety of trade associations that provide educational guidance, support, conferences, and information to members. These might include the American Library Association, the American Society for Information Science and Technology, the Association for Library Collections and Technical Services (ALCTS), the Library and Information Technology Association (LITA), the Council on Library and Media Technology, the Library and Information Technology Association, or the Association of College and Research Libraries.

Tips for Entry

1. Make contacts. Often, part-time jobs open up unexpectedly and need to be filled quickly. There may not even be time to advertise the job. If you have joined various professional organizations for Librarians and if you have kept in touch with your library friends, you will have a network through which you may hear about part-time opportunities when they arise.
2. To learn about the profession's current activities and to make useful contacts, consider joining a professional association such as the American Society for Information Science and Technology (www.asis.org).
3. Because positions in public libraries are often advertised locally, read classified ads in the cities where you are interested in working, or monitor the on-line classifieds in these areas.
4. Visit the Placement Service job list on the website of the American Society for Information Science and Technology (www.asis.org/Jobline).
5. Attend annual conferences of library associations, where job listings are often posted.
6. E-mail discussion groups are a good source for job postings. Many local jobs are advertised on the Internet. Find out what lists advertise jobs, and join them. Try LIBJOBS (www.ifla.org/II/lists/libjobs.htm), one of the more popular discussion groups. Topical groups are also a good place for finding advertisements for Systems Librarians.
7. Use job websites, such as www.Lisjobs.com; the daily job postings on "Hot Jobs Online" at the website of the American Library Association (www.ala.org); or

www.libraryjobpostings.org. Or check out *Jobs for Librarians and Information Professionals,* a comprehensive guide to on-line job resources for librarians and information professionals.

8. Another place to check is the major library trade publications, such as *Library Journal* (www.libraryjournal.com). There are also related publications, such as the *Chronicle of Higher Education* (http://chronicle.com/jobs) for academic library postings.

9. Visit the ALISE website, which has links to all library schools, each of which has state and national employment listings (www.alise.org). Libweb (http://sunsite.berkeley.edu/Libweb) can help you locate library homepages.

INTERLIBRARY LOAN ASSISTANT

CAREER PROFILE

Duties: After training is complete, work with minimal supervision from the interlibrary loan coordinator on support services for the interlibrary loan services

Alternate Title(s): Interlibrary Loan Assistant Librarian

Salary Range: $16,800 to $25,000

Employment Prospects: Excellent

Advancement Prospects: Good

Best Geographical Location(s): Positions in rural areas may be more plentiful, since competition is stiff for jobs in large metropolitan areas. Still, libraries throughout the country should have positions for Interlibrary Loan Assistants

Prerequisites:

Education or Training—High school diploma; college degree helpful but not usually required

Experience—Experience working in a library is helpful; computer skills are needed

Special Skills and Personality Traits—Good people skills; attention to detail; neatness; organizational skills; aptitude for computers; good English writing and speaking skills; willingness to attend conferences and workshops; willingness to learn new skills

CAREER LADDER

```
┌─────────────────────────────────────┐
│    Interlibrary Loan Assistant at    │
│         Larger Library or            │
│    Interlibrary Loan Coordinator     │
└─────────────────────────────────────┘

┌─────────────────────────────────────┐
│      Interlibrary Loan Assistant     │
└─────────────────────────────────────┘

┌─────────────────────────────────────┐
│            Entry Level               │
└─────────────────────────────────────┘
```

Position Description

Interlibrary loan is a service through which a borrower in one library can acquire material from other libraries' collections. In many states, interlibrary loan is a free service for library card holders. When a borrower makes a request, the library identifies other libraries that own items needed, asks to borrow them, and then notifies the borrower when they are available. There is not usually any limit to the number of requests that may be submitted for books. When the item has been received and is ready to be checked out, the borrower is notified by the library.

The Interlibrary Loan Assistant provides a range of support services, including downloading and updating interlibrary loan lending requests on computer and searching CLICnet (the Shared Catalog of Cooperating Libraries in Consortium) for periodical holdings, book call numbers, and locations. The Assistant retrieves books and periodicals from the library stacks and helps copy articles and package books and articles for delivery. The Assistant retrieves mail and handles courier deliveries, sorts and processes items, and prepares items received from other libraries for patrons. The Assistant also takes materials to the circulation desk for patron pickup, or places materials in courier pouches for delivery to other libraries.

In addition, the Interlibrary Loan Assistant handles borrowing requests received from patrons. For periodical articles, the Assistant may search an on-line database to verify potential lenders from libraries owning the correct issue, and sends routine article requests to other libraries in the region. Finally, the Assistant may perform other tasks (such as filing, photocopying forms, and so on) as needed.

Work schedules for Interlibrary Loan Assistants at larger libraries may be busy and even stressful, since keeping up with incoming and outgoing materials can be a never-ending process. Assistants typically work a five-day, 35-to-40-hour workweek, which may include evenings and weekends.

Salaries

Salaries for this position vary a great deal depending on specific job responsibilities and the location of the library. Workers with college degrees are likely to start at higher salaries and advance more easily than those without degrees. Average annual earnings of Interlibrary Loan Assistants is $17,980. Salaries range from a low of $16,800 to $25,000.

Employment Prospects

The job outlook is good for Interlibrary Loan Assistants, and there are many opportunities for flexible schedules; more than half of all Assistants have part-time schedules. Opportunities should be good for people interested in jobs as Interlibrary Loan Assistants through 2012. Turnover of these workers is quite high, reflecting the limited investment in training and subsequent weak attachment to this occupation. Many openings will become available each year to replace workers who transfer to another occupation or as Assistants move within the organization.

Efforts to contain costs may result in more hiring of library support staff. Also, due to changing roles within libraries, Interlibrary Loan Assistants are taking on more responsibility. Assistants are not directly affected by the ups and downs of the business cycle, but some workers may lose their jobs if there are cuts in library budgets.

Because many public library positions are advertised only locally, it's worth checking the classified ad sections of newspapers. Many times, the on-line classified version will be more convenient than the print, because you can frequently search the classifieds by keyword. Ads are usually posted whenever a job comes open, and will mention a title and brief description of the position. In most cases, public library positions are filled at the local level, and Interlibrary Loan Assistants working for public libraries are usually considered employees of the city or town where the library is located.

Advancement Prospects

Advancement usually comes by transfer to a position with more responsibilities or by promotion to a supervisory position. Interlibrary Loan Assistants can be promoted to library technicians, and eventually reach supervisory positions in public service or technical service areas. Advancement opportunities are better in large libraries and may be more limited in small ones. Most libraries fill administrative support positions by promoting individuals within their organization, so Assistants who acquire new skills, experience, and training improve their advancement opportunities. However, in a number of libraries, a college degree may be required for advancement to management ranks or to a position of Interlibrary Loan Coordinator.

Education and Training

Although many employers prefer to hire Interlibrary Loan Assistants with a college background, it is only required in a few positions. Orientation and training for Assistants usually takes place on the job, and new employees often learn job tasks through on-the-job training under the guidance of a supervisor or an experienced technician. Most Assistants continue to receive instruction on new procedures and library policies after their initial training ends. Some formal classroom training also may be necessary, such as training in specific computer software.

Many libraries require some experience in a library setting and the ability to demonstrate capabilities with computer software (including Microsoft Word and Microsoft Excel), and automated library systems. Interlibrary Loan Assistants participate in continuing training once they are on the job to keep abreast of new information systems brought about by changing technology.

Experience, Skills, and Personality Traits

The Interlibrary Loan Assistant must be able to work with diverse individuals and groups. The Assistant must be self-motivated, with the ability to recognize and prioritize tasks that need to be done, and able to work with minimal supervision once trained. Excellent organizational and basic computer and keyboarding skills are important, along with curiosity, attention to detail, a love of books, research, and education.

Unions and Associations

Interlibrary Loan Assistants may belong to a variety of trade associations that provide educational guidance, support, conferences, and information to members. These might include the American Library Association, the Association of Part-Time Librarians, the American Society for Information Science and Technology, the Reference and User Services Association, the Association for Library Collections and Technical Services, the Council on Library and Information Resources, the Library and Information Technology Association, or the Special Libraries Association.

Tips for Entry

1. Get experience. Take every opportunity to volunteer in the type of library that interests you most. Library administrators are likely to select a candidate with some relevant experience over one with none.
2. Make contacts. Join various professional organizations and keep in touch with your library friends to provide a network through which you may hear about job opportunities.

3. Send out your résumé. Find out the name and address of every library in your area where you might like to work (the telephone book is helpful; call to find out to whom to address your cover letter). When openings occur, administrators often pull out their collection of unsolicited résumés and contact the candidates.

4. Look for jobs on the Internet, such as on www. Lisjobs.com. *Jobs for Librarians and Information Professionals* is a comprehensive guide to on-line job resources for librarians and information professionals. Check daily job postings on "Hot Jobs Online" at the website of the American Library Association (www. ala.org); investigate other websites that list library jobs, such as http://www.libraryjobpostings.org or the American Society of Information Science job line (http://www.asis.org/Jobline).

5. E-mail discussion groups such as LIBJOBS and LIS-JOBS are a good source for job postings. Topical groups are also a good place for finding advertisements in a particular field of librarianship. For example, Web4Lib often receives library Webmaster-type job postings.

6. Check the classified ads in your local newspapers. Often, library administrators who have time to advertise for Assistants choose this method.

7. If you're targeting a specific institution or geographic area, take a look at individual websites for postings. The Folger Shakespeare Library, in Washington, D.C., for example, has an employment opportunities page.

INTERLIBRARY LOAN COORDINATOR

CAREER PROFILE

Duties: Provides complex support services for the interlibrary loan services of the library

Alternate Title(s): Interlibrary Loan Librarian

Salary Range: $24,510 to $66,590+

Employment Prospects: Excellent

Advancement Prospects: Good

Best Geographical Location(s): Positions in rural areas may be more plentiful, since competition is stiff for jobs in large metropolitan areas

Prerequisites:

Education or Training—Master's degree in library or information science (M.L.S.)

Experience—Student internships in another library, or volunteer experience is helpful

Special Skills and Personality Traits—Good people skills, communications skills; organizational ability; excellent computer skills; attention to detail; willingness to work independently; organizational ability

CAREER LADDER

```
┌─────────────────────────────────────┐
│ Library Director or Interlibrary Loan│
│   Coordinator at Larger Library or   │
│  Head of Interlibrary Loan Department│
└─────────────────────────────────────┘

┌─────────────────────────────────────┐
│    Interlibrary Loan Coordinator     │
└─────────────────────────────────────┘

┌─────────────────────────────────────┐
│ Assistant Interlibrary Loan Coordinator│
└─────────────────────────────────────┘
```

Position Description

Interlibrary loan is a service through which a borrower in one library can acquire material from other libraries' collections. In many states, interlibrary loan is a free service for library card holders.

When a borrower makes a request, the library identifies other libraries that own items needed, asks to borrow them, and then notifies the borrower when they are available. There is not usually any limit to the number of requests that may be submitted for books. When the item has been received and is ready to be checked out, the borrower is notified by the library.

The Interlibrary Loan Coordinator provides these complex support services for the interlibrary loan services of the library. On a typical day, the Interlibrary Loan Coordinator might receive and verify loan requests and search for libraries that own needed material. The Coordinator is responsible for monitoring requests from lending libraries, receiving items through the mail, and notifying patrons when their requested materials have arrived.

In addition, the Interlibrary Loan Coordinator may collect all loaned material and update records related to these transactions. When material is requested by other libraries, the Coordinator must verify that the library owns the material, create a record of the loan, package the material, and send it to the requesting library.

The Coordinator also must bill the appropriate institutions and create and store records of all transactions. This person also works not just with other libraries but also with the public, providing information and help to patrons, answering questions, receiving requests, and providing instructions and directions. The Coordinator also may supervise staff, volunteers, and student interns and assistants.

Work schedules for Interlibrary Loan Coordinators at larger libraries may be busy, demanding, and even stressful, since keeping up with incoming and outgoing materials while answering questions and interacting with patrons can be taxing. Coordinators typically work a five-day, 35-to-40-hour workweek, which may include evenings and weekends. In addition, the job may require a great deal of standing, stooping, bending, and reaching.

Salaries

Salaries for this position vary widely depending on the responsibilities and location of the library. Beginning full-time Coordinators with a master's degree in library and information studies accredited by the ALA but with no professional experience can expect a salary range of $30,126 to $37,580. Median annual earnings of Interlibrary Loan Coordinators are $43,090; salaries can range from less than $24,510 to more than $66,590.

Employment Prospects

Employment of Interlibrary Loan Coordinators is expected to grow about as fast as the average through 2012. The increasing use of computerized information storage and retrieval systems continues to contribute to moderate growth in the demand for Interlibrary Loan Coordinators. Computerized systems make keeping track of loan requests easier, so that interlibrary loan assistants can now handle the task. In addition, many libraries are equipped for users to access library computers directly from their homes or offices. These systems allow users to bypass the library and conduct research on their own.

However, Interlibrary Loan Coordinators will still be needed to manage staff, help patrons locate materials, address complicated requests, and define users' needs. Despite expectations of slower-than-average employment growth, the need to replace Coordinators as they retire will result in additional job openings. Moreover, the continuing demand for accurate and computer-delivered materials has increased the need for Coordinators with information management skills, which can improve the job prospects.

Applicants for Interlibrary Loan Coordinator jobs in large metropolitan areas, where most graduates prefer to work, usually face competition; those willing to work in rural areas should have better job prospects.

Advancement Prospects

Interlibrary Loan Coordinators can advance to administrative positions such as department head or library director with more experience and administrative skills, knowledge of automated systems, and additional training. Advancement opportunities are better in larger library systems.

Education and Training

A master's degree in library and information science or an equivalent combination of relevant experience and education is required for this position. In addition, many libraries require a minimum of two years' experience in a library setting and the ability to demonstrate capabilities with computer software (including Microsoft Word and Microsoft Excel), automated library systems, and budget/expenditure tracking. In fact, computer-related coursework is an increasingly important part of an M.L.S. degree. Some programs offer interdisciplinary degrees combining technical coursework in information science with traditional training in library science. Interlibrary Loan Coordinators participate in continuing training once they are on the job to keep abreast of new information systems brought about by changing technology.

Experience, Skills, and Personality Traits

The Interlibrary Loan Coordinator must be able to work independently a good deal of the time, but also be able to work collaboratively with diverse individuals and groups. Excellent organizational and computer skills are important, along with curiosity, attention to detail, a love of books, research, and education.

Unions and Associations

Interlibrary Loan Coordinators may belong to a variety of trade associations that provide educational guidance, support, conferences, and information to members. These might include the American Library Association, the American Society for Information Science and Technology, the Reference and User Services Association, the Association for Library Collections and Technical Services, the Council on Library and Information Resources, the Library and Information Technology Association, or the Special Libraries Association.

Tips for Entry

1. Get experience. If you are attending library school, take every opportunity available to work as a student assistant in the university libraries, do a practicum or internship in another library, or volunteer in the type of library which interests you most. Library administrators are likely to select a candidate with some relevant experience over one with none.
2. Make contacts. Join various professional organizations and keep in touch with your library friends to provide a network through which you may hear about job opportunities.
3. Attend library conventions (local, state, and national); check out the placement service that lists library-related jobs at annual ALA conventions.
4. Send out your résumé. Find out the name and address of every library in your area where you might like to work (the telephone book is helpful; call to find out to whom to address your cover letter). When openings occur, administrators often pull out their collection of unsolicited résumés and contact the candidates.
5. Look for jobs on the Internet, such as on www. Lisjobs.com. *Jobs for Librarians and Information*

Professionals is a comprehensive guide to on-line job resources for librarians and information professionals. Check daily job postings on "Hot Jobs Online" at the website of the American Library Association (www.ala.org); investigate other websites that list library jobs, such as http://www.libraryjobpostings.org or the American Society of Information Science job line (http://www.asis.org/Jobline).

6. E-mail discussion groups such as LIBJOBS and LIS-JOBS are a good source for job postings. Topical groups are also a good place for finding advertisements in a particular field of librarianship. For example, Web4Lib often receives library Webmaster-type job postings.

7. Check the classified ads in your local newspapers. Often, administrators who have time to advertise choose this method.

8. Visit the ALISE website, which has links to all library schools, each of which has state and national employment listings (www.alise.org).

9. Subscribe to major library trade publications, such as *Library Journal* and *American Libraries*.

10. If you're targeting a specific institution or geographic area, take a look at individual websites for postings. The Folger Shakespeare Library, in Washington, D.C., for example, has an employment opportunities page.

USER SUPPORT COORDINATOR

CAREER PROFILE

Duties: Coordinate and evaluate all user support activities

Alternate Title(s): None

Salary Range: $40,000 to $70,000+

Employment Prospects: Good

Advancement Prospects: Good

Best Geographical Location(s): Positions in rural areas may be more plentiful, since competition is stiff for jobs in large metropolitan areas.

Prerequisites:

Education or Training—Master's degree in information or library sciences.

Experience—Experience with productivity software; supervisory experience helpful

Special Skills and Personality Traits—Patience, good communication skills, detail oriented, excellent organizational skills

CAREER LADDER

```
┌─────────────────────────────────┐
│   Library Director or Librarian  │
└─────────────────────────────────┘

┌─────────────────────────────────┐
│    User Support Coordinator      │
└─────────────────────────────────┘

┌─────────────────────────────────┐
│     User Support Assistant       │
└─────────────────────────────────┘
```

Position Description

The User Support Coordinator must evaluate all user support activities related to computers including developing plans, budgets, policies, procedures, schedules, and reports to address all areas of responsibility within available resources and strategic library goals. The Coordinator may help users with problems, work with patrons using web-based tools, and provide "help desk" support. The Coordinator may plan training sessions and provide guidance to staff on resolving computer problems. The Coordinator also may help devise user manuals and work with and monitor support staff.

Salaries

Salaries for this position vary a great deal depending on the responsibilities and location of the library. User Support Coordinators with several years of experience may expect a minimum starting salary of $60,000, commensurate with training and experience. Salaries may range from $40,000 to more than $70,000.

Employment Prospects

Employment of User Support Coordinators is expected to grow more slowly than the average for all occupations through 2010, but Coordinators will still be needed to manage staff, help with outreach for patrons, and define users' needs. Despite expectations of slower-than-average employment growth, the need to replace User Support Coordinators as they retire will result in numerous additional job openings. Applicants for jobs in large metropolitan areas, where most graduates prefer to work, usually face competition; those willing to work in rural areas should have better job prospects.

Advancement Prospects

User Support Coordinators can advance to administrative positions such as department head, library director, or chief information officer, with more experience and administrative skills, knowledge of automated systems, and additional training. Advancement opportunities are better in larger library systems.

Education and Training

A User Support Coordinator must have a master's degree in information and library science from a library program accredited by the American Library Association. In addition, libraries often require several years of progressively responsible professional library-related experience involving one or more of the following areas: acquisitions, cataloging, circulation, reference, serials, and interlibrary loan (ILL)/document delivery. Many libraries also require several years of recent experience with an integrated library system and web-based library services. Experience in user support delivery is preferred and project management experience is desirable. Supervisory experience is usually required.

Experience, Skills, and Personality Traits

Strong interpersonal and communication skills are required. In addition, excellent organizational and computer skills are important, along with curiosity, attention to detail, a love of books, research, and education.

Working in a public library is a career for those who can wear many hats and work as a team player, working with all age groups and all types of requests for information.

Unions and Associations

User Support Coordinators may belong to a variety of trade associations that provide educational guidance, support, conferences and information to members. These might include the American Library Association, the Reference and User Services Association, the American Society for Information Science and Technology, the Association for Library Collections and Technical Services, the Council on Library and Information Resources, the Library and Information Technology Association, or the Special Libraries Association.

Tips for Entry

1. Get experience. If you are attending library school, take every opportunity available to work as a student assistant in the university libraries, do a practicum or internship in another library, or volunteer in the type of library which interests you most. Library administrators are likely to select a candidate with some relevant experience over one with none.

2. Make contacts. Join various professional organizations and keep in touch with your library friends to provide a network through which you may hear about job opportunities.

3. Attend library conventions (local, state, and national); check out the placement service that lists library-related jobs at annual ALA conventions.

4. Send out your résumé. Find out the name and address of every library in our area where you might like to work (the telephone book is helpful; call to find out to whom to address your cover letter). When openings occur, administrators often pull out their collection of unsolicited résumés and contact the candidates.

5. Look for jobs on the Internet, such as on www.Lisjobs.com. *Jobs for Librarians and Information Professionals* is a comprehensive guide to on-line job resources for librarians and information professionals. Check daily job postings on "Hot Jobs Online" at the website of the American Library Association (www.ala.org); investigate other websites that list library jobs, such as (http://www.libraryjobpostings).org or the American Society of Information Science job line (http://www.asis.org/Jobline).

6. E-mail discussion groups such as LIBJOBS and LIS-JOBS are a good source for job postings. Topical groups are also a good place for finding advertisements in a particular field of librarianship. For example, Web4Lib often receives library Webmaster-type job postings.

7. Check the classified ads in your local newspapers. Often, administrators who have time to advertise choose this method.

8. Visit the ALISE website, which has links to all library schools, each of which has state and national employment listings (www.alise.org).

9. Subscribe to major library trade publications, such as *Library Journal* and *American Libraries*.

10. If you're targeting a specific institution or geographic area, take a look at individual websites for postings. The Folger Shakespeare Library, in Washington, D.C., for example, has an employment opportunities page.

CIRCULATION DEPARTMENT DIRECTOR

CAREER PROFILE

Duties: Plans, organizes, and supervises the activities of the circulation unit and oversees circulation staff

Alternate Title(s): Circulation Department Head

Salary Range: $30,126 to $67,000+

Employment Prospects: Good

Advancement Prospects: Good

Best Geographical Location(s): Libraries throughout the country hire Circulation Directors; positions in rural areas may be more plentiful, since competition is stiff for jobs in large metropolitan areas

Prerequisites:

Education or Training—Master's degree in library or information science (M.L.S.)

Experience—Several years of experience in library circulation departments is helpful

Special Skills and Personality Traits—Good people skills and the ability to supervise others; communication skills; organizational ability; excellent computer skills; attention to detail; willingness to work independently

CAREER LADDER

```
┌─────────────────────────────────┐
│       Directory of Library       │
└─────────────────────────────────┘

┌─────────────────────────────────┐
│  Circulation Department Director │
└─────────────────────────────────┘

┌─────────────────────────────────┐
│  Assistant Circulation Director  │
└─────────────────────────────────┘
```

Position Description

The Circulation Department Director supervises the circulation of the library collection of books and nonbook materials; plans, organizes, and supervises the activities of the circulation unit; oversees staff; helps library patrons use library services, facilities, and equipment; interprets library policies; and coordinates activities with other unit directors. The Director performs routine circulation desk duties as necessary, oversees return of books and materials to shelves or storage places, oversees billing and collections operations, and helps out in other library divisions as needed.

Personnel activities are an important part of the job for the Director, who establishes and administers procedures for the operation of the circulation department and helps interview, train, and evaluate circulation and shelving staff. The Director also prepares weekly schedules for circulation, reference, children's services, and shelving personnel. In addition, the Director keeps track of vacation and meeting schedules for various staff members in order to insure proper coverage at all times in all areas, and recommends hiring and promotion of unit staff members. The Director participates in periodic employee evaluations, provides training exercises for circulation unit employees, and reviews and resolves personnel problems within the unit.

The Circulation Department Director also is aware of all events, shows, and classes taking place at the library and disseminates that information to all members of the circulation staff so they can respond to any questions the public may have and be able to register interested patrons.

Efficient operation of the circulation desk is also an important part of the Director's job. The Director must evaluate circulation operating procedures and make adjustments as needed to improve efficiency. The Director also oversees the enrollment of new patrons to the library and provides service and book and media collection information and advice to new and current patrons. The Director also supervises the book reserve system and is responsible for the appearance and order of the adult collection.

Problem solving is another aspect of the job; the Director supervises the receiving and recording of overdue fines and inspects damaged circulation materials, including books and equipment. The Director also identifies cataloging errors, oversees the performance and repair of circulation equipment, and recommends equipment improvements.

Recordkeeping is still another aspect of this job, including maintaining circulation data and preparing regular statistical reports.

Salaries

Salaries for this position vary a great deal depending on the responsibilities and location of the library. Beginning full-time Circulation Directors with a master's degree in library and information studies accredited by the American Library Association (ALA) but with no professional experience can expect a salary range of $30,126 to $37,580. The median annual salary of Circulation Directors is about $41,700, but the highest 10 percent earn more than $67,000.

Employment Prospects

It is expected that there will be a growing need for Circulation Directors because of the increasing diversity and growing population of library users, and because more Circulation Directors will reach retirement age in the next 10 years. Applicants for Director jobs in large metropolitan areas where most graduates prefer to work usually face stiff competition; those willing to work in rural areas should have better job prospects.

Advancement Prospects

Circulation Directors can advance to senior administrative positions such as library director or chief information officer, with more experience and administrative skills, knowledge of automated systems, and additional training. Advancement opportunities are better in larger library systems.

Education and Training

Although many colleges and universities offer M.L.S. programs, employers often prefer graduates of the approximately 56 schools accredited by the American Library Association (ALA). A Circulation Director must have a master's degree in information or library science (either an M.S.I. or M.L.S.), and several years of increasingly responsible professional library work, preferably with experience in library circulation control.

Experience, Skills, and Personality Traits

The Circulation Director is usually expected to have some experience with library circulation departments and should be able to relate effectively to library patrons and coworkers and have the ability to supervise staff, prepare clear and concise statistical and narrative reports, and oversee and operate word and data processing equipment. The Director should have a proven ability to deal with the public, manage a department, organize tasks, and initiate service improvements.

Unions and Associations

Circulation Directors may belong to a variety of trade associations that provide educational guidance, support, conferences, and information to members. These might include the American Library Association, the American Society for Information Science and Technology, Library Administration and Management Association, Reference and User Services Association, Association for Library Collections and Technical Services, or the Special Libraries Association.

Tips for Entry

1. Make contacts. Often, part-time jobs open up unexpectedly and need to be filled quickly. There may not even be time to advertise the job. If you have joined various professional organizations for librarians and if you have kept in touch with your library friends, you will have a network through which you may hear about part-time opportunities when they arise.

2. To learn about current job openings and to make useful contacts, consider joining a professional association such as the American Society for Information Science and Technology (www.asis.org). Attend annual conferences of library associations, where job listings are often posted.

3. E-mail discussion groups are a good source for job postings. Many local jobs are advertised on the Internet. Find out what lists advertise jobs, and join them. Try LIBJOBS (www.ifla.org/II/lists/libjobs.htm), one of the more popular discussion groups. Topical groups are also a good place for finding advertisements for Circulation Directors.

4. Use job websites such as www.Lisjobs.com, the daily job postings on "Hot Jobs Online" at the website of the American Library Association (www.ala.org) or (www.libraryjobpostings.org). Or check out *Jobs for Librarians and Information Professionals,* a comprehensive guide to on-line job resources for librarians and information professionals.

5. Another place to check is the major library trade publications, such as *Library Journal* (www.libraryjournal.com). There are also related publications, such as the *Chronicle of Higher Education* (http://chronicle.com/jobs) for academic library postings.

6. Visit the ALISE website, which has links to all library schools, each of which has state and national employment listings (www.alise.org). Libweb (http://sunsite.berkeley.edu/Libweb) can help you locate library homepages.

CHILDREN'S OUTREACH LIBRARIAN

CAREER PROFILE

Duties: Introduce children to interesting children's books, magazines, and games that stimulate thought, provide entertainment, and promote learning

Alternate Title(s): Youth Outreach Librarian

Salary Range: $35,719 to $55,494

Employment Prospects: Excellent

Advancement Prospects: Excellent

Best Geographical Location(s): All geographical areas offer possibilities

Prerequisites:

Education or Training—Master's degree in library and information science, or in education

Experience—Computer experience and several years of classroom or primary school library experience

Special Skills and Personality Traits—Excellent interpersonal, oral, and written communication skills; attention to detail; commitment to working with children

CAREER LADDER

```
┌─────────────────────────────────────┐
│          Library Director            │
└─────────────────────────────────────┘

┌─────────────────────────────────────┐
│     Children's Outreach Librarian    │
└─────────────────────────────────────┘

┌─────────────────────────────────────┐
│  Assistant Librarian, Children's Services  │
└─────────────────────────────────────┘
```

Position Description

Unfortunately, not every child has the opportunity to visit a public library. The Children's Outreach department in a library is responsible for introducing children with little library experience to interesting children's books, magazines, and games that stimulate thought, provide entertainment, and promote learning.

A Children's Outreach Librarian can perform a wide variety of tasks, including developing story time programs, training caregivers to develop story-sharing skills, and preparing programs specifically for children in schools, hospitals, and other settings. The Outreach Librarian may also be involved in coordinating the bookmobile service and setting up programs for parents to help their children read.

During the first three years of life, important intellectual and emotional development takes place in young children that has a profound impact on their success later in life. Libraries have long recognized the importance of serving these young children, and many libraries have adopted a "preschooler's door to learning" program. In addition, the Children's Outreach Librarian extends the library beyond traditional boundaries by offering services in remote locations and to patrons with limited circumstances.

In addition, Outreach Services often offers large print books, regular print books, books-on-tape, videos, and research upon request. They often perform bimonthly visits at local nursing care and hospital centers to visit patrons who cannot travel to the library.

In addition, Children's Outreach Librarians work in the local community, especially with teachers and other group leaders, as well as with the children, to make the library's collection better known and to organize visits so that the children experience the full impact and benefit of these exhibitions. The Librarian also conceives, implements, oversees, and evaluates the program of sponsored visits by organized groups of children.

An important aspect of the job lies in building ties to the community to help make the collection a visible resource, important in the education of young people throughout the area. Duties of the Children's Outreach Library may range from preparing a manual for the operation of the program, drafting a teacher's guide, preparing for group visits, consulting area teachers and those who work with children, presenting exhibitions to children, and evaluating programs.

Salaries

Salaries for this position vary a great deal depending on the responsibilities and location of the library, but they can range from a starting salary of $35,719 to more than $55,494 per year.

Employment Prospects

Employment of Children's Outreach Librarians is expected to grow about as fast as the average for all occupations through 2012. Librarians will be needed to manage staff, help with outreach for children, and define users' needs. The need to replace Children's Outreach Librarians as they retire will result in many new job openings. Applicants for jobs in large metropolitan areas, where most graduates prefer to work, usually face competition; those willing to work in rural areas should have better job prospects.

Advancement Prospects

Children's Outreach Librarians can advance to administrative positions such as department head, library director, or chief information officer, with more experience and administrative skills, knowledge of automated systems, and additional training. Advancement opportunities are better in larger library systems.

Education and Training

A Children's Outreach Librarian should have a B.A. degree in a humanistic discipline, (preferably with a literary emphasis) and a master's degree in education or library and information science. In addition, many libraries look for at least two years of classroom or school library experience in the primary or secondary grades (especially primary grade experience). Experience with using computers is also desirable.

Experience, Skills, and Personality Traits

The Children's Outreach Librarian should have excellent interpersonal, oral, and written communication skills, and exemplary organizational abilities, including the capacity to maintain daily responsibilities while implementing longer-term projects. This Librarian also should have a commitment to working with children and being responsive to their needs, and be an experienced educator.

Unions and Associations

Children's Outreach Librarians may belong to a variety of trade associations that provide educational guidance, support, conferences, and information to members. These might include the American Library Association, the American Association of School Librarians, the Association for Library Services to Children, EduCause, and the Special Libraries Association.

Tips for Entry

1. Get experience. If you are attending library school, take every opportunity available to work as a student assistant in the university libraries, do a practicum or internship in another library, or volunteer in the type of library which interests you most. Library administrators are likely to select a candidate with some relevant experience over one with none.

2. Make contacts. Join various professional organizations and keep in touch with your library friends to provide a network through which you may hear about job opportunities.

3. Attend library conventions (local, state, and national); check out the placement service that lists library-related jobs at annual ALA conventions.

4. Send out your résumé. Find out the name and address of every library in our area where you might like to work (the telephone book is helpful; call to find out to whom to address your cover letter). When openings occur, administrators often pull out their collection of unsolicited résumés and contact the candidates.

5. Look for jobs on the Internet, such as on www. Lisjobs.com. *Jobs for Librarians and Information Professionals* is a comprehensive guide to on-line job resources for librarians and information professionals. Check daily job postings on "Hot Jobs Online" at the website of the American Library Association (www.ala.org). Investigate other websites that list library jobs, such as http://www.libraryjobpostings. org or the American Society of Information Science job line (http://www.asis.org/Jobline).

6. E-mail discussion groups such as LIBJOBS and LIS-JOBS are a good source for job postings. Topical groups are also a good place for finding advertisements in a particular field of librarianship. For example, Web4Lib often receives library Webmaster-type job postings.

7. Check the classified ads in your local newspapers. Often, administrators who have time to advertise choose this method.

8. Visit the ALISE website, which has links to all library schools, each of which has state and national employment listings (www.alise.org).

9. Subscribe to major library trade publications, such as *Library Journal* and *American Libraries*.

10. If you're targeting a specific institution or geographic area, take a look at individual websites for postings. The Folger Shakespeare Library, in Washington, D.C., for example, has an employment opportunities page.

BOOKMOBILE DRIVER

CAREER PROFILE

Duties: Drive the bookmobile; answer patrons' questions; receive and check out books; collect fines; maintain the book collection; shelve materials; sometimes operate audiovisual equipment to show slides or films

Alternate Title(s): Library Assistant, Library Technician

Salary Range: $16,400 to $20,000

Employment Prospects: Good

Advancement Prospects: Fair

Best Geographical Location(s): Jobs are found throughout the country, but less populated areas tend to have more need for bookmobiles

Prerequisites:

Education or Training—High school diploma, good computer skills, and (often) a commercial driver's license

Experience—Library experience is helpful but not required; computer experience may be very important for one-person bookmobiles

Special Skills and Personality Traits—Good driving skills; good organizational skills; attention to detail; good people skills; ability to work independently; computer skills

CAREER LADDER

```
┌─────────────────────────────┐
│     Library Technician      │
└─────────────────────────────┘

┌─────────────────────────────┐
│     Bookmobile Driver       │
└─────────────────────────────┘

┌─────────────────────────────┐
│    Entry-Level Position     │
└─────────────────────────────┘
```

Position Description

To extend library services to more patrons, many libraries operate bookmobiles, trucks stocked with books that travel to designated sites on a regular schedule. Typically, bookmobiles serve community organizations such as shopping centers, apartment complexes, schools, and nursing homes, and also may be used to extend library service to patrons living in remote areas.

Depending on local conditions, Drivers may operate a bookmobile alone or may be accompanied by another library employee. When working alone, the Driver performs many of the same functions as a library assistant, answering patrons' questions, receiving and checking out books, collecting fines, maintaining the book collection, shelving materials, and occasionally operating audiovisual equipment to show slides or films. They may help plan programs sponsored by the library, such as reader advisory programs, used book sales, or outreach programs.

There is a fair amount of paperwork involved with operating a bookmobile, so attention to detail is important for this position. Bookmobile Drivers must keep track of their mileage, the materials they have lent out, and the amount of fines collected. They record statistics on circulation and the number of people visiting the bookmobile. Drivers also may record requests for special items from the main library and arrange for the materials to be mailed or delivered to a patron during the next scheduled visit.

In some areas, Bookmobile Drivers are responsible for maintaining their vehicle and any photocopiers or other equipment they carry in it. (Many bookmobiles are equipped with personal computers and CD-ROM systems linked to the main library system; this allows bookmobile drivers to reserve or locate books immediately. Some book-mobiles now offer Internet access to users.)

The schedule of a Bookmobile Driver depends on the size of the area being served. Some Drivers go out on their routes every day, while others go to different routes and locations on different days. When not out on their routes, they work at the library.

Some Bookmobile Drivers also work evenings and week-ends, to give patrons as much access to the library as possible. Because these employees may be the only link some people have to the library, much of their work involves helping the public. They also may help handicapped or elderly patrons to the bookmobile, or shovel snow to make sure they can reach the bookmobile safety. They may enter hospitals or nursing homes to deliver books to patrons who are bedridden.

The Bookmobile Driver is usually responsible to the librarian or library director. While some of the duties can be tedious, there is often a feeling of satisfaction in bringing books to those who otherwise might not have access to them. There is plenty of opportunity for flexible schedules, since more than half of these workers are on part-time schedules.

Salaries

Salaries for this position vary a great deal depending on the region of the country, size of city, and type and size of the library. The level of industry or technical expertise required and the complexity of the driver's responsibilities may also affect earnings. In general, the average salary for a Book-mobile Driver is about $16,400. Many Bookmobile Driver jobs are offered at part time or flextime.

Employment Prospects

Opportunities should be good for Bookmobile Drivers. Turnover among these workers is quite high; this work tends to attract retirees and others who prefer a part-time schedule. For this reason, there is a lot of movement into and out of the occupation, so thousands of openings will become available each year to replace workers who transfer to another occupa-tion or leave the labor force. Because most Bookmobile Dri-vers work in public libraries, they are not generally directly affected by the ups and downs of the business cycle.

Advancement Prospects

Bookmobile Drivers may advance to librarian assistants or technicians if they are willing to take extra courses in this field. Advancement prospects depend on how much the individual is willing to work toward a career goal.

Education and Training

A college degree is not required for this position, although there is a formal training/certification program in many cases. Many Bookmobile Drivers are required to have a commercial driver's license.

Regardless of the type of work being done, most employ-ers prefer that their Bookmobile Drivers be computer liter-ate; knowledge of word processing is especially valuable. This is particularly important for those Drivers who work alone in the bookmobile.

Experience, Skills, and Personality Traits

Good driving skills are important, since Bookmobile Dri-vers must maneuver their large vehicles in all kinds of traf-fic and weather conditions. In addition, the Bookmobile Driver must be good at dealing with people and interested in working in a service field. Attention to detail and very good organizational skills are needed, as is resourcefulness and the ability to work independently with minimal supervision.

The Bookmobile Driver is much more than a driver; he or she must also have a good understanding of librarianship. The person must also be quite familiar with new technology, as computers or CD-ROMs may be on board and duties may include helping patrons learn how to use these devices.

Unions and Associations

Bookmobile Drivers working in libraries do not usually belong to unions, but they can belong to a variety of trade associations that provide educational guidance, support, conferences, and information to members, such as the American Library Association.

Tips for Entry

1. Consult the classified section of your daily paper, where these positions are often advertised.
2. Check with local libraries, which may post available positions.
3. Get experience. Volunteer in the type of library or bookmobile that interests you most. Library adminis-trators are more likely to select a candidate with some relevant experience.
4. Send out your résumé. Find out the name and address of every library in your area where you might like to work (the telephone book is helpful; call to find out to whom to address your cover letter). When openings occur, administrators often pull out their collection of unsolicited résumés and contact the candidates.

SPECIAL LIBRARIES

ART LIBRARIAN

CAREER PROFILE

Duties: Collect, organize, and make accessible material relating to the visual arts, architecture, and design, including slides, videos, graphic material, and artists' books, as well as the more conventional books and journals

Alternate Title(s): Director of Art Library

Salary Range: $32,891 to $50,000+

Employment Prospects: Fair

Advancement Prospects: Fair

Best Geographical Location(s): Larger cities may offer more possibilities, but many art libraries exist throughout the country

Prerequisites:

Education or Training—A master's degree in art history and a master's of library science

Experience—French, German, and other languages are helpful and may be necessary; volunteering in an art library can be helpful

Special Skills and Personality Traits—Good people skills; good communication and writing skills; excellent administration/management skills; good computer and image technology skills; attention to detail; interest in and aptitude for art

CAREER LADDER

```
┌─────────────────────────────┐
│   Director of Art Library   │
└─────────────────────────────┘

┌─────────────────────────────┐
│       Art Librarian         │
└─────────────────────────────┘

┌─────────────────────────────┐
│   Assistant Art Librarian   │
└─────────────────────────────┘
```

Position Description

Art libraries introduce information about art and design to those seeking it, including professional researchers, students, and the general public. Art libraries collect, organize, and make accessible material relating to the visual arts, architecture and design, including slides, videos, graphic material and artists books as well as the more conventional books and journals. Art Librarians are responsible for establishing, anticipating, and meeting the specific information needs of these users, helping them to research, understand, and enjoy the diverse world of the visual arts.

Most major public libraries and some smaller ones have dedicated visual arts collections with staff to support them; these collections are used by specialists, students, teachers, and dealers, as well as the general public. They may relate to local institutions and include some special collections and archival materials. Museum libraries are research libraries for museum staff, and also offer facilities to outside researchers.

Just as academic librarians interact with academic subject departments, Art Librarians interact with curatorial staff about library services and possible acquisitions. Opportunities often exist to research and prepare museum exhibitions, and some Art Librarians are also involved with object photography and courier work.

An Art Librarian's work includes identifying, acquiring, and organizing information about art, architecture, and design; advising and supporting library users; and investigating and developing new applications for the visual arts. Art Librarians also may manage and train staff to provide the best service and make the best use of resources.

Salaries

Salaries for this position vary a great deal depending on job responsibilities and location of the library. Although beginning Art Librarians may start at $32,891, the average salary of an Art Librarian without supervisory responsibilities ranges from $42,704 to $50,000 and above.

Employment Prospects

Art librarianship is a specialized area where regular job opportunities occur. Many Art Librarians find that they can combine this job with a part-time second career in art. Most Art Librarians work either in full-time public service positions or as a part-time responsibility shared with their other work.

Advancement Prospects

Starting salaries may be modest, but opportunities for progression do exist and job satisfaction is potentially high. Art Librarians may move into a broad range of administrative and supervisory positions. While smaller art collections may be administered by a single professional Art Librarian plus a small support staff, in large public libraries Art Librarians may hold management positions as assistant heads or department heads, and have budget, personnel, facilities, and collection management responsibilities. Some Art Librarians go on to specialize and get more education and training, becoming a conservator or curator in a large library or museum.

Education and Training

In addition to master's degrees in art and library science, the Art Librarian should have some basic knowledge in an art- or design-related area. Some library schools offer special courses or internships in art librarianship. Other than that, training for art librarianship should include as broad an education as possible in both art and the liberal arts. Training in art must be the equivalent of at least substantial undergraduate work. Undergraduate education should include a wide background in the humanities, as Art Librarians need to be familiar with the relationship of art to other disciplines. Art and art-related literature are produced in many countries and languages; basic cataloging and bibliographic research require a working knowledge of German and at least one Romance language.

A master's degree in library or information science is required by most employers. Because Art Librarians need a thorough knowledge of art history, a second master's degree in art or art history is required or strongly preferred for some positions.

Experience, Skills, and Personality Traits

In addition to formal training, other useful skills include familiarity with word-processing packages, keyboarding skills, knowledge of languages, and a pleasant and confident manner in dealing with the public.

Unions and Associations

Art Librarians working in libraries do not usually belong to unions, but they can belong to a variety of trade associations that provide educational guidance, support, conferences, and information to members. These might include the Arts Libraries Society of North America, American Institute for Conservation of Historic and Artistic Works, the American Library Association, or the Special Libraries Association.

Tips for Entry

1. Networking and professional involvement are key ways to make useful contacts and be aware of what's going on. Visit the job listings on the Arts Libraries Society of North America website (www.arlisna.org/jobs.html).
2. Jobs in this field may be found in the job listings for other related trade associations, including the American Library Association.
3. Look for job ads in *American Libraries* magazine.
4. Check daily job postings on "Hot Jobs Online" at the website of the American Library Association (www.ala.org), www.libraryjobpostings.org, or the American Society of Information Science website job line at http://www.asis.org/Jobline.
5. Subscribe to library journals and periodicals.
6. Attend library conventions or conferences and check job boards, and don't miss the placement service that lists library-related jobs at annual ALA conventions.
7. Visit the ALISE website, which has links to all library schools, each of which has state and national employment listings (www.alise.org).
8. Unpaid voluntary work or student placements can provide experience, which may lead to paid work. You should approach the Arts Librarians of individual institutions with a detailed résumé and an outline of the time you would be prepared to donate.
9. Short-term contracts may also be worth considering. Look out for advertised vacancies or contact recruitment agencies.

CORPORATE LIBRARIAN

CAREER PROFILE

Duties: Corporate librarians find and analyze data relevant to their company, troubleshoot, and often oversee a research staff

Alternate Title(s): Corporate Information Specialist

Salary Range: $24,510 to $66,590+

Employment Prospects: Excellent

Advancement Prospects: Excellent

Best Geographical Location(s): Corporations throughout the country maintain libraries and have information needs requiring the assistance of a librarian

Prerequisites:

Education or Training—Master's degree in library science

Experience—Experience in a public library or in the business world is helpful

Special Skills and Personality Traits—Computer skills; attention to detail; good organizational ability; good people skills; curiosity

CAREER LADDER

```
┌─────────────────────────────┐
│   Corporate Librarian for   │
│       Larger Company        │
└─────────────────────────────┘

┌─────────────────────────────┐
│     Corporate Librarian     │
└─────────────────────────────┘

┌─────────────────────────────┐
│ Corporate Library Technician │
└─────────────────────────────┘
```

Position Description

Corporate Librarians build and arrange an organization's information resources, which usually are limited to subjects of special interest to the company. These special Librarians can provide vital information services by preparing abstracts and indexes of current periodicals, organizing bibliographies, or analyzing background information and preparing reports on areas of particular interest. For example, a Librarian working for a corporation could provide the sales department with information on competitors or new developments affecting their field.

Corporate Librarians may perform manual and computer-assisted searches, including on-line searches; maintain and troubleshoot automated library systems and CD-ROM databases; key information into a computer to search for or store selected library materials; train other workers engaged in cataloging, entering data, locating, filing, or copying selected material; and support business information needs of the organization's management.

The Corporate Librarian is involved in much more than archiving company information. Today's Corporate Librarians are technologically savvy information scientists who use the latest technology to gather, analyze, and disseminate knowledge for corporate decision making. Corporate Librarians can research technology trends, study consumer issues, and profile various companies and industry sectors for employees.

Corporate Librarians usually work normal business hours, but in fast-paced industries, such as advertising or legal services, they can work longer hours during peak times.

Salaries

Salaries for this position vary a great deal depending on the specific job responsibilities and location of the library. Starting salaries begin at about $30,000 and may rise to more than $80,000 for librarians who manage large corporate departments.

Employment Prospects

The Internet has created unprecedented new demand for highly trained Corporate Librarians who can take all this information and organize it for easy corporate consumption. As demand for information-sorting expertise has grown, the role of the Corporate Librarian has evolved. As a result, there are almost limitless possibilities for Corporate Librarians, especially if the individual is willing to relocate for a job.

Advancement Prospects

As the growth of corporate libraries has exploded in the wake of the technology revolution, the opportunities for Corporate Librarians have likewise exploded. Corporate Librarians can parlay their experience and skills into a wide range of related jobs, but many corporate information specialists are going into business for themselves, serving as freelancers who work with a wide variety of companies.

Education and Training

Most corporate library positions require a master of library science (M.L.S.) degree, preferably from a school accredited by the American Library Association (ALA). Undergraduate degrees in almost any subject area are appropriate, but special expertise in business or the company's area of specialization is helpful.

Most M.L.S. programs take one to two years to complete. A typical graduate program includes courses in the foundations of library and information science, including the history of books and printing, intellectual freedom and censorship, and the role of libraries and information in society. Other basic courses cover material selection and processing, the organization of information, reference tools and strategies, and user services. Courses are adapted to educate librarians to use new resources brought about by advancing technology such as on-line reference systems, Internet search methods, and automated circulation systems. Course options can include classification, cataloging, indexing, and abstracting; library administration; and library automation.

Computer-related coursework is an increasingly important part of an M.L.S. degree. Some programs offer interdisciplinary degrees combining technical coursework in information science with traditional training in library science. Librarians participate in continuing training once they are on the job to keep abreast of new information systems brought about by changing technology.

Experience, Skills, and Personality Traits

Corporate Librarians spend a great deal of their time working with employees of the company, so strong interpersonal and communication skills are required. In addition, excellent organizational and computer skills and the ability to work unsupervised are important.

Unions and Associations

Corporate Librarians do not usually belong to unions, but they can belong to a variety of trade associations that provide educational guidance, support, conferences, and information to members. These include the American Library Association, the Association for Library Collections and Technical Services, the American Society for Information Science, and the Special Libraries Association.

Tips for Entry

1. Jobs in this field may be found in the job listings for all related trade associations, beginning with the American Library Association.
2. Look for job ads in *American Libraries* magazine.
3. Check daily job postings on "Hot Jobs Online" at the website of the American Library Association (www.ala.org).
4. Subscribe to library journals and periodicals.
5. Attend library conventions or conferences and check job boards, especially the placement service that lists library-related jobs at annual ALA conventions.
6. Investigate other websites that list library job postings, such as http://www.libraryjobpostings.org or the American Society of Information Science website job line (http://www.asis.org/Jobline).
7. Visit the ALISE website, which has links to all library schools, each of which has state and national employment listings (www.alise.org).

CORPORATE MEDICAL LIBRARIAN

CAREER PROFILE

Duties: Provide health information about new medical treatments, clinical trials, and standard trials procedures, tests, and equipment to corporate employees, such as those of a pharmaceutical firm

Alternate Title(s): Corporate Medical Information Specialist

Salary Range: $45,000 to $100,000+

Employment Prospects: Good

Advancement Prospects: Good

Best Geographical Location(s): Major cities or nearby suburbs are usually the primary location for large pharmaceutical firms and other medical companies large enough to maintain a medical library

Prerequisites:

Education or Training—Graduate degree in library or information science

Experience—A background in science, health sciences, or allied health is helpful

Special Skills and Personality Traits—Strong oral and written communication skills; good interpersonal skills; and solid computer skills

CAREER LADDER

```
┌─────────────────────────────────────┐
│  Director of Corporate Medical Library │
└─────────────────────────────────────┘

┌─────────────────────────────────────┐
│     Corporate Medical Librarian       │
└─────────────────────────────────────┘

┌─────────────────────────────────────┐
│     Medical Librarian Assistant       │
└─────────────────────────────────────┘
```

Position Description

A Medical Librarian at a health-related corporation is responsible for retrieving, selecting, organizing, and disseminating health information to employees. Librarians may evaluate advanced information technologies, teach users how to find health care information, develop content and design materials for instructional purposes, and design and manage digital access.

The Corporate Medical Librarian also provides general and subject reference assistance and develops and manages the collection. Administrative responsibilities include supervising support staff. In addition, they must be sure to provide employees from a variety of disciplines with the latest information on diseases, procedures, treatments, and research. Corporate Medical Librarians also select and maintain medical books, journals, and audiovisual materials, and provide computer database searches for users.

Medical Librarians also must be familiar with key databases that cover biomedical literature, such as MEDLINE, a huge index of some 7 million articles published since 1966 that is the standard searching tool for medical literature, and Dialog, a database vendor that allows a user to search through numerous databases such as Biosis (abstracts of scientific articles) and Science Citation Index (abstracts of articles in diverse magazines and journals). In addition, Medical Librarians train corporate employees to do their own searches and teach search strategies.

Salaries

Salaries vary according to the size and location of the company, the level of responsibility, and the length of employment. Salaries range from $45,000 to more than $100,000.

Employment Prospects

Employment of Medical Librarians in the corporate world is especially strong as the need for organization grows amidst the technological information explosion. While corporations housing medical libraries can be found throughout the country, they tend to be located in or near large cities; competition for these positions is therefore more competitive.

Advancement Prospects

There is a variety of opportunities for Medical Librarians in the corporate world, depending on the interests and expertise of the individual Librarian. The more time, experience, and additional education an individual has, the better the advancement prospects. Because Medical Librarians have a number of marketable skills, they can move on to a variety of positions such as Web manager for a medical center, medical informatics expert, or chief information officer. A Medical Librarian may move into work as a community outreach coordinator for a public health agency, reference librarian at a hospital, electronic resources cataloger for an Internet startup company, director of a nursing school library, user education specialist at a consumer health library, or information architect for a pharmaceutical company.

Education and Training

A master's of library or information science from an ALA-accredited school is required for any position as a Medical Librarian. Many medical libraries also require a background in science, health sciences, or allied health, or graduate courses in medical informatics or medical librarianship. The Medical Librarian should learn everything possible related to the medical field (for example, understanding biomedical references, principles of organization of information in the biomedical sciences, and on-line computer databases such as MEDLINE, from the National Library of Medicine.)

Experience, Skills, and Personality Traits

Because Medical Librarians spend most of their day working with company employees, strong interpersonal and communication skills are required. In addition, excellent organizational and computer skills are important, along with a solid understanding of and interest in medicine or health-related issues. Librarians working in medical libraries need to be well organized with strong attention to detail. Because the Medical Librarian is expected to work with employees from all areas of the company, the ability to communicate effectively with diverse clients, and to maintain clients' privacy is vital.

Unions and Associations

Medical Librarians working in the corporate world do not usually belong to unions, but they can belong to a variety of trade associations that provide educational guidance, support, conferences, and information to members. These might include the Medical Library Association, the American Library Association, the American Society for Information Science, the Medical Librarian Association, or the Special Libraries Association.

Tips for Entry

1. Check out the job listings on the Medical Librarian Association website (www.mlanet.org/jobs/index.html).
2. Attend the annual May convention of the Medical Librarian Association and check out the jobs posted.
3. Jobs in this field also may be found in the job listings for all related trade associations, beginning with the American Library Association.
4. Look for job ads in *American Libraries* magazine.
5. Check daily job postings on "Hot Jobs Online" at the website of the American Library Association (www.ala.org).
6. Subscribe to library journals and periodicals.
7. Check out the placement service that lists library-related jobs at annual ALA conventions.
8. Investigate other websites that list library job postings, such as http://www.libraryjobpostings.org.
9. Visit the ALISE website, which has links to all library schools, each of which has state and national employment listings (www.alise.org).
10. Visit the American Society of Information Science website job line (http://www.asis.org/Jobline).

CORPORATE LAW LIBRARIAN

CAREER PROFILE

Duties: Develop and direct information programs and systems at a corporate law library to ensure information is organized to meet users' needs; provide reference help for attorneys, clerks, and partners; prepare and shelve new materials; supervise technicians

Alternate Title(s): Law Library Information Specialist

Salary Range: $38,000 to $100,000+

Employment Prospects: Good

Advancement Prospects: Good

Best Geographical Location(s): All locations may hold employment possibilities

Prerequisites:

Education or Training—Master's degree in library science; a law degree is also helpful (and may be required at some firms)

Experience—Experience working in a law library is helpful

Special Skills and Personality Traits—Good people skills and superior organizational skills; attention to detail; flexibility; good written and verbal communication skills

CAREER LADDER

```
┌─────────────────────────────────┐
│     Director of Law Library     │
└─────────────────────────────────┘

┌─────────────────────────────────┐
│     Corporate Law Librarian     │
└─────────────────────────────────┘

┌─────────────────────────────────┐
│     Law Library Technician      │
└─────────────────────────────────┘
```

Position Description

Corporate Law Librarians are employed in law firms of all sizes in cities and towns throughout the country. They fill many of the same positions that can be found at other libraries. They are in technical services, cataloging, public services, collection development, and reference services.

The Corporate Law Librarian's primary duty is to help the firm's attorneys with their research. In some cases, this could be as little as helping the attorney locate research materials, but often the Librarian may do the bulk of the research alone, and prepare a report for the attorney's use. When information is needed quickly and cost is not a problem, electronic resources such as Lexis-Nexis or Westlaw can be used. Many of these database services are expensive, so the Librarian needs to be able to do the research using both print and electronic media.

Most Corporate Law Librarians juggle many different duties and projects. In a given week, a Law Librarian might do research for a clerk or partner, serve on a committee, edit a newsletter, or conduct a training session. Other duties might include cataloging some books (in smaller firm libraries), supervising paraprofessionals checking in serials, and negotiating contracts.

An essential feature of library work is that it involves organizing. Librarians catalog and classify material and organize information, people and projects. Librarians also tend to think institutionally about policies and procedures—for example, setting up a checkout system for a firm library that is likely to be used by all the attorneys. They build and arrange an organization's information resources, which usually are limited to subjects of special interest to the organization. These special Librarians can provide vital information services by preparing abstracts and indexes of current periodicals, organizing bibliographies, or analyzing background information and preparing reports on areas of particular interest. Most Law Librarians are involved in setting library policy and making decisions about personnel and resources.

The Corporate Law Librarian of the future will be expected to work with an increasing number of electronic services, within a short time period and under a great deal of pressure. Space is a very important factor within the confines of a law firm office, and often the library facilities are not at the top of the priority list. As a result, an increasing number of law firm libraries have a small collection of books and heavily rely on electronic resources. The desktop computer, electronic databases, and the Internet are becoming the primary tools of the Corporate Law Librarian.

Salaries

Salaries for this position vary a great deal depending on the specific job responsibilities and location of the library. The median salary for a Law Librarian in a one-person library is about $39,681. The median for a director/chief Law Librarian is $63,636, but can reach $107,900 or above.

Employment Prospects

Law Librarians can apply for—and might even be recruited for—jobs in other parts of the country. It is often true that a Law Librarian needs to move in order to get a desired position. However, in larger cities there are plenty of opportunities with corporate law firm libraries, which usually are advertised and filled locally.

Advancement Prospects

Experienced Librarians can advance to administrative positions, such as department head, library director, or chief information officer.

Education and Training

To qualify for virtually any professional job in a professional law library, a Librarian usually must have a graduate degree in library science. There are a few exceptions. Some people work as Law Librarians without formal training in librarianship. For instance, a paralegal in a small firm might have responsibility for filing the looseleafs and pocket parts; as the firm grows, the responsibilities grow to include reference, budgeting, and other duties—at which point the paralegal is called the "firm librarian." Some law libraries hire lawyers with good research skills to work as reference librarians; they pick up on-the-job knowledge about other library operations.

Most jobs require a master's degree from an American Library Association (ALA)–accredited institution. The names of the degrees vary (B.M.L.S., M.L.I.S., M.S.I.S., M.L., M.A. in L.S.B.) but all reflect an appropriate entry-level educational requirement for careers in the law librarianship profession.

Although corporate law firms do not usually require a law degree (less than 20 percent of the Law Librarian jobs being filled require both degrees), almost 30 percent of all Law Librarians have a J.D. or L.L.B. degree. If such a degree is required, most positions stipulate that this degree be earned from a law school accredited by the American Bar Association (ABA). Some jobs state a preference for the law degree in addition to a graduate degree in library science.

A law degree is less important for other positions in law libraries—for example, in cataloging, acquisitions, circulation, government documents, and computer services—although some people in those positions do have law degrees. Court librarians may or may not have law degrees.

Experience, Skills, and Personality Traits

Corporate Law Librarians need top-notch information management skills, since they must direct staff members to the right resources. Networking skills are vital, as are effective interpersonal skills. Technical skills are important, since the importance of new technology in the corporate legal world cannot be overemphasized.

Unions and Associations

Corporate Law Librarians working in libraries do not usually belong to unions, but they can belong to a variety of trade associations that provide educational guidance, support, conferences, and information to members. These might include the American Association of Law Libraries (AALL), the American Library Association, the American Society for Information Science, or the Special Libraries Association.

Tips for Entry

1. There are many jobs posted each year for Law Librarians. Jobs in law libraries are almost always advertised nationally, but jobs in court and county law libraries and firms may only be advertised locally.
2. Contact the placement committee of the AALL, which coordinates personal interviews at the association's annual meeting each July.
3. Check the job database on the AALL webpage, which is updated regularly and includes jobs in all kinds of law libraries.
4. Check AALL chapter listservs and websites.
5. Check the job lists as advertised on the websites of the Special Library Association and the ALA.
6. A J.D./M.L.S. degree combination does increase job options, but it is not a requirement.

CURATOR (SPECIAL LIBRARY)

CAREER PROFILE

Duties: Preserve, conserve, and document an institution's collections, archives, and objects on loan.

Alternate Title(s): Curator of Archives

Salary Range: $20,010 to $70,100+

Employment Prospects: Fair

Advancement Prospects: Fair

Best Geographical Location(s): Large cities are more likely to provide more types of varied collections

Prerequisites:

Education or Training—Master's degree in library science from an ALA-accredited library and information studies program

Experience—Many curators work in archives or museums while completing their formal education to gain the hands-on experience that many employers seek when hiring

Special Skills and Personality Traits—Good people skills; detail oriented; flexibility; good written and verbal communication skills

CAREER LADDER

```
┌─────────────────────────┐
│    Museum Director       │
└─────────────────────────┘

┌─────────────────────────┐
│       Curator            │
└─────────────────────────┘

┌─────────────────────────┐
│   Assistant Curator      │
└─────────────────────────┘
```

Position Description

Curators oversee collections in a wide variety of institutions, including museums, zoos, aquariums, botanical gardens, nature centers, and historic sites. They acquire items through purchases, gifts, field exploration, intermuseum exchanges, or (in the case of some plants and animals) reproduction. Curators also plan and prepare exhibits. In natural history museums, Curators collect and observe specimens in their natural habitat, describing and classifying species.

Curators help develop their collections and provide researchers, media and the general public with information and assistance. They try to improve donor relations, provide reference and research services, create exhibits, oversee the development and arrangement of the archives, and support digital preservation efforts.

Depending on the institution, the collections may include historical documents, audiovisual materials, institutional records, works of art, coins, stamps, minerals, clothing,

maps, living and preserved plants and animals, buildings, computer records, or historic sites. Curators usually handle objects found in cultural, biological, or historical collections, such as sculptures, textiles, and paintings, while archivists mainly handle valuable records, documents, or objects that are retained because they originally accompanied and relate specifically to a document.

Most Curators specialize in a particular field, such as botany, art, paleontology, or history; those working in large institutions may be highly specialized. Curators who work in large institutions may travel extensively to evaluate potential additions to the collection, organize exhibitions, and conduct research in their area of expertise. However, travel is rare for Curators employed in small institutions.

Some Curators maintain collections while others do research, and others perform administrative tasks. Registrars, for example, keep track of and move objects in the collection. In small institutions, with only one or a few

Curators, one Curator may be responsible for multiple tasks, from maintaining collections to directing the affairs of museums. Curators also organize records of storage, transport, insurance, and loans, conduct periodic inventories, and prepare reports.

Most Curators use computer databases to catalog and organize their collections. Many also use the Internet to make information available to other Curators and the public. Increasingly, Curators are expected to participate in grantwriting and fund-raising to support their projects.

Salaries

Earnings of Curators vary considerably by specialty and size of institution. Salaries in large, well-funded museums can be several times higher than those in small ones. The average annual salary for museum Curators was $35,270; other Curators' earnings range from a low of $20,010 to a high of more than $70,100.

Employment Prospects

Competition for jobs as Curators is expected to be keen as qualified applicants outnumber job openings. A Curator job is attractive to many people, and many applicants have the necessary training and subject knowledge, but there are only a few openings. Consequently, candidates may have to work part time, as an intern, or even as a volunteer assistant curator or research associate after completing their formal education. Job opportunities for Curators should be best in art and history museums. Although jobs are expected to grow at an average pace, the high competition will continue.

Substantial work experience in collection management, exhibit design, restoration, and database management skills are required to obtain a position with an institution.

Advancement Prospects

Competition for advancement is strong. In large institutions, Curators may be promoted to a position of museum director. Curators in smaller institutions usually advance by moving into bigger museums or institutions for a job with more responsibility.

Education and Training

Because only a few graduate program in museum conservation exist in the United States, competition for these schools is fierce. Most museums require a master's degree in an appropriate discipline of the museum's specialty (art, history, or archaeology) or museum studies. Many employers prefer a doctoral degree, particularly for Curators in natural history or science museums. Earning two graduate degrees—in museum studies (museology) and a specialized subject—gives a candidate a distinct advantage in this competitive job market. For most positions, experience in a full-time internship is required, and additional courses in business administration, marketing, and fund-raising are helpful.

Curators are often required to be knowledgeable in a number of fields. For historic and artistic conservation, courses in chemistry, physics, and art are desirable. Curators with administrative and managerial responsibilities may find courses in business administration, public relations, marketing, and fund-raising to be helpful.

Significant knowledge of digital technology and the ability to ensure an effective digital presence are important. Curators need computer skills and the ability to work with electronic databases. Curators also need to be familiar with digital imaging, scanning technology, and copyright infringement, since many are responsible for posting information on the Internet.

Experience, Skills, and Personality Traits

Many Curators work in archives or museums while completing their formal education, to gain the hands-on experience that many employers seek when hiring.

Curators must be able to communicate effectively with patrons, as they answer questions and provide reference help. Being personable and able to work well with others is a plus, and computer knowledge is absolutely necessary. Curators must be flexible because of their wide variety of duties. They need design ability to present exhibits and, in small museums, manual dexterity to build exhibits or restore objects. Leadership and business skills are important for museum directors, while marketing skills are valuable for increasing museum attendance and fund-raising.

Unions and Associations

Curators can belong to a variety of trade associations that provide educational guidance, support, conferences, and information to members. These might include the Independent Curators International, Institute of Museum and Library Services, American Library Association, the American Society for Information Science, or the Special Libraries Association.

Tips for Entry

1. Take every opportunity available to work as a curator intern, do a curator practicum, or volunteer in the type of institution that interests you most. Library administrators look for candidates with some relevant experience.

2. Make contacts. Join various professional organizations for librarians to provide a network through which you may hear about job opportunities.

3. E-mail discussion groups such as LIBJOBS and LIS-JOBS are a good source for job postings. Topical groups are also a good place for finding advertisements in a particular field of librarianship.

4. Look for jobs on the Internet, such as on www. Lisjobs.com.
5. Check daily job postings on "Hot Jobs Online" at the website of the American Library Association (www. ala.org), investigate other websites that list library job postings, or visit the American Society of Information Science website job line (http://www.asis.org/Jobline).
6. Visit the ALISE website, which has links to all library schools, each of which has state and national employment listings (www.alise.org).
7. Attend library conventions or conferences and check out the placement service that lists library-related jobs at annual ALA conventions.

SPECIAL LIBRARY TECHNICIAN

CAREER PROFILE

Duties: Conduct literature searches, compile bibliographies, and prepare abstracts, usually on subjects of particular interest to the organization

Alternate Title(s): Library Assistant, Media Aide, Library Technical Assistant

Salary Range: $14,410 to $38,000+

Employment Prospects: Excellent

Advancement Prospects: Excellent

Best Geographical Location(s): Larger cities may offer more possibilities, but special libraries throughout the country use Library Technicians

Prerequisites:

Education or Training—High school diploma, associate or bachelor's degree, or diploma from library technician course

Experience—Experience working in a library is helpful; computer skills are needed for many jobs

Special Skills and Personality Traits—Good people skills; attention to detail; neatness; organizational skills; aptitude for computers; good English writing and speaking skills; willingness to attend conferences and workshops; willingness to learn new skills

CAREER LADDER

```
┌─────────────────────────────────┐
│           Librarian             │
└─────────────────────────────────┘

┌─────────────────────────────────┐
│   Special Library Technician    │
└─────────────────────────────────┘

┌─────────────────────────────────┐
│          Entry Level            │
└─────────────────────────────────┘
```

Position Description

Library Technicians may work in all sorts of special libraries maintained by corporations, advertising agencies, museums, professional societies, and research laboratories, where they conduct literature searches, compile bibliographies, and prepare abstracts, usually on subjects of particular interest to the organization.

The Library Technician helps the librarian manage convenient and cost-effective information services that support the interests of the organization, such as developing specialized lists of indexing terms for databases. The Technician also helps the librarian teach employees how to find information related to current business goals and provides troubleshooting service for employees accessing information from the desktop. The Technician may create databases of in-house documents such as reports, technical manuals, or resource materials used for special projects, or create searchable document files and on-line technical manuals. The Technician could be asked to create a home page on the Internet for the organization, or link an existing home page to other sites of interest on the Internet.

Depending on the employer, Library Technicians can have other title(s), such as library technical assistant or media aide. Library Technicians direct library users to standard references, organize and maintain periodicals, prepare volumes for binding, handle interlibrary loan requests, prepare invoices, perform routine cataloging and coding of library materials, retrieve information from computer databases, and supervise support staff. Many libraries now offer self-service registration and circulations with computers, so that Library Technicians spend less time recording information manually.

Some Library Technicians are also responsible for maintaining special equipment such as projectors, tape recorders, videocassette recorders, copiers, and microfilm or microfiche readers. They also design posters, bulletin boards, or displays. Library Technicians in special libraries usually work normal business hours, although they often work overtime as well.

Salaries

Salaries for this position vary a great deal depending on the responsibilities and location of the library. Starting salaries begin at $14,410. Median annual earnings of Library Technicians in special libraries are $21,170; earnings may exceed $38,000.

Employment Prospects

Employment of Library Technicians in special libraries is particularly strong and growing because of the increase in the number of special libraries. Because computerized library systems have made cataloging easier, Library Technicians are now being given these job responsibilities. In addition to employment growth, some job openings will occur when Library Technicians transfer to other fields or leave the labor force.

Advancement Prospects

Library Technicians usually advance by assuming added responsibilities, such as involvement in budget, scheduling, and personnel matters in their department. Some Library Technicians are eventually promoted to supervisory positions and are in charge of the day-to-day operation of their department.

Education and Training

Training requirements for Special Library Technicians vary, from a high school diploma to specialized postsecondary training. Library Technicians need at least a high school diploma, and many more are now obtaining a diploma from a library technician course. Some Technicians also have an associate or bachelor's degree.

More and more two-year colleges are offering an associate of arts degree in library technology, in both liberal arts and library-related study. In these courses, students learn about library and media organization and operation, and how to order, process, catalog, locate, and circulate library materials and work with library automation. Libraries and associations offer continuing education courses to keep Technicians abreast of new developments in the field.

Some special libraries hire individuals with work experience or other training (especially in the library's area of speciality). For example, a Library Technician with extra training or work experience in the field of psychology would be of great interest to the special library of a psychology professional association.

Other special libraries prefer to train inexperienced workers for their particular job; a few special libraries require that technicians have an associate or bachelor's degree.

Given the widespread use of technology in special libraries, computer skills are just about required for most of these jobs—and the more computer experience a person has, the better. An understanding of databases, library automation systems, on-line library systems, on-line public access systems, and circulation systems is valuable.

Experience, Skills, and Personality Traits

Library Technicians need to feel a commitment to working with people; the ability to pay close attention to details; neatness; organizational skills, aptitude for computers; good English writing and speaking skills; willingness to attend conferences and workshops, and an interest in learning new skills.

Unions and Associations

Librarian Technicians working in special libraries do not usually belong to unions, but they can belong to a variety of trade associations that provide educational guidance, support, conferences and information to members. These might include the Special Libraries Association, the Library Assistants and Technicians Group, the American Library Association, or the American Society for Information Science.

Tips for Entry

1. Visit the local special library of your choice (corporation, museum, and so on) to check out job openings.
2. Information about a career as a Library Technician can be obtained from the Council on Library/Media Technology, P.O. Box 951, Oxon Hill, MD 20750.
3. For information on training programs for library/media technical assistants, write to the American Library Association, Office for Library Personnel Resources, 50 East Huron Street, Chicago, IL 60611.
4. Check newspaper classified ads under "library technician" for openings in local special libraries.
5. Look for job ads in *American Libraries* magazine.
6. Check daily job postings on "Hot Jobs Online" at the website of the American Library Association (www.ala.org), www.libraryjobpostings.org, or the American Society of Information Science website job line (www.asis.org/Jobline).
7. Attend the Special Library Association conferences and check job boards, or the placement service that lists library-related jobs at annual ALA conventions.
8. Visit the ALISE website, which has links to all library schools, each of which has state and national employment listings (www.alise.org).

SPECIAL CATALOGER

CAREER PROFILE

Duties: Describe special library, archive, or museum materials in catalogs by author, title, subject, or keyword

Alternate Title(s): None

Salary Range: $40,000 to $62,000

Employment Prospects: Good

Advancement Prospects: Good

Best Geographical Location(s): Most positions are available in special libraries, museums, and archives in cities and urban areas, but job openings are available throughout the United States

Prerequisites:

Education or Training—Master's degree in library or information science and a second master's degree in another area

Experience—Coursework in special collections and/or archives; knowledge of AACR2, LCRI, LCSH, LC, and APPM classification systems

Special Skills and Personality Traits—Attention to detail; ability to work independently; foreign language skills; patient; decisive; good communication and organizational skills

CAREER LADDER

```
┌─────────────────────────────────┐
│   Cataloger in Larger Library   │
└─────────────────────────────────┘

┌─────────────────────────────────┐
│           Cataloger             │
└─────────────────────────────────┘

┌─────────────────────────────────┐
│     Assistant Cataloger or      │
│      Entry Level Position       │
└─────────────────────────────────┘
```

Position Description

Special Catalogers classify a wide range of material for special libraries, museums, or archives, describing materials by subject, publication date, format, author, title, and many other characteristics. Catalogers spend all their time acquiring and preparing materials for use, and often do not deal directly with the public. As part of their daily job, they perform original and complex copy cataloging; establish, review, and revise cataloging policies and procedures; and manage daily cataloging workflow, which can be at times overwhelming. Catalogers in special libraries also perform database management or enrichment functions as required and collect cataloging statistics and contribute to department reports. They may be required to supervise, train, and evaluate graduate interns, student workers, and volunteers, and track current trends in the profession. Keeping track of information management, bibliographic control, and emerging technologies is an important part of their job. In addi-

tion, the Special Cataloger may research, identify, plan, and implement initiatives to advance the resources and tools within the museum, university, and broader community.

On a daily basis, a Special Cataloger records the title, author's name, publication information, and a short summary of each item, making distinctions about individual materials. Certain items that are valuable or important may be photographed and assigned a code linked to their location. The codes are then recorded in a computerized reference database.

The sheer volume of the tasks can be overwhelming, as materials often come into the library faster than they can be cataloged; this type of library job can be highly stressful.

Salaries

Salaries for this position vary a great deal depending on the responsibilities and location of the museum, special library, or archive, but generally range between $40,000 and

$62,000. Catalogers in large museums, archives, or special libraraies in metropolitan areas can expect to earn more.

Employment Prospects

The number of jobs is projected to grow about 5 percent as modern technology continues to require unique methods of data management in special libraries, archives, and museums.

Advancement Prospects

Catalogers can become archivists, reference librarians, or take on administrative positions in public, private, or university libraries, or become catalogers in museums. They can apply their methodical and analytical skills to other fields, such as history, bibliography, and data entry. Promotions usually come with experience and administrative skills, knowledge of automated systems, and additional training. Advancement opportunities are greater in larger library systems.

Education and Training

Catalogers generally need a master's degree in library or information studies, along with a bachelor's degree in general arts. Prospective Catalogers should supplement this education with courses in computers and business studies. It is also a good idea to volunteer with a library, archive, or museum, as any experience in the field will be beneficial in the long run.

Experience, Skills, and Personality Traits

Special Catalogers need to have experience in special collections cataloging using Online Computer Library Center (OCLC) and Data Research Associates (DRA) automated library system, knowledge of archival practice and management and bibliographic control, and knowledge of computer applications in the special collections/archival environment. Catalogers in special libraries also need to understand emerging technologies.

Catalogers should enjoy research, love books, and be comfortable working alone. An analytical mind and a thorough, methodical approach to tasks are important qualities.

Unions and Associations

Catalogers working in special libraries, archives, and museums can belong to a variety of trade associations that provide educational guidance, support, conferences, and information to members. These might include the Special Libraries Association, American Institute for Conservation of Historic and Artistic Works, the Independent International Curators, Institute of Museum and Library Services, Society of American Archivists, the American Library Association, the American Society for Information Science, or American Association of Museums.

Tips for Entry

1. Get experience. If you are attending library school, take every opportunity available to work as a student assistant in the university library, do a practicum or internship in another library, or volunteer in the cataloging department of the library. Library administrators are likely to select a candidate with some relevant experience over one with none.

2. Make contacts. Join professional organizations for librarians and keep in touch with your library friends to provide a network through which you may hear about job opportunities.

3. Send out your résumé. Find out the name and address of every library in your area where you might like to work (the telephone book is helpful; call to find out to whom to address your cover letter). When openings occur, administrators often pull out their collection of unsolicited résumés and contact the candidates.

4. E-mail discussion groups such as LIBJOBS and LIS-JOBS are a good source for job postings. Topical groups are also a good place for finding advertisements in a particular field of librarianship. For example, Web4Lib often receives library Webmaster-type job postings.

5. Look for jobs on the Internet, such as on www.Lisjobs. com. *Jobs for Librarians and Information Professionals* is a comprehensive guide to online job resources for librarians and information professionals. Check daily job postings on "Hot Jobs Online" at the website of the American Library Association (www.ala.org). Investigate other websites that list library job postings, such as: www.libraryjobpostings.org.

6. Visit the ALISE website, which has links to all library schools, each of which has state and national employment listings (www.alise.org), or the American Society of Information Science website job line (www.asis.org/Jobline).

7. Subscribe to major library trade publications, such as *Library Journal* and *American Libraries*.

8. If you're targeting a specific institution or geographic area, take a look at individual websites for postings. The Folger Shakespeare Library, in Washington, D.C., for example, has an employment opportunities page.

9. Attend library conventions or conferences and check job boards.

10. Check out the placement service that lists library-related jobs at annual ALA conventions.

LEGAL SERVICES INFORMATION BROKER

CAREER PROFILE

Duties: Perform online searching, competitive intelligence, and law library research for law firms

Alternate Title(s): Independent Researcher, Legal Information Research Consultant

Salary Range: $55 to $100 per hour

Employment Prospects: Excellent

Advancement Prospects: Good

Best Geographical Location(s): Because Legal Services Information Brokers generally use computerized networks, location is relatively unimportant; however, proximity to a variety of legal clients is better near urban areas

Prerequisites:

Education or Training—Master's in library science plus law experience or advanced degree

Experience—Experience working in a law library setting is helpful

Special Skills and Personality Traits—Research skills; organizational skills; computer literacy; ability to work well with others; ability to work well under pressure

CAREER LADDER

```
┌─────────────────────────────────────┐
│  Director of Legal Services Information │
│         Brokerage Firm               │
└─────────────────────────────────────┘

┌─────────────────────────────────────┐
│  Legal Services Information Broker   │
└─────────────────────────────────────┘

┌─────────────────────────────────────┐
│         Information Broker           │
└─────────────────────────────────────┘
```

Position Description

Legal Services Information Brokers are often independent consultants who are usually affiliated with law firms, and who perform legal research and writing, manage law libraries, and offer litigation support. They search cases, statutes and other sources of law, and are able to draft legal memoranda, pleadings, motions, and briefs. Searching of on-line legal databases is also provided as needs arise.

Legal services information professionals also maintain and update law library collections, organize and arrange law libraries, monitor expenditures, plan and implement law library relocations, and recommend acquisitions. For example, the library of a growing law firm may expand to the extent that its members can no longer keep it organized and up to date. If the firm does not want to hire a full-time law librarian, it might instead hire an information management firm that provides a law librarian two days a week.

Through a combination of on-line and manual research, Legal Services Information Brokers also find information about products, assets of judgment debtors, ownership of subsidiaries, and expert witnesses. The Legal Services Information Broker provides crucial information for clients who can't find it on their own, charging for their expertise at locating, analyzing, and interpreting information for their clients.

Usually, freelance legal services information brokering involves a fixed project with a deadline and a specific budget, although some Information Brokers work on a continuing basis. Typical clients include the smaller law firm without a staff researcher; it is far more cost effective for such a firm to hire an information professional on an as-needed basis.

The Information Broker must take the raw data and present only that which is pertinent to the client. An Information Broker can expect to spend a great deal of time researching questions on CD-ROM databases or the Internet, either in the Broker's office or in libraries, courthouses, or government records depositories.

Salaries

An independent Legal Services Information Broker may charge between $45 and $100 per hour, depending on the specific type of information being sought. However, many of the services and databases used by Information Brokers incur separate hourly fees, which must be deducted from the broker's fee.

Employment Prospects

The demand for legal information continues to rise, and the sheer amount of available information creates a demand for information professionals who are adept at finding the correct data and presenting it in the client's desired format. The explosion of information on the Internet has caused many law firms to turn to the services of the information broker. An experienced librarian with research skills and computer know-how can turn those assets into a thriving business.

Advancement Prospects

Many Information Brokers start out working for an information broker company, and gradually move into consulting or freelancing and set up their own businesses. Initially, Information Brokers who go out on their own must spend time focusing on marketing and business development. An Information Broker can build the business slowly while generating income from other sources, but at some point, most Information Brokers find it difficult to operate part time. As the Information Broker's client load increases, clients tend to expect that the Information Broker will be available throughout the day.

Education and Training

Many Legal Services Information Brokers have an advanced degree in library and information science, as well as some legal experience or time spent working in a law library. Increasingly, Information Brokers have advanced degrees in law.

Experience, Skills, and Personality Traits

The most important attribute of the Legal Services Information Broker is top-notch research skills. Organizational skills and computer literacy are next in importance. Because the Legal Services Information Broker is usually running an independent business, the ability to work well with customers is extremely important. Running a business also requires additional skills, including marketing, promotion, and financial planning.

Unions and Associations

Legal Services Information Brokers may belong to a variety of trade associations that provide educational guidance, support, conferences, and information to members. These might include the Association for Information Professionals, the Society for Competitor Intelligence Professionals, the Public Record Retrievers Network, the American Society for Information Science and Technology, the Library and Information Technology Association, the American Association of Law Libraries, or the National Information Standards Organization.

Tips for Entry

1. Before going into business for yourself, consider first working for an information brokerage firm. Check out the *Burwell World Directory of Information Brokers* (www.burwellinc.com), which lists more than 1,800 information brokerage companies.
2. Contact local law firms and present your résumé, discussing how your skills may benefit the company.
3. After you have a few years of experience, consider striking out on your own. First, set up a website to advertise your services as an information broker.
4. Join e-mail discussion groups such as LIBJOBS and LIS-JOBS for a good source for job postings.
5. Look for jobs on the Internet, such as www.Lisjobs.com, the daily job postings on "Hot Jobs Online" at the website of the American Library Association (www.ala.org), the American Society of Information Science website job line (www.asis.org/Jobline), or www.libraryjobpostings.org.
6. Check out *Jobs for Librarians and Information Professionals,* a comprehensive guide to on-line job resources for librarians and information professionals and subscribe to major library trade publications, such as *Library Journal* and *American Libraries.*
7. Visit the ALISE website, which has links to all library schools, each of which has state and national employment listings (www.alise.org).

HEALTH SERVICES INFORMATION BROKER

CAREER PROFILE

Duties: On-line searching and library research in health topics for businesses, industry, hospitals, and medical schools

Alternate Title(s): Health Information Research Consultant

Salary Range: $55 to $100 per hour

Employment Prospects: Excellent

Advancement Prospects: Good

Best Geographical Location(s): Urban areas provide the widest choice of potential clients; however, because Information Brokers generally use computerized networks, location is relatively unimportant

Prerequisites:

Education or Training—Master's in library science

Experience—Experience working in a health library setting is helpful

Special Skills and Personality Traits—Medical knowledge; research and organizational skills; computer literacy; ability to work well under pressure

CAREER LADDER

```
┌─────────────────────────────────┐
│           Director of           │
│  Information Brokerage Firm      │
└─────────────────────────────────┘

┌─────────────────────────────────┐
│ Health Services Information Broker │
└─────────────────────────────────┘

┌─────────────────────────────────┐
│        Information Broker        │
└─────────────────────────────────┘
```

Position Description

Although a few Health Services Information Brokers began their businesses in the 1980s, it is only since the 1990s that the growth in on-line databases, personal computers, and telecommunications technology reached the point where all kinds of information can be accessed on a freelance basis.

The Health Services Information Broker provides crucial information for clients who can't find it on their own, charging for their expertise at locating, analyzing, and interpreting information. An Information Broker can expect to spend a great deal of time researching questions on CD-ROM databases or the Internet. They can perform health-related on-line searching, library research, competitor intelligence, and similar services for health-related businesses, corporations, universities, and medical centers, taking raw data and presenting only that which is pertinent to the client.

The entire health care industry is built on a framework of information, enabling doctors and nurses to provide appropriate care and manufacturers to produce safe and effective drugs and devices. The information is available from the U.S. government, associations, books, journals, electronic databases, and the Internet, and generally requires an understanding of medical terminology. Health Services Information Brokers have been trained to access all of these sources and organize the resulting data into a meaningful form.

Typical clients include smaller medical corporations or drug companies without staff researchers; it is far more cost effective for such a firm to hire an information professional on an as-needed basis. For example, a medical products company might hire a Health Services Information Broker to research background information on a device the company wants to sell to hospitals. The broker must first learn from the U.S. Food and Drug Administration what regulations govern its sale in the United States, and then might conduct a complete search of the medical literature for evidence of the safety and effectiveness of similar devices. A Health Services Information Broker also might review FDA files for any relevant reports of adverse incidents associated with these devices, or he or she could research the toxicity of the materials used in the device.

A Health Services Information Broker also might consult with a pharmaceutical company working on a drug with potential for treating a number of different disorders. Since the government regulates specific indications for drugs, the company must identify which disorder to approach first, before tackling the others. The Health Services Information Broker could research the number of patients afflicted with each disorder, plus the current methods and costs of treatment, so that the company can determine if the current treatments are lacking and if their new idea will be more cost effective.

Salaries

An independent Health Services Information Broker may charge between $55 and $100 per hour, depending on the specific type of information being sought. Usually, a self-employed Health Services Information Broker works on a case-by-case basis with a deadline and a specific budget, although some information brokers are hired on retainer.

Employment Prospects

As the medical and health care fields have undergone profound changes, Health Services Information Brokers have found ways to serve clients in a wide range of areas. As the demand for health information continues to rise, the sheer amount of available data creates a demand for information professionals who are adept at finding the facts and presenting them in the right format. The explosion of health-related on-line information is the major reason why many medical-related companies are turning to the services of the Information Broker.

Advancement Prospects

Many Health Services Information Brokers start their careers by working for larger, established information broker companies. Eventually, many choose self-employment, running their businesses out of a small office or their home. Initially, self-employed Health Service Information Brokers spend a great deal of time concentrating on marketing and business development. A Health Services Information Broker can build a business slowly while keeping a regular job, but at some point clients will expect that the Information Broker be available throughout the day.

Education and Training

Many Health Services Information Brokers have an advanced degree in library and information science, as well as some medical experience or time spent working in a medical library setting. Increasingly, Health Services Information Brokers have advanced degrees in some area related to health or medicine. Some Health Services Information Brokers sign up with various on-line database vendors and commit to on-line database training and documentation collections.

Experience, Skills, and Personality Traits

The key to success as a Health Services Information Broker centers on the ability to market the business and develop a client base while honing top-notch research skills. Health Services Information Brokers must be able to define and implement goals, be willing to take calculated risks, be open to new ideas and potential business relationships, be creative, and have determination, discipline, dedication and drive. Liking research and being good at it, being comfortable with computers, and even being good at spelling and typing are important skills. To be an intermediary is by definition the ability to be effective as a middleman, going between the information source and the client. This requires knowing how to ask questions effectively, so that they intrigue, rather than threaten.

In addition to specific research skills, those who run their own small businesses must be able to market and sell their services, develop research skills, and be able to help clients find solutions through the use of information.

Unions and Associations

Health Services Information Brokers may belong to a variety of trade associations that provide educational guidance, support, conferences, and information to members. These might include the Association of Independent Information Professionals (AIIP), Society for Competitor Intelligence Professionals, the Public Record Retrievers Network, the American Society for Information Science and Technology, the Library and Information Technology Association, the Medical Library Association, or the National Information Standards Organization.

Tips for Entry

1. Before going into business for yourself, consider first working for an information brokerage firm. Check out the *Burwell World Directory of Information Brokers* (www.burwellinc.com), which lists more than 1,800 information brokerage companies.
2. After you have a few years of experience, consider striking out on your own. Outline your marketing and business plan.
3. Set up a website to advertise your services as an information broker.
4. Contact local medical-related companies or drug companies and present your resume, discussing how your skills may benefit the company.
5. Consider a listing in the Burwell directory, which lists Information Brokers from around the world. It is considered the world's most comprehensive guide to independent information experts.

6. Sign up for a few classes on information brokering, marketing, and business planning.

7. Consult the Information Professionals Institute seminar schedule and the seminar schedules at major online conferences, such as National Online Meeting (NOM) or Online World for additional classes, and investigate continuing education seminars at local universities or community colleges.

8. Check out *The Information Brokers Handbook,* available in bookstores.

FINANCIAL SERVICES INFORMATION BROKER

CAREER PROFILE

Duties: Perform on-line searching and competitive intelligence for banks and financial institutions

Alternate Title(s): Independent Researcher

Salary Range: $55 to $100 per hour

Employment Prospects: Excellent

Advancement Prospects: Good

Best Geographical Location(s): Proximity to financial and banking clients is better near urban areas, but Financial Services Information Brokers generally use computerized networks so location is relatively unimportant

Prerequisites:

Education or Training—Master's in library science plus financial experience or advanced business degree

Experience—Experience working in business or finance is helpful

Special Skills and Personality Traits—Research skills; organizational skills; computer literacy; ability to work well with others; ability to work well under pressure

CAREER LADDER

```
┌─────────────────────────────────┐
│   Director of Financial Services │
│   Information Brokerage Firm     │
└─────────────────────────────────┘

┌─────────────────────────────────┐
│ Financial Services Information Broker │
└─────────────────────────────────┘

┌─────────────────────────────────┐
│      Information Broker          │
└─────────────────────────────────┘
```

Position Description

Financial Services Information Brokers can offer a variety of services to consumer banks, investment banks, and brokerage firms. As financial institutions become more complex, they need people who can identify problems, figure out how to solve them, and then do so in a way that is understandable to the rest of the group—tasks that are uniquely designed for the Information Broker.

Financial Services Information Brokers can provide expertise in locating data, and can offer fast turnaround information for merger and acquisition efforts. They can locate and analyze detailed financial information about competitors, providing a strategic advantage in new product development or market planning. The Information Broker can offer the additional benefit of anonymity in such high-stakes issues.

The Information Broker sifts through raw data, presenting only that which is pertinent to the client. An informa-

tion broker can expect to spend a great deal of time researching questions on CD-ROM databases or the Internet, either in the broker's office or in libraries and government records depositories.

For example, if one bank believes that there is no longer a local market for a financial service, a Financial Services Information Broker can perform a zip code analysis of direct mail and in-branch promotions. The result of this data mining can reveal a new market segment on which to focus future promotions. This analysis can create new avenues for the bank to generate profits, while identifying the demographics of potential customers.

Among the most valuable resources a financial institution has are its own market analyses, forecasts, and other expert research. However, many firms don't have this information readily available. Often it is sprinkled throughout many different offices, on different servers, and is inaccessible to those who might put it to profitable use. Financial

Services Information Brokers can apply their organizational skills to create a library integrating all the data sources in one company, and help with drafting a routing policy for print materials.

Alternatively, a Financial Services Information Broker might provide information about trends, innovative products, new types of services, or delivery methods required by small businesses for brokerage firm analysts. The information professional could deliver a report containing news, fundamental data, analyses, and forecasts.

Some Financial Services Information Brokers combine information brokering with other services; for example, some Brokers with existing freelance businesses expand their services by offering consulting, financial technical writing, or translation services to existing clients. Many Financial Services Information Brokers are generalists and provide all kinds of financial information.

Salaries

A Financial Services Information Broker may earn between $55 and $100 per hour, depending on the specific type of information being sought. Self-employed Information Brokers must take time to build a client base; a profitable business depends on the Broker's business skills. Usually, freelance Financial Services Information Brokering involves a fixed project with a deadline and a specific budget, although some information brokers work on a continuing basis.

Independent Information Brokers may gross anywhere from $15,000 to $100,000 or more for an established one-person business. Higher incomes are the result of a long-term investment in the business. How well a Financial Services Information Broker does depends on how much time is spent on the business, whether the Broker is capable of building a business profitably, and the Broker's long-term commitment to the business.

Employment Prospects

The sheer amount of available financial information—either outside a company or inside—creates a demand for information professionals who are adept at finding the correct data and presenting it in the client's desired format. The explosion of information on the Internet has caused many brokerage firms and banks to turn to Financial Services Information Brokers. An experienced librarian with research and computer skills can turn those assets into a thriving business.

Advancement Prospects

Many Information Brokers moonlight for the first few years, maintaining a regular job (often in library services) before striking out as an Information Broker. They may begin their own brokerage on a part-time basis and build their client base slowly, sometimes taking a few years before they are ready to work full time. This way, a Broker can build the business slowly while generating income from other sources. At some point, most Information Brokers find it difficult to operate part time, as clients demand that a Broker be available throughout the day, and most will at that point operate full time. Once a Financial Services Information Broker decides to freelance full time, he or she must at first focus a great deal of time on marketing and business development.

Education and Training

Many Financial Services Information Brokers have an advanced degree in library and information science, as well as a business degree or some financial experience. Some Information Brokers sign up with various on-line database vendors and commit to on-line database training and documentation collections to further develop their business.

Experience, Skills, and Personality Traits

The most important attribute of the Financial Services Information Broker is top-notch research skills. Organizational skills and computer literacy are next in importance. Working as an Information Broker basically means acting as an intermediary between an information source and a client. This requires knowing how to ask questions effectively so that they intrigue, rather than threaten. A good Financial Services Information Broker must know how to charm the information from the source without boring or alarming him or her.

Because the Information Broker is usually running an independent business, the ability to work well with customers is extremely important. Running a business also requires a separate set of skills such as advertising, marketing, writing business plans, and so on.

Unions and Associations

Financial Services Information Brokers may belong to a variety of trade associations that provide educational guidance, support, conferences, and information to members. These might include the Association for Information Professionals, the Society for Competitor Intelligence Professionals, the Public Record Retrievers Network, the American Society for Information Science and Technology, the Library and Information Technology Association, or the National Information Standards Organization.

Tips for Entry

1. Before going into business for yourself, consider first working for an information brokerage firm. Check out the *Burwell World Directory of Information Brokers* (www.burwellinc.com), which lists more than 1,800 information brokerage companies.
2. After you have a few years of experience, consider striking out on your own; first, develop a comprehensive business plan.

3. Set up a website to advertise your services as a Financial Services Information Broker.
4. Contact local banks and financial services firms to present your résumé, discussing how your skills may benefit the company.
5. Sign up for a few classes on information brokering, marketing, and business planning.
6. Consult the Information Professionals Institute seminar schedule and the seminar schedules at major online conferences, such as National Online Meeting (NOM) or Online World for additional classes, and investigate continuing education seminars at local universities or community colleges.
7. Check out *The Information Brokers Handbook,* available in bookstores.

SCIENCE/TECHNOLOGY INFORMATION BROKER

CAREER PROFILE

Duties: Perform on-line searching and competitive intelligence for scientific and technical corporations

Alternate Title(s): Independent Researcher

Salary Range: $55 to $100 per hour

Employment Prospects: Excellent

Advancement Prospects: Good

Best Geographical Location(s): Because Science/Technology Information Brokers generally use computerized networks, location is relatively unimportant, but proximity to an urban area—especially a highly technical urban area, such as the greater Boston area around Route 128, or Silicon Valley in California—may provide access to more clients

Prerequisites:

Education or Training—Master's in library science plus an advanced degree in science or technology

Experience—Experience working in science or technology helpful

Special Skills and Personality Traits—Research skills; organizational skills; computer literacy and comfort with technology; ability to work well with others; ability to work well under pressure

CAREER LADDER

```
┌─────────────────────────────────────────┐
│  Director of Information Brokerage Firm  │
└─────────────────────────────────────────┘

┌─────────────────────────────────────────┐
│  Science/Technology Information Broker   │
└─────────────────────────────────────────┘

┌─────────────────────────────────────────┐
│           Information Broker             │
└─────────────────────────────────────────┘
```

Position Description

Science/Technology Information Brokers serve clients in a variety of fields, often specializing in patent searching, engineering, chemistry, or computer programming and software design. Clients include consultants, other research firms, laboratories, petrochemical and energy companies, and high-tech companies. As scientific or technology companies become more complex, they need to find people who can identify problems, figure out how to solve them, and do so in a way which is understandable to the rest of the group. Most information professionals who provide such services have a scientific background themselves, in addition to library science training, and combine their specific subject expertise with research skills.

Science and Technology Information Brokers collect resources, not answers. This ability to know where to find specific scientific information distinguishes information professionals from many others who collect facts, rather than learning where to find them again when needed. Science/Technology Information Brokers provide summaries and evaluations of scientific literature, interpreting jargon and helping their clients understand technical materials. They also search patent literature, which contains a great deal of information not published anywhere else. Reviewing the patent documents of others is useful in the patent application process, as well as in competitive intelligence.

With access to more than 2,500 international databanks and information centers worldwide, the Information Broker provides information-on-demand and consulting services for clients interested in science and technology issues. Brokers also usually provide document delivery services in addition to consulting services, and they use traditional research techniques when needed.

A Science/Technology Information Broker may provide all kinds of information in a variety of formats. For example, if a customer is injured by a collapsing walkway, and an engineering consultant hired to perform a failure analysis needs to know the relevant regulations and industry standards in order to determine whether substandard workmanship factored into the accident, an Information Broker can locate and provide this information, along with articles on similar incidents. Background research on the contracting company also could be included.

The Science/Technology Information Broker provides crucial information for their clients who can't find it on their own, charging for their expertise at locating, analyzing, and interpreting information. They also may provide the ability to index full-text documents in changing technical fields. Building and maintaining a pertinent, up-to-date index can make the difference between accessible and inaccessible information. Information Brokers are trained and uniquely suited to this work.

Salaries

A Science/Technology Information Broker may charge between $55 and $100 per hour, depending on the specific type of information being sought. Independent Brokers may earn up to $100,000 a year. However, many of the services and databases used by Information Brokers incur separate hourly fees, which must be deducted from the broker's fee.

Employment Prospects

The sheer amount of available technical information— either outside a company or inside—creates a demand for information professionals who are adept at finding the correct data and presenting it in the client's desired format. In fact, the fastest-growing segment in the information brokerage business is in the fields of science and technology, which accounted for more than $2 billion in information brokering spending in 2003.

Brokers interested in starting their own businesses may develop independence quickly, depending on how much time and money they put into the process and whether they can identify potential sales opportunities—and then follow through on such opportunities.

Advancement Prospects

Many Science/Technology Information Brokers begin by signing up with a large science and technology information brokerage, eventually moving into their own independent consulting business. Initially, Science and Technology Brokers must spend a lot of time developing their business while maintaining a full-time job elsewhere. Eventually, most Information Brokers focus on their own business full time, as their client load increases and their responsibilities multiply.

Education and Training

Many Science/Technological Information Brokers have an advanced degree in library and information science, as well as a degree in science or technology. Additional courses in information brokering may be added.

Experience, Skills, and Personality Traits

The most important attribute of the Science/Technology Information Broker is top-notch research skills. Organizational skills and computer literacy are next in importance. Because many Information Brokers run independent businesses, the ability to work well with customers is extremely important. Successful Brokers must develop the ability to serve as a tactful intermediary between an information source and a client. This requires knowing how to ask questions effectively, being able to wheedle information from a source without being threatening.

Running a business also requires skills such as financial and business management beyond those needed for the information profession. For those who love the idea of working at home, information brokering offers a way to reach out to clients and colleagues throughout the world while maintaining a home-based business.

Unions and Associations

Science and Technology Information Brokers may belong to a variety of trade associations that provide educational guidance, support, conferences, and information to members. These might include the Association for Information Professionals, the Society for Competitor Intelligence Professionals, the Public Record Retrievers Network, the American Society for Information Science and Technology, the Library and Information Technology Association, or the National Information Standards Organization.

Tips for Entry

1. Consider starting your information brokerage career by working for a large, established firm. Check out the *Burwell World Directory of Information Brokers* (www.burwellinc.com), which lists more than 1,800 information brokerage companies.
2. After you have a few years of experience, consider going into business on your own. First, develop a comprehensive business plan.
3. Set up a website to advertise your services as an Information Broker.

4. Contact local scientific or technical firms and present your résumé, discussing how your skills may benefit the company.

5. Sign up for classes on information brokering, marketing, and business planning.

6. Consult the Information Professionals Institute seminar schedule and the seminar schedules at major online conferences, such as National Online Meeting (NOM) or Online World for additional classes, and investigate continuing education seminars at local universities or community colleges.

7. Check out *The Information Brokers Handbook,* available in bookstores.

APPENDIXES

APPENDIX I
ASSOCIATIONS

American Association of Law Libraries
53 West Jackson Boulevard
Suite 940
Chicago, IL 60604
Phone: (312) 939-4764
http://www.aallnet.org
Founded in 1906, the association aims to promote and enhance the value of law libraries to the legal and public communities, to foster the profession of law librarianship, and to provide leadership in the field of legal information. Today, with more than 4,600 members, the association represents law librarians and related professionals who are affiliated with a wide range of institutions: law firms, law schools, corporate legal departments, courts, and local, state, and federal government agencies.

American Association of Museums (AAM)
1575 I Street, NW
Suite 400
Washington, DC 20005
http://www.aam-us.org
This organization is dedicated to promoting excellence within the museum community through advocacy, professional education, information exchange, accreditation, and guidance on current professional standards of performance. AAM assists museum staff, boards, and volunteers across the country to better serve the public, and is the only organization representing the entire scope of museums and professionals and nonpaid staff who work for and with museums.

American Association of School Librarians (AASL)
American Library Association
50 East Huron Street
Chicago, IL 60611
http://www.ala.org/aasl
An association that advocates excellence and develops leaders in the school library media field, AASL works to ensure that all members of the school library media field provide leadership in the total education program, participate as active partners in the teaching/learning process, connect learners with ideas and information, and prepare students for lifelong learning, informed decision-making, a love of reading, and the use of information technologies.

American Institute for Conservation of Historic and Artistic Works
1717 K Street, NW
Suite 200
Washington, DC 20006
Phone: (202) 452-9545
http://aic.stanford.edu
The institute is a national membership organization of conservation professionals dedicated to preserving art and historic artifacts for future generations. It provides a forum for the exchange of ideas on conservation, and advances the practice and promotes the importance of the preservation of cultural property by coordinating the exchange of knowledge, research, and publications.

American Library Association (ALA)
50 East Huron Street
Chicago, IL 60611
http://www.ala.org
The oldest and largest library association in the world, with more than 64,000 members. Its mission is to promote the highest quality library and information services and public access to information. ALA offers professional services and publications to members and nonmembers. ALA sponsors 11 divisions, including the American Association of School Librarians (AASL); Association of College and Research Libraries (ACRL); Association for Library Collections and Technical Services (ALCTS); Association for Library Service to Children (ALSC); Association for Library Trustees and Advocates (ALTA); Association of Specialized and Cooperative Library Agencies (ASCLA); Library Administration and Management Association (LAMA); Library and Information Technology Association (LITA); Public Library Association (PLA); Reference and User Services Association
(RUSA); and Young Adult Library Services Association (YALSA).

Asian/Pacific American Librarians Association
3735 Palomar Centre
Suite 150 PMB 26
Lexington, KY 40513
Phone: (859) 257-5679
http://www.apalaweb.org
Founded in 1980, the Asian/Pacific Librarians Association (APALA) was incorporated in Illinois in 1981 and formally affiliated with the American Library Association (ALA) in 1982. A predecessor of APALA, the Asian American Librarians Caucus (AALC), was organized in 1975 as a discussion group of the ALA Office for Library Outreach Services, reflecting the interest in library services to minority communities and professional support of librarians of minority ancestry that prevailed in the ALA in the 1960s and 1970s. APALA and AALC were organized/founded by librarians of diverse Asian/Pacific ancestries committed to working together toward a common goal: to create an organization that would address the needs of Asian/Pacific American librarians and those who serve Asian/Pacific American communities.

American Society for Information Science and Technology (ASIST)
1320 Fenwick Lane
Suite 510
Silver Spring, MD 20910
Phone: (301) 495-0900
http://www.asis.org
This society for information professionals leads the search for new and better theories, techniques, and technologies to improve access to information. ASIST counts among its membership some 4,000 information specialists from such fields as computer science, linguistics, management, librarianship, engineering, law, medicine, chemistry, and education; they are individuals who share a common interest in improving the ways society stores, retrieves, analyzes, manages, archives, and disseminates information.

American Society of Indexers (ASI)

10200 West 44th Avenue
Suite 304
Wheat Ridge, CO 80033
Phone: (303) 463-2887
http://www.asindexing.org
ASI is the only professional organization in the United States devoted solely to the advancement of indexing, abstracting, and database building. This nonprofit organization was founded in 1968 to promote excellence in indexing and increase awareness of the value of well-written indexes.

American Theological Library Association

250 South Wacker Drive
Suite 1600
Chicago, IL 60606
Phone: (888) 665-ATLA
http://www.atla.com
Established in 1946, the American Theological Library Association (ATLA) is a professional association of more than 800 individual, institutional, and affiliate members providing programs, products, and services in support of theological and religious studies libraries and librarians. ATLA's ecumenical membership represents many religious traditions and denominations.

Archivists and Librarians in the History of the Health Sciences

Louise M. Darling Biomedical Library
UCLA12-077 CHS
Box 951798
Los Angeles, CA 90095
Phone: (310) 825-6940
http://www.alhhs.org
This association was established exclusively for educational purposes, to serve the professional interests of librarians, archivists, and other specialists actively engaged in the librarianship of the history of the health sciences by promoting the exchange of information and by improving standards of service.

Art Libraries Society of North America

232-329 March Road
Box 11
Ottawa, Ontario
Canada K2K 2E1
Phone: (800) 817-0621
http://www.arlisna.org
This organization promotes the interests of nearly 1,500 members, including architecture and art librarians, visual resources

professionals, artists, curators, educators, publishers, and others interested in visual arts information.

Association for Library and Information Science Education

1009 Commerce Park Drive
Suite 150
Oak Ridge, TN 37830
Phone: (865) 425-0155
http://www.alise.org

Association for Library Collections & Technical Services (ALCTS)

American Library Association
50 East Huron Street
Chicago, IL 60611
Phone: (800) 545-2433 ext. 5038
E-mail: alcts@ala.org
http://www.ala.org/alcts
ALCTS is responsible for acquisition, identification, cataloging, classification, and preservation of library materials; the development and coordination of U.S. library resources; and those areas of selection and evaluation involved in the acquisition of library materials and pertinent to the development of library resources.

Association for Library Service to Children (ALSC)

American Library Association
50 East Huron Street
Chicago, IL 60611
Phone: (800) 545-2433 ext. 2163
E-mail: alsc@ala.org
http://www.ala.org/alsc
The ALSC is a network of more than 3,700 children's and youth librarians, children's literature experts, and publishers committed to improving and ensuring the future of the nation through exemplary library service to children, their families, and others who work with children.

Association for Library Trustees and Advocates (ALTA)

American Library Association
50 East Huron Street
Chicago, IL 60611
Phone: (800) 545-2433
http://www.ala.org/alta
ALTA promotes outstanding library service through educational programs that develop excellence in trusteeship and actions that advocate access to information for all.

Association of Records Managers and Administrators

ARMA International
13725 West 109th Street
Suite 101
Lenexa, KS 66215
Phone: (913) 341-3808 or (800) 422-2762 (U.S. and Canada)
http://www.arma.org
A not-for-profit association serving more than 10,000 information management professionals in the United States, Canada, and more than 30 other nations. ARMA International members include records and information managers, archivists, corporate librarians, imaging specialists, legal professionals, knowledge managers, consultants, and educators. The mission of ARMA International is to provide education, research, and networking opportunities to information professionals, enabling them to use their skills and experience to leverage the value of records, information, and knowledge as corporate assets and as contributors to organizational success.

Association of Academic Health Sciences Libraries (AAHSL)

2150 North 107th Street
Suite 205
Seattle, WA 98133
Phone: (206) 367-8704
http://www.aahsl.org
This association is composed of the directors of libraries of 142 accredited U.S. and Canadian medical schools belonging to the Association of American Medical Colleges. AAHSL's goals are to promote excellence in academic health science libraries and to ensure that the next generation of health practitioners is trained in information-seeking skills that enhance the quality of health care delivery, education, and research. AAHSL was founded in 1977 and is a member of the Council of Academic Societies of the Association of American Medical Colleges.

Association of Architecture School Librarians

www.library.njit.edu/archlib/aasl
A nonprofit association established to advance academic architectural librarianship, to develop and enhance the roll of architecture school librarians in the advancement of architectural education, and to promote a spirit of cooperation among members of the profession.

Association of College and Research Libraries

American Library Association
50 East Huron Street
Chicago, IL 60611
Phone: (800) 545-2433 ext. 2523
http://www.ala.org/acrl
This group enhances the effectiveness of academic and research librarians to advance learning, teaching, and research in higher education.

Association of Independent Information Professionals (AIIP)

8550 United Plaza Boulevard
Suite 1001
Baton Rouge, LA 70809
Phone: (225) 408-4400
http://www.aiip.org
An international association of owners of information businesses, the AIIP includes a description of the independent information professional as well as the Code of Ethical Business Practice.

Association of Jewish Libraries (AJL)

15 East 26th Street
Room 1034
New York, NY 10010
Phone: (212) 725-5359 (voice mail)
http://www.jewishlibraries.org
AJL is dedicated to supporting the production, collection, organization, and dissemination of Judaic resources and library and media information services in the United States, Canada, and more than 23 other countries. The association promotes Jewish literacy through enhancement of libraries and library resources and through leadership for the profession and practitioners of Judaica librarianship. It fosters access to information, learning, teaching, and research relating to Jews, Judaism, the Jewish experience, and Israel.

Association of Part-Time Librarians

www2.canisius.edu/~huberman/aptl.html
The Association of Part-Time Librarians was founded in 1988 by Marianne Eimer to communicate with other part-time colleagues and provide interesting programs for a group that is often excluded from other opportunities for professional development.

Association of Research Libraries (ARL)

21 Dupont Circle
Suite 800
Washington, DC 20036
Phone: (202) 296-2296
http://www.arl.org

A nonprofit membership organization comprising the leading research libraries in North America whose mission is to shape and influence forces affecting the future of research libraries in the process of scholarly communication. ARL programs and services promote equitable access to and effective use of recorded knowledge in support of teaching, research, scholarship, and community service. The association articulates the concerns of research libraries and their institutions, forges coalitions, influences information policy development, and supports innovation and improvements in research library operations. ARL operates as a forum for the exchange of ideas and as an agent for collective action. Proceedings of the biannual ARL meetings are available on-line.

Association of Specialized and Cooperative Library Agencies (ASCLA)

American Library Association
50 East Huron Street
Chicago, IL 60611
Phone: (800) 545-2433 ext. 4398
http://www.ala.org/ascla
An association that focuses on evolving issues that cut across library boundaries. Emphasizing the future, ASCLA supports individuals in their personal development and career growth. ASCLA enhances the development and effectiveness of library service through its diverse professional and service constituencies, including state library agencies, specialized library agencies, multitype library organizations, and independent librarians.

Association of Vision Science Librarians

6 North Michigan Avenue
Suite 300
Chicago, IL 60602
http://spectacle.berkeley.edu/~library/ AVSL.HTM
This association is an international organization composed of professional librarians whose collections and services include the literature of vision. Among current members are individuals who work in libraries that serve educational institutions, eye clinics and hospitals, and private companies with an interest in eye- or vision-related products and services. The association is a special interest group of both the Association of Schools and Colleges of Optometry and the Medical Library Association.

Beta Phi Mu: The International Library and Information Studies Honor Society

School of Information Studies
101 Louis Shores Building
Florida State University
Tallahassee, FL 32306
Phone: (850) 644-3907
http://www.beta-phi-mu.org
The organization was founded in 1948 by a group of librarians and library educators as a way to recognize and encourage scholastic achievement among library and information studies students. Eligibility for membership in Beta Phi Mu is by invitation of the faculty from an American Library Association–accredited professional degree program.

Bibliographical Society of America

P.O. Box 1537
Lenox Hill Station
New York, NY 10021
Phone: (212) 452-2710
http://www.bibsocamer.org
The only scholarly society in the United States whose primary focus is the study of books and manuscripts as physical objects. It was organized in 1904 to promote bibliographical research and issue bibliographical publications. The group offers meetings, lectures, and fellowship programs, as well as publishing books and the *Papers of the Bibliographical Society of America (PBSA),* North America's leading bibliographical journal. The society is open to all those interested in bibliographical problems and projects, and its membership includes bibliographers, librarians, professors, students, and collectors worldwide. Libraries are welcome as institutional members.

Canadian Association for Information Science (CAIS)

School of Library and Information Studies
Faculty of Management
Dalhousie University
6225 University Avenue
Halifax, Nova Scotia
Canada B3H 3J5
Phone: (902) 494-2473
http://www.cais-acsi.ca
CAIS was incorporated in 1970 to promote information science in Canada and encourage the exchange of information about the use, access, retrieval, organization, management, and dissemination of information. CAIS achieves these goals through its journal, the *Canadian Journal*

of Information and Library Science, and its annual conference. CAIS members include information scientists and archivists, librarians, computer scientists, documentalists, economists, educators, journalists, psychologists, and others who support its objectives.

Catholic Library Association
100 North Street
Suite 224
Pittsfield, MA 01201-5109
Phone: (413) 443-2252
http://www.cathla.org
Established in 1921, the CLA is an international membership organization, providing its members with professional development through educational and networking experiences, publications, scholarships, and other services. The association coordinates the exchange of ideas, provides a source of inspirational support and guidance in ethical issues related to librarianship, and offers fellowship for those who seek, serve, preserve, and share the word in all its forms.

Chief Officers of State Library
Agencies
167 West Main Street
Suite 600
Lexington, KY 40507
Phone: (859) 514-9151
http://www.cosla.org
An independent organization of the chief officers of state and territorial agencies designated as the state library administrative agency and responsible for statewide library development. Its purpose is to identify and address issues of common concern and national interest, to further state library agency relationships with federal government and national organizations, and to initiate cooperative action for the improvement of library services to the people of the United States. Its membership consists solely of these top library officers of the states and territories, variously designated as state librarian, director, commissioner, or executive secretary. It provides a continuing mechanism for dealing with the problems and challenges faced by the heads of the state agencies that are responsible for statewide library development.

Chinese American Librarians
Association (CALA)
http://www.cala-web.org
CALA started in 1973 as Mid-West Chinese American Librarians Association, a

regional organization in Illinois. A year later, in 1974, the Chinese Librarians Association was formed in California. In 1976, Mid-West Chinese American Librarians Association was expanded to a national organization as Chinese American Librarians Association. Chinese American Librarians Association and Chinese Librarians Association merged in 1983. With the establishment of the Florida chapter in 1998, CALA now has six chapters and members throughout the United States, as well as in Canada, China, Hong Kong, Singapore, and Taiwan.

Church and Synagogue Library
Association (CSLA)
P.O. Box 19357
Portland, OR 97280-0357
Phone: (503) 244-6919 or (800) 542-2752 (LIB-CSLA)
http://www.worldaccessnet.com/~csla
CSLA serves religious librarians through publications, a network of religious libraries, and training sessions offered at regional and national workshops. The association also provides counseling and guidance for individual libraries through its Library Services Committee, composed of experienced congregational librarians.

It establishes chapters to provide ongoing service and fellowship in local areas and sponsors an annual three-day conference providing the opportunity for continuing education in library practice and sharing experience in the field. The association publishes a bimonthly publication, *Church & Synagogue LIBRARIES,* and a series of guides on many aspects of library science targeted at the religious library.

Council of Planning Librarians
(CPL)
101 North Wacker Drive
Suite CM-190
Chicago, IL 60606
Phone: (312) 409-3349
http://www.west.asu.edu/mmyers/cpl
An international professional organization of librarians, information specialists, planners, researches, and educators in the field of planning librarianship.

Council on Library and Information
Resources (CLIR)
1755 Massachusetts Avenue, NW
Suite 500
Washington, DC 20036-2124
Phone: (202) 939-4750
http://www.clir.org

CLIR is an independent nonprofit organization that works to maintain and improve access to information for generations to come through projects, programs, and publications. CLIR works to expand access to information, however recorded and preserved, as a public good. In partnership with other organizations, CLIR helps create services that expand the concept of "library" and supports the providers and preservers of information. CLIR is supported by fees from sponsoring institutions, grants from public and private foundations, contracts with federal agencies, and donations from individuals.

EDUCAUSE
1150 18th Street, NW
Suite 1010
Washington, DC 20036
Phone: (202) 872-4200
http://www.educause.edu
This organization is dedicated to advancing higher education by promoting the intelligent use of information technology. Membership is open to institutions of higher education, corporations serving the higher education information technology market, and other related associations and organizations. Educause programs include professional development activities, print and electronic publications, strategic policy initiatives, research, awards for leadership and exemplary practices, and a wealth of on-line information services. The current membership comprises more than 1,800 colleges, universities, and education organizations, including more than 180 corporations. Educause has offices in Boulder, Colorado, and Washington, D.C.

Independent Curators International
(ICI)
799 Broadway
Suite 205
New York, NY 10003
Phone: (212) 254-8200
http://www.ici-exhibitions.org
ICI's mission is to improve the understanding and appreciation of contemporary art through traveling exhibitions and other activities that will reach a diverse national and international audience. Collaborating with a wide range of eminent curators, ICI develops its program of innovative traveling exhibitions and substantial catalogs to introduce and document sometimes challenging new work in all media by younger as well as more established artists from the United States

and abroad. Since its founding in 1975, ICI has created almost 90 exhibitions that collectively have included the work of more than 2,000 artists. ICI exhibitions have been presented by more than 400 museums, university art galleries, art centers, and alternative spaces in the United States and abroad. Each year, ICI exhibitions are on view in 30 to 40 cities throughout the United States, Canada, Mexico, and Europe.

Institute of Museum and Library Services (IMLS)

Office of Library Services
1100 Pennsylvania Avenue, NW
Room 802
Washington, DC 20506
Phone: (202) 606-8536
http://www.imls.gov
An independent grant-making federal agency that fosters leadership, innovation and lifetime learning by supporting all types of museums, libraries, and archives, from public and academic to research and school. IMLS expands the educational benefit of these institutions by encouraging partnerships. Created by the Museum and Library Services Act of 1996, IMLS administers the Library Services and Technology Act and the Museum Services Act. The institute receives policy advice from the National Commission for Libraries and Information Science and the National Museum Services Board.

International Federation of Library Associations and Institutions (IFLA)

P.O. Box 95312
2509 CH The Hague
Netherlands
Phone: +31 70 3140884
http://www.ifla.org
IFLA is the leading international body representing the interests of library and information services and their users, the global voice of the library and information profession. Founded in Edinburgh, Scotland, in 1927 at an international conference, IFLA now boasts members in 150 countries. Its headquarters is located at the Royal Library, the national library of the Netherlands, in The Hague.

Library Administration and Management Association (LAMA)

American Library Association
50 East Huron Street
Chicago, IL 60611
Phone: (800) 545-2433 ext.5036
E-mail: lama@ala.org
http://www.ala.org/lama
LAMA provides an organizational framework for encouraging the study of administrative theory, for improving the practice of administration in libraries, and for identifying and fostering administrative skill. The division is responsible for all elements of general administration that are common to more than one type of library.

Library and Information Technology Association (LITA)

American Library Association
50 East Huron Street
Chicago, IL 60611
Phone: (800) 545-2433 ext.4270
E-mail: lama@ala.org
http://www.ala.org/lita
LITA is concerned with planning, development, design, application, and integration of technology within the library and information environment, with the impact of emerging technologies on library service, and with the effect of automated technologies on people. Its major focus is on interdisciplinary issues and emerging technologies. Within these areas, the association fosters research, promotes the development of appropriate technical standards, monitors new technologies having potential application in library and information science, develops models for library systems and networks, and disseminates information.

Library Technicians and Assistants Interest Group

c/o British Columbia Library Association
900 Howe Street
Suite 150
Vancouver, British Columbia
Canada V6Z 2M4
Phone: (604) 683-5354
http://www.bcla.bc.ca/ltaig
This group is an inclusive, province-wide organization that supports and promotes the role of library technicians and assistants through education, communication, and advocacy.

Lutheran Church Library Association (LCLA)

275 South Third Street
Suite 101-A
Stillwater, MN 55082
Phone: (651) 430-0770
http://www.lclahq.org
LCLA is a nonprofit national organization that provides direction, support, and resources to church librarians. LCLA was founded in 1958. Today all Christian denominations are welcomed into membership as the LCLA carries on a tradition of building successful church libraries. Membership in the LCLA is open to individuals or churches who need help with church library development. LCLA membership provides free resources and information, including the LCLA quarterly publication, book lists, guidelines, creative ideas, and how-to information on developing, maintaining, and promoting a library.

Medical Library Association (MLA)

65 East Wacker Place
Suite 1900
Chicago, IL 60601
Phone: (312) 419-9094
http://www.mlanet.org
Founded in 1898, MLA is a nonprofit, educational organization of more than 1,100 institutional and 3,600 individual members in the health sciences information field, committed to educating health information professionals, supporting health information research, promoting access to the world's health sciences information, and working to ensure that the best health information is available to all.

Music Library Association

8551 Research Way
Suite 180
Middleton, WI 53562
Phone: (608) 836-5825
http://www.musiclibraryassoc.org
As a professional organization in the United States devoted to music librarianship and to all aspects of music materials in libraries, MLA provides a forum for study and action on issues that affect music libraries and their users. Founded in 1931, MLA (and its members) make significant contributions to librarianship, publishing standards, scholarship, and the development of new information technologies. In the forefront of contemporary librarianship, MLA assures that users of music materials will be well served by their libraries.

National Association of Government Archives and Records Administrators (NAGARA)

48 Howard Street
Albany, NY 12207
Phone: (518) 463-8644
http://www.nagara.org
NAGARA champions good management of government archives and records

programs for the benefit of government and its citizens. The association provides a forum for government archives and records professionals, develops professional standards for government archives and records administration, fosters greater awareness of the value of government archives and records programs, and represents the government archives and records community on important issues.

National Association to Promote Library and Information Services to Latinos and the Spanish-Speaking

P.O. Box 25963
Scottsdale, AZ 85255
Phone: (480) 471-7452
http://www.reforma.org
REFORMA is committed to improving library and information services for the 56.2 million Spanish-speaking and Latino people in the United States. Established in 1971 as an affiliate of the American Library Association, REFORMA seeks to promote the development of library collections to include Spanish-language and Latino-oriented materials; the recruitment of more bilingual and bicultural library professionals and support staff; the development of library services and programs that meet the needs of the Latino community; the establishment of a national information and support network; the education of the U.S. Latino population in regards to the availability and types of library services; and lobbying efforts to preserve existing library resource centers serving the interests of Latinos.

National Commission on Libraries and Information Science (NCLIS)

1110 Vermont Avenue, NW
Suite 820
Washington, DC 20005
Phone: (202) 606-9200
http://www.nclis.gov
NCLIS is a permanent independent agency of the federal government charged with advising the executive and legislative branches and other public and private organizations on national library and information policies and plans. It was established in 1970 with the enactment of Public Law 91-345. The Museum and Library Services Act of 1996 established that the commission shall have the responsibility to advise the director of the Institute of Museum and Library Services (IMLS) on general policies with respect to

the duties, powers and authority of the IMLS relating to library services.

National Federation of Abstracting and Information Services (NFAIS)

1518 Walnut Street
Suite 1004
Philadelphia, PA 19102
Phone: (215) 893-1564
http://www.nfais.org
NFAIS serves those groups that aggregate, organize, and facilitate access to information. To improve member capabilities and contribute to their ongoing success, NFAIS provides opportunities for education and advocacy and offers a forum to address common interests. NFAIS seeks to be recognized globally as the premier membership organization for groups that aggregate, organize, and facilitate access to information.

National Information Standards Organization (NISO)

4733 Bethesda Avenue
Suite 300
Bethesda, MD 20814
Phone: (301) 654-2512
http://www.niso.org
NISO is a nonprofit association accredited by the American National Standards Institute (ANSI) that identifies, develops, maintains, and publishes technical standards to manage information. NISO standards apply both traditional and new technologies to the full range of information- related needs, including retrieval, repurposing, storage, metadata, and preservation. Founded in 1939, incorporated as a not-for-profit education association in 1983, and assuming its current name the following year, NISO draws its support from the communities it serves. The leaders of more than 70 organizations in the fields of publishing, libraries, information technology, and media serve as its voting members. Hundreds of experts and practitioners serve on NISO committees and as officers of the association.

Public Library Association (PLA)

American Library Association
50 East Huron Street
Chicago, IL 60611
Phone: (800) 545-2433 ext. 5752
E-mail: pla@ala.org
http://www.ala.org/pla
With more than 9,500 members, this is one of the fastest growing divisions of the American Library Association, the oldest

and largest library association in the world. PLA enhances the development and effectiveness of public library staff and services and provides a diverse program of publication, advocacy, continuing education, and programming. PLA's priority concerns are funding for public libraries, better public library management, recognition of the importance of all library staffers, recruitment, education, training, and compensation of public librarians, intellectual freedom, improved access to library resources, and effective communication with the nonlibrary world.

Reference and User Services Association (RUSA)

American Library Association
50 East Huron Street
Chicago, IL 60611
Phone: (800) 545-2433 ext. 4398
E-mail: rusa@ala.org
http://www.ala.org/rusa
RUSA is the foremost organization of reference and information professionals who make the connections between people and the information sources and services they need. The association is responsible for stimulating and supporting in every type of library the delivery of reference/information services to all groups, regardless of age, and of general library services and materials to adults. This involves facilitating the development and conduct of direct service to library users, the development of programs and guidelines for service to meet the needs of these users, and assisting libraries in reaching potential users.

Research Libraries Group (RLG)

330 Madison Avenue
6th Floor
New York, NY 10017
Phone: (800) 537-7546
http://www.rlg.org
A nonprofit corporation of more than 160 universities, national libraries, archives, historical societies, and other institutions. Rooted in collaborative work that addresses members' shared goals for these collections, RLG develops and operates information resources used by members and nonmembers around the world. Founded in 1974 by Columbia, Harvard, and Yale Universities and the New York Public Library, RLG was conceived to help achieve the economies and power of service that come from pooling resources, expertise, and operations. The organization became a pioneer in devel-

oping cooperative solutions to the problems that research collections and their users face in the acquisition, delivery, and preservation of information. Today RLG is an international member alliance, including universities and colleges, national libraries, archives, historical societies, museums and independent research collections, and public libraries. To develop, coordinate, and operate their joint initiatives, RLG provides a highly skilled staff, sophisticated technical resources, and a long, successful track record in managing and supporting interactions among its members.

Society of American Archivists

527 South Wells Street
5th Floor
Chicago, IL 60607-3922
Phone: (312) 922-0140
http://www.archivists.org
Founded in 1936, the Society of American Archivists (SAA) is North America's oldest and largest national archival professional association. SAA's mission is to serve the educational and informational needs of more than 3,400 individual and institutional members and to provide leadership to ensure the identification, preservation, and use of records of historical value.

Special Libraries Association (SLA)

331 South Patrick Street
Alexandria, VA 22314
Phone: (703) 647-4900
http://www.sla.org
Headquartered in Washington, D.C., the SLA is the international association representing the interests of thousands of information professionals in more than 70 countries. Special librarians are information resource experts who collect, analyze, evaluate, package, and disseminate information to facilitate accurate decision-making in corporate, academic, and government settings. The Association offers a variety of programs and services designed to help its members serve their customers more effectively and succeed in an increasingly challenging environment of information management and technology. SLA is committed to the professional growth and success of its membership.

Special Libraries Association Legal Division

211 North Broadway
Suite 3300
St. Louis, MO 63102
Phone: (703) 647-4900
http://www.slalegal.org
Founded June 11, 1993, the Special Libraries Association Legal Division serves as a forum for the exchange of information, ideas, and knowledge among law and regulatory affairs librarians. It addresses concerns unique to librarians practicing in law firms, businesses, and government libraries.

Theatre Library Association

Shubert Archive
149 West 45th Street
New York, NY 10036
http://tla.library.unt.edu
This nonprofit educational organization was established in 1937 to promote the collection, preservation, and use of theatrical and performing arts materials. Membership includes librarians, scholars, curators, archivists, performers, writers, designers, historians, collectors, and students.

Urban Libraries Council

1603 Orrington Avenue
Suite 1080
Evanston, IL 60201
Phone: (847) 866-9999
http://www.urbanlibraries.org
Founded in 1971, the Urban Libraries Council is an association of public libraries in metropolitan areas and the corporations that serve them. Believing that thriving public libraries are a result of collaborative leadership, the trustees, library directors, and corporate officers of member institutions work together to address shared issues, grasp new opportunities, and conduct research that improves professional practice.

Young Adult Library Services Association (YALSA)

American Library Association
50 East Huron Street
Chicago, IL 60611
Phone: (800) 545-2433
E-mail: yalsa@ala.org
http://www.ala.org/yalsa
With more than 3,500 members, this association is a division of the American Library Association. Founded in 1957, YALSA strengthens service to young adults ages 12 through 18 as part of the continuum of total library services, and supports those who provide library service to this population. Based in Chicago, YALSA provides a diverse program of continuing education, publications, and youth advocacy for its members.

APPENDIX II
ACCREDITED LIBRARY AND INFORMATION SCIENCE DEGREE PROGRAMS

A. THE UNITED STATES AND PUERTO RICO

ALABAMA

University of Alabama
School of Library and Information Studies
Box 870252
Tuscaloosa, AL 35487
Phone: (205) 348-4610
http://www.slis.ua.edu
Degrees accredited by the American
Library Association (with date of next
review):
Master of Library and Information
Studies (2009)
Educational Specialist in Library and
Information Studies
Master of Fine Arts—Book Arts
Ph.D.—Library and Information
Studies

ARIZONA

University of Arizona
School of Information Resources and
Library Science
1515 East First Street
Tucson, AZ 85719
Phone: (520) 621-3565
http://www.sir.arizona.edu
Degrees accredited by the American
Library Association (with date of next
review):
Master of Arts (2005)
Other degrees or certificates:
Ph.D.
Distance education opportunities:
Internet

CALIFORNIA

San Jose State University
School of Library and Information Science
One Washington Square
San Jose, CA 95192
Phone: (408) 924-2490
http://slisweb.sjsu.edu
Degrees accredited by the American
Library Association (with date of next
review):

Master of Library and Information
Science (2007)

University of California, Los Angeles
Department of Information Studies
Graduate School of Education and
Information Studies
2320 Moore Hall
Mailbox 951520
Los Angeles, CA 90095
Phone: (310) 825-8799
http://is.gseis.ucla.edu
Degrees accredited by the American
Library Association (with date of next
review):
Master of Library and Information
Science (2004)
Other degrees or certificates:
M.L.I.S./M.A.—History
M.L.I.S./M.A.—Latin American
Studies
M.L.I.S./M.B.A.
Ph.D.
Post-M.L.I.S.

CONNECTICUT

Southern Connecticut State University
School of Communication, Information,
and Library Science
Department of Information and Library
Science
501 Crescent Street
New Haven, CT 06515
Phone: (888) 500-7278 ext. 4;
(203) 392-5781
http://www.southernct.edu/departments/ils
Degrees accredited by the American
Library Association (with date of next
review):
Master of Library Science (2003)
Other degrees or certificates:
M.L.S./J.D.
M.L.S./M.S.—Chemistry
M.L.S./M.S.—English
M.L.S./M.S.—Foreign Languages
M.L.S./M.S.—History

M.L.S./M.S.—Instructional Technology
M.S. Instructional Technology/M.S.—
Chemistry
M.S. Instructional Technology/M.S.—
History
School Media Specialist certification
Sixth-Year Diploma in Library
Information Studies: Art of the
Oral Tradition
School Media Specialist Certification

DISTRICT OF COLUMBIA

Catholic University of America
School of Library and Information
Science
620 Michigan Avenue, NE
2nd Floor, Marist Hall
Washington, DC 20064
Phone: (202) 319-5085
http://slis.cua.edu
Degrees accredited by the American
Library Association (with date of next
review):
Master of Science in Library Science
(2005)
Other degrees or certificates:
M.S.L.S./J.D.
M.S.L.S./M.A.—English
M.S.L.S./M.A.—Greek and Latin
M.S.L.S./M.A.—History
M.S.L.S./M.A.—Musicology
M.S.L.S./M.A.—Religious Studies
M.S.L.S./M.S.—Biology
Post-Master's Certificate

FLORIDA

Florida State University
School of Information Studies
101 Louis Shores Building
Tallahassee, FL 32306
Phone: (850) 644-5775
http://www.lis.fsu.edu
Degrees accredited by the American
Library Association (with date of next
review):

Master of Science (2005)
Master of Arts (2005)
Other degrees or certificates:
B.S.—Information Studies
School Media Certification
M.S./J.D.
Specialist
Certificate in Museum Studies and
Information Studies

University of South Florida
School of Library and Information
Science
4202 East Fowler Avenue, CIS 1040
Tampa, FL 33620
Phone: (813) 974-3520
Fax: (813) 974-6840
http://www.cas.usf.edu/lis
Degrees accredited by the American
Library Association (with date of next
review):
Master of Arts (2009)
Other degrees or certificates:
Educational Media Certification
Distance education opportunities:
Fort Lauderdale, Gainesville,
Lakeland, Miami, Orlando, Palm
Beach, Sarasota (Internet)

GEORGIA

Clark Atlanta University
School of Library and Information
Studies
300 Trevor Arnett Hall
223 James P. Brawley Drive
Atlanta, GA 30314
Phone: (404) 880-8697
http://www.cau.edu
Degrees accredited by the American
Library Association (with date of next
review):
Master of Science in Library Service
(2005)
Other degrees or certificates:
Specialist in Library Service
State of Georgia Certification for
School Media Center Services

HAWAII

University of Hawaii
Library and Information Science Program
2550 The Mall
Honolulu, HI 96822
Phone: (808) 956-7321
http://www.hawaii.edu/slis
Degrees accredited by the American
Library Association (with date of next
review):
Master of Library and Information
Science (2006)

Other degrees or certificates:
Ph.D.—Interdisciplinary Program in
Communications and Information
Sciences
Certificate in Advanced Library and
Information Science
Distance education opportunities:
Hawaii Interactive Television System
(HITS) limited to the islands of
Hawaii, Kauai, Lanai, Maui,
Molokai, and Oahu

ILLINOIS

Dominican University
Graduate School of Library and
Information Science
7900 West Division Street
River Forest, IL 60305
Phone: (708) 524-6845
http://www.dom.edu/gslis
Degrees accredited by the American
Library Association (with date of next
review):
Master of Library and Information
Science (2004)
Other degrees or certificates:
M.S.K.M.—Master of Science in
Knowledge Management
M.L.I.S./M.A.—Public History
M.L.I.S./M.B.A.
M.L.I.S./Master of Divinity
M.L.I.S./Master of Music—Music
History
Certificate of Special Studies
Illinois Standard Special Certificate in
Media Specialist (K–12)
B.A./M.L.I.S.
Distance education opportunities:
Chicago, Lake County, Pekin, Vernon
Hills, Illinois; St. Paul, Minnesota

University of Illinois at Urbana-Champaign
Graduate School of Library and
Information Science
Library and Information Science Building
501 East Daniel Street, MC-493
Champaign, IL 61820
Phone: (217) 333-3280; (800) 982-0914
http://www.lis.uiuc.edu
Degrees accredited by the American
Library Association (with date of next
review):
Master of Science (2004)
Other degrees or certificates:
Ph.D.
Certificate of Advanced Study
Undergraduate Minor in Information
Technology Studies

Illinois Media Specialist Certification
(K–12)
Distance education opportunities:
Internet

INDIANA

Indiana University
School of Library and Information Science
Main Library LI-011
1320 East 10th Street
Bloomington, IN 47405
Phone: (812) 855-2018
http://www.slis.indiana.edu
Degrees accredited by the American
Library Association (with date of next
review):
Master of Information Science (2005)
Master of Library Science (2005)
Other degrees or certificates:
Ph.D.—Information Science
Sp.L.I.S.—Specialist in Library and
Information Science (post-master's)
M.I.S./M.A.—Folklore and
Ethnomusicology
M.I.S./M.A.—Russian and East
European Studies
M.I.S./M.A.—Folklore and
Ethnomusicology
M.I.S./M.P.A.-S.P.E.A. (Public Affairs)
M.L.S./J.D.
M.L.S./M.A.—African American and
African Diaspora
M.L.S./M.A.—Art History
M.L.S./M.A.—Comparative Literature
M.L.S./M.A.—English
M.L.S./M.A.—Folklore and
Ethnomusicology
M.L.S./M.A.—History
M.L.S./M.A.—History and
Philosophy of Science
M.L.S./M.A.—Journalism
M.L.S./M.A.—Latin American and
Caribbean Studies
M.L.S./M.A.—Musicology or Music
Theory
M.L.S./M.A.—Russian and East
European Studies
M.L.S./M.P.A.-S.P.E.A. (Public
Affairs)
Public Library Certification
School Library Media and Information
Technology Certification

IOWA

University of Iowa
School of Library and Information Science
3087 Main Library
Iowa City, IA 52242

Phone: (319) 335-5707
http://www.uiowa.edu/~libsci
Degrees accredited by the American
    Library Association (with date of next
    review):
    Master of Arts (2009)
Other degrees or certificates:
    M.A./J.D.
    M.A./M.B.A.
Distance education opportunities:
    Various sites within Iowa

KANSAS

Emporia State University
School of Library and Information
    Management
1200 Commercial Street
P.O. Box 4025
Emporia, KS 66801
Phone: (620) 341-5465
http://slim.emporia.edu
Degrees accredited by the American
    Library Association (with date of next
    review):
    Master of Library Science (2005)
Other degrees or certificates:
    Ph.D.—Library and Information
        Management
    M.L.S./History, English, Music, and
        Business
    School Library Media Specialist
    Information Management Certification
    B.S. Information Resource Studies
        (interdisciplinary)
Distance education opportunities:
    Denver, Colorado; Overland Park,
        Kansas; Portland, Oregon; Salt
        Lake City, Utah; Boise, Idaho;
        Fargo, North Dakota; interactive
        video, Internet

KENTUCKY

University of Kentucky
College of Communications and
    Information Studies
School of Library and Information Science
105 Grehan Building
Lexington, KY 40506
Phone: (859) 257-4839
http://www.uky.edu/CommInfoStudies
Degrees accredited by the American
    Library Association (with date of next
    review):
    Master of Arts (2004)
    Master of Science in Library Science
        (2004)
Other Degrees or Certificates:
    Ph.D. (L.I.S.—tract in
        Communication)

Distance Education Opportunities:
    Covington, Elizabethtown, Highland
        Heights, Louisville, Kentucky;
        Cincinnati, Ohio; interactive video,
        Internet

LOUISIANA

Louisiana State University
School of Library and Information Science
267 Coates Hall
Baton Rouge, LA 70803
Phone: (225) 578-3158
http://slis.lsu.edu
Degrees accredited by the American
    Library Association (with date of next
    review):
    Master of Library and Information
        Science (2005)
Other degrees or certificates:
    M.L.I.S./M.A.—History
    M.L.I.S./M.S.—Systems Science
    Certificate of Advanced Study in
        Library and Information Science
    Certification in School Librarianship
        for the State of Louisiana
Distance education opportunities:
    Alexandria, Eunice, Lafayette, Lake
        Charles, Monroe, New Orleans,
        Shreveport, Thibodeaux, Louisiana;
        two-way interactive video, Internet
        (selected courses)

MARYLAND

University of Maryland
College of Information Studies
4105 Hornbake Library Building
College Park, MD 20742
Phone: (301) 405-2038
http://clis.umd.edu
Degrees accredited by the American
    Library Association (with date of next
    review):
    Master of Library Science (2006)
Other degrees or certificates:
    Ph.D.—Library and Information
        Science
    M.L.S./Ge.L.S.—Geography
    M.L.S./Hi.L.S.—History

MASSACHUSETTS

Simmons College
Graduate School of Library and
    Information Science
300 The Fenway
Boston, MA 02115
Phone: (617) 521-2800;
http://www.simmons.edu/gslis

Degrees accredited by the American
    Library Association (with date of next
    review):
    Master of Science (2003)
Other degrees or certificates:
    D.A.
    Master of Competitive Intelligence
    M.S./M.A.—History
    M.S./M.S.—Education
Distance education opportunities:
    Master of Science at Mount Holyoke
        College, South Hadley,
        Massachusetts

MICHIGAN

University of Michigan
School of Information
304 West Hall Building
550 East University Avenue
Ann Arbor, MI 48109
Phone: (734) 763-2285
http://www.si.umich.edu
Degrees accredited by the American
    Library Association (with date of next
    review):
    Master of Science in Information (2003)
Other degrees or certificates:
    M.S.I./M.S.N. (Nursing)
    M.S.I./M.B.A. (Business
        Administration)
    M.S.I./J.D. (Law)
    M.S.I./M.P.P. (Public Policy)
    M.S.I./M.S.W. (Social Work)
    Ph.D. (Information)

Wayne State University
Library and Information Science Program
106 Kresge Library
Detroit, MI 48202
Phone: (877) 263-2665
http://www.lisp.wayne.edu
Degrees accredited by the American
    Library Association (with date of next
    review):
    Master of Library and Information
        Science (2009)
Other degrees or certificates:
    Specialist certificate
    Archival Administration certificate
Distance education opportunities:
    Farmington, Flint, Grand Rapids,
        Kalamazoo, Lansing, Saginaw,
        Michigan

MISSISSIPPI

University of Southern Mississippi
School of Library and Information Science
118 College Drive
Box 5146
Hattiesburg, MS 39406

Phone: (601) 266-4228
http://www.usm.edu/~slis
Degrees accredited by the American
    Library Association (with date of next
    review):
    Master of Library and Information
        Science (2005)
Other degrees or certificates:
    Specialist in Library and Information
        Science
    M.L.I.S./M.A.—Anthropology
    M.L.I.S./M.A.—History
    M.L.I.S. with School Library Media
        Licensure
    B.A. with major in Library and
        Information Science
    B.A. in L.I.S. with School Library
        Media Licensure
Distance education opportunities:
    online and interactive video

MISSOURI

University of Missouri–Columbia
School of Information Science and
    Learning Technologies
303 Townsend Hall
Columbia, MO 65211
Phone: (573) 884-1391; (877) 747-5868
http://sislt.missouri.edu
Degrees accredited by the American
    Library Association (with date of next
    review):
    Master of Arts (2005)
Distance education opportunities:
    Kansas City, Springfield, St. Louis,
        Missouri; Wyoming, Nebraska;
        Internet

NEW JERSEY

Rutgers University
School of Communication, Information
    and Library Studies
4 Huntington Street
New Brunswick, NJ 08901-1071
Phone: (732) 932-7917; (732) 932-7916
http://www.scils.rutgers.edu
Degrees accredited by the American
    Library Association (with date of next
    review):
    Master of Library and Information
        Science (2004)
Other degrees or certificates:
    Ph.D.—Communication, Information
        and Library Studies, Sixth-Year
        Specialist Program

NEW YORK

Long Island University
Palmer School of Library and
    Information Science
C. W. Post Campus

720 Northern Boulevard
Brookville, NY 11548-1300
Phone: (516) 299-2866
http://palmer.cwpost.liu.edu
Degrees accredited by the American
    Library Association (with date of next
    review):
    Master of Science in Library and
        Information Science (2005)
Other degrees or certificates:
    Ph.D.—Information Studies
    B.S.—Information Management and
        Technology
    Certificate in Archives and Records
        Management
Distance education opportunities:
    Brentwood; Manhattan; Suffolk
        County; and Purchase (Westchester
        County), New York

Pratt Institute
Pratt Manhattan Center
School of Information and Library Science
144 West 14th Street
6th Floor
New York, NY 10011
Phone: (212) 647-7682
http://www.pratt.edu/sils
Degrees accredited by the American
    Library Association (with date of next
    review):
    Master of Science in Library and
        Information Science (2008)
Other degrees or certificates:
    M.S./J.D.
    M.S.L.I.S./M.S.—Art History
    Advanced Certificate

Queens College
City University of New York
Graduate School of Library and
    Information Studies
65-30 Kissena Boulevard
Flushing, NY 11367
Phone: (718) 997-3790
http://www.qc.edu/gslis
Degrees accredited by the American
    Library Association (with date of next
    review):
    Master of Library Science (2004)
Other degrees or certificates:
    Post-Master's Certificate Program

St. John's University
Division of Library and Information
    Science
8000 Utopia Parkway
Jamaica, NY 11439
Phone: (718) 990-6200
http://new.stjohns.edu

Degrees accredited by the American
    Library Association (with date of next
    review):
    Master Library Science (2004)
Other degrees or certificates:
    M.L.S./M.A.—Government and
        Politics
    M.L.S./M.S.—Pharmaceutical Sciences
    Advanced Certificate in Library and
        information Studies

State University of New York–Albany
School of Information Science and Policy
135 Western Avenue
Draper Hall, Room 113
Albany, NY 12222
Phone: (518) 442-5110
http://www.albany.edu/sisp
Degrees accredited by the American
    Library Association (with date of next
    review):
    Master of Library Science (2003)
    Master of Science in Information
        Science (2003)
Other degrees or certificates:
    Ph.D.—Information Science
        (interdisciplinary program)
    M.L.S./M.A.—English
    M.L.S./M.A.—History
    Certificate of Advanced Study
Distance education opportunities:
    Selected courses held in
        Poughkeepsie, New York

State University of New York–Buffalo
Department of Library and Information
    Studies
School of Informatics
528 Baldy Hall
Buffalo, NY 14260-1020
Phone: (716) 645-6481
http://www.informatics.buffalo.edu/lis
Degrees accredited by the American
    Library Association (with date of next
    review):
    Master of Library Science (2006)
Other degrees or certificates:
    M.A.—Master of Arts in Informatics
    M.L.S./J.D.—Legal Information
        Management and Analysis
    M.L.S./M.A.—Music History/Music
        Librarianship
    Ph.D.—Communication with Cognate
        in Library and Information Studies
    Post Master's Certificate
Distance education opportunities:
    Satellite: Rochester, New York
        (selected courses), Internet (selected
        courses), Two-way interactive video
        to Fredonia and Rochester, New
        York (selected courses)

Syracuse University
School of Information Studies
4-206 Center for Science and Technology
Syracuse, NY 13244
Phone: (315) 443-2911
http://istweb.syr.edu
Degrees accredited by the American
    Library Association (with date of next
    review):
    Master of Library Science (2008)
Other degrees or certificates:
    Ph.D.—Information Transfer
    M.S.—Information Management
    M.S.—Telecommunications and
        Network Management
    B.S.—Information Management and
        Technology
    Certificate in Information Systems and
        Telecommunications Management
    Certification in Strategic Information
        Resources Management in the
        Federal Government
Distance education opportunities:
    Washington, DC (M.S.—Information
        Management)
    Internet-based coursework combined
        with limited on-campus residencies
        for the master's programs.

NORTH CAROLINA

North Carolina Central University
School of Library and Information
    Sciences
1801 Fayetteville Street
P.O. Box 19586
Durham, NC 27707
Phone: (919) 530-6485
Phone: (919) 560-5211
http://www.nccuslis.org
Degrees accredited by the American
    Library Association (with date of next
    review):
    Master of Library Science (2009)
Other degrees or certificates:
    M.L.S./J.D.
    M.I.S.
    M.B.A./M.I.S.
    Media Coordinator Certificate
Distance education opportunities:
    Fayetteville, Greenville, Hickory,
        Pembroke, Wilmington, North
        Carolina

**University of North Carolina–Chapel
    Hill**
School of Information and Library Science
CB #3360
100 Manning Hall
Chapel Hill, NC 27599
Phone: (919) 962-8366
http://www.ils.unc.edu

Degrees accredited by the American
    Library Association (with date of next
    review):
    Master of Science in Library Science
        (2006)
    Master of Science in Information
        Science (2006)
Other degrees or certificates:
    Ph.D.—Information and Library
        Science
    Certificate of Advanced Study
    Bachelor of Science in Information
        Science

**University of North
    Carolina–Greensboro**
Department of Library and Information
    Studies
349 Curry Building
P.O. Box 26170
Greensboro, NC 27402
Phone: (336) 334-3477
http://www.uncg.edu/lis
Degrees accredited by the American
    Library Association (with date of next
    review):
    Master of Library and Information
        Studies (2005)
Other degrees or certificates:
    Media Coordinator Certificate
    Media Supervisor Certificate
Distance education opportunities:
    Asheville, Charlotte, North Carolina

OHIO

Kent State University
School of Library and Information Science
Room 314 University Library
P.O. Box 5190
Kent, OH 44242
Phone: (330) 672-2782
http://www.slis.kent.edu
Degrees accredited by the American
    Library Association (with date of next
    review):
    Master of Library and Information
        Science (2004)
Other degrees or certificates:
    Certificate of Advanced Study in
        Library and Information Science
    Information Architecture/Knowledge
        Management

OKLAHOMA

University of Oklahoma
School of Library and Information Studies
401 West Brooks
Room 120
Norman, OK 73019
Phone: (405) 325-3921
http://www.ou.edu/cas/slis

Degrees accredited by the American
    Library Association (with date of next
    review):
    Master of Library and Information
        Studies (2007)
Other degrees or certificates:
    M.L.I.S./M.A.—History of Science
    M.L.I.S./Master of Education
    Generic Dual Master's Degree
    Certificate of Advanced Studies
    Bachelor of Arts in Information Studies
Distance education opportunities:
    Tulsa, Oklahoma

PENNSYLVANIA

Clarion University of Pennsylvania
Department of Library Science
222 Carlson Library
840 Wood Street
Clarion, PA 16214-1232
Phone: (814) 393-2271
http://www.clarion.edu/libsci
Degrees accredited by the American
    Library Association (with date of next
    review):
    Master of Science in Library Science
        (2003)
Other degrees or certificates:
    Certificate of Advanced Studies in
        Library Science
    B.S.Ed. Library Science
Distance education opportunities:
    Harrisburg, Southpointe, Philadelphia,
        Pennsylvania; interactive
        television, Internet

Drexel University
College of Information Science and
    Technology
3141 Chestnut Street
Philadelphia, PA 19104
Phone: (215) 895-2474
http://www.cis.drexel.edu
Degrees accredited by the American
    Library Association (with date of next
    review):
    Master of Science (2003)
Other degrees or certificates:
    Ph.D.
    M.S.I.S.
    M.S.S.E.
    Certificate of Advanced Study
    Competitive Intelligence Certificate
    B.S.I.S.
    B.S.S.E.
    Pennsylvania School Library Media
        Certification, K–12
    Pennsylvania Teacher Certification,
        Library Science, K–12
Distance education opportunities:
    Internet

University of Pittsburgh
School of Information Sciences
135 North Bellefield Avenue
Pittsburgh, PA 15260
Phone: (412) 624-5230
Fax: (412) 624-5231
http://www.sis.pitt.edu
Degrees accredited by the American
    Library Association (with date of next
    review):
    Master of Library and Information
        Science (2006)
Other degrees or certificates:
    Ph.D.—Library and Information
        Science
    Ph.D.—Information Science and
        Telecommunications
    M.S.I.S.
    M.S.T.—Telecommunications
    C.A.S.—Library and Information
        Science
    B.S.I.S.

PUERTO RICO

University of Puerto Rico
Graduate School of Information Sciences
    and Technologies
P.O. Box 21906
San Juan, PR 00931-1906
Phone: (787) 763-6199
http://egcti.upr.edu
Degrees accredited by the American
    Library Association (with date of next
    review):
    Master of Library Science (2008)

RHODE ISLAND

University of Rhode Island
Graduate School of Library and
    Information Studies
Rodman Hall
94 West Alumni Avenue
Suite 2
Kingston, RI 02881
Phone: (401) 874-2947
http://www.uri.edu/artsci/lsc
Degrees accredited by the American
    Library Association (with date of next
    review):
    Master of Library and Information
        Studies (2007)
Other degrees or certificates:
    M.L.I.S./M.A.—English
    M.L.I.S./M.A.—History
    M.L.I.S./M.P.A.—Public
        Administration
Distance education opportunities:

Amherst, Boston, Worcester,
    Massachusetts; Durham, New
    Hampshire; Internet

SOUTH CAROLINA

University of South Carolina
College of Library and Information
    Science
Davis College
Columbia, SC 29208
Phone: (803) 777-3858
http://www.libsci.sc.edu
Degrees accredited by the American
    Library Association (with date of next
    review):
    Master of Library and Information
        Science (2009)
Other degrees or certificates:
    M.L.I.S./Applied History
    M.L.I.S./English
    Certificate of Graduate Study in
        Library and Information Science

TENNESSEE

University of Tennessee
School of Information Sciences
451 Communications Building
1345 Circle Park Drive
Knoxville, TN 37996-0341
Phone: (865) 974-2148
http://www.sis.utk.edu
Degrees accredited by the American
    Library Association (with date of next
    review):
    Master of Science (2009)
Other degrees and certificates:
    Ph.D. in Communications with a
        primary concentration in
        Information Sciences
    School Librarianship Endorsement
        (Tennessee)
Distance education opportunities:
    Web-based M.S.

TEXAS

Texas Woman's University
School of Library and Information
    Sciences
P.O. Box 425438
Denton, TX 76204
Phone: (940) 898-2602
http://www.libraryschool.net
Degrees accredited by the American
    Library Association (with date of next
    review):
    Master of Library Science (2003)
    Master of Arts in Library Science
        (2003)

Other degrees or certificates:
    Ph.D.
    Learning Resources Endorsement
Distance education opportunities:
    Full degree available on-line with
        optional face-to-face sessions three
        times per semester

University of North Texas
School of Library and Information
    Sciences
P.O. Box 311068
NT Station
Denton, TX 76203
Phone: (940) 565-2445
http://www.unt.edu/slis
Degrees accredited by the American
    Library Association (with date of next
    review):
    Master of Science (2006)
Other degrees or certificates:
    Ph.D.—Information Science
        (interdisciplinary)
    Certificate of Advanced Study
    School Librarianship
    Graduate Academic Certificate in
        Storytelling
    Graduate Academic Certificate in
        Youth Services
    Graduate Academic Certificate in
        Advanced Management of LIbrary
        and Information Agencies
Distance education opportunities:
    Master's program via Internet with
        nine days of required on-site
        institutes held in various cities,
        including Denton and Houston,
        Texas; Minneapolis, Minnesota;
        Las Vegas, Nevada.
    Site-based master's in Denton, Dallas,
        and Houston, Texas.

University of Texas–Austin
School of Information
Sanchez Building 564
1 University Station D700
Austin, TX 78712
Phone: (512) 471-3821
http://www.gslis.utexas.edu
Degrees accredited by the American
    Library Association (with date of next
    review):
    Master of Science in Information
        Studies (2007)
Other degrees or certificates:
    Ph.D.—Library and Information
        Science
    Certificate of Advanced Study
    Standard School Library Certificate
    Endorsement of Specialization
Distance education opportunities:
    Interactive television

WASHINGTON

University of Washington
The Information School
Mary Gates Hall
Suite 370
Box 352840
Seattle, WA 98195
Phone: (206) 685-9937
http://www.ischool.washington.edu
Degrees accredited by the American
    Library Association (with date of next
    review):
    Master of Library and Information
        Science (2006)
Other degrees or certificates:
    Certificate, Data Resource
        Management
    Certificate, Geneology and Family
        History
    Certificate, Information and Records
        Management
    Certificate, Law Librarianship
    Certificate, School Library Media
    B.S.—Informatics
    M.S.—Information Management
    Ph.D.—Information Science

Distance education opportunities:
    dMLIS—Distance Master of Library
        and Information Science

WISCONSIN

University of Wisconsin–Madison
School of Library and Information
    Studies
Helen C. White Hall, Room 4217
600 North Park Street
Madison, WI 53706
Phone: (608) 263-2900
http://www.slis.wisc.edu
Degrees accredited by the American
    Library Association (with date of next
    review):
    Master of Arts (2007)
Other degrees or certificates:
    Ph.D. Specialist Degree
Distance education opportunities:
    Noncredit continuing education via
        Educational Teleconferencing
        Network and the World Wide
        Web

University of Wisconsin–Milwaukee
School of Information Studies
P.O. Box 413
Milwaukee, WI 53201
Phone: (414) 229-4707
http://www.uwm.edu/Dept/SOIS
Degrees accredited by the American
    Library Association (with date of next
    review):
    Master of Library and Information
        Science (2003)
Other degrees or certificates:
    Ph.D. (multidisciplinary)
    M.L.I.S./M.A.—Geography, History,
        English, Foreign Language, and
        Literature
    M.L.I.S./M.M.—Music
    M.L.I.S./M.S.—Anthropology
    M.L.I.S./M.S.—Urban Studies
    Certificate of Advanced Study
    B.S.—Information Resources
Distance education opportunities:
    Internet

B. CANADA

ALBERTA

University of Alberta
School of Library and Information Studies
3-20 Rutherford South
Edmonton, Alberta
Canada T6G 2J4
Phone: (780) 492-4578
http://www.slis.ualberta.ca
Degrees accredited by the American
    Library Association (with date of next
    review):
    Master of Library and Information
        Studies (2004)

BRITISH COLUMBIA

University of British Columbia
School of Library, Archival and
    Information Studies
6190 Agronomy Road
Suite 301
Vancouver, British Columbia
Canada V6T 1Z3
Phone: (604) 822-2404
http://www.slais.ubc.ca
Degrees accredited by the American
    Library Association (with date of next
    review):

Master of Library and Information
    Studies (2006)
Other degrees or certificates:
    Certificate of Advanced Study (post-
        master)
    Master of Archival Studies
    First Nations Curriculum
        Concentration (master's program)
    Master of Archival Studies/Master of
        Library and Information Studies
    Master of Arts in Children's Literature
    Master of Arts/Master of Education
        (Teacher-Librarianship)
    Ph.D.

NOVA SCOTIA

Dalhousie University
School of Library and Information Studies
Killam Library, Room 3621
6225 University Avenue
Halifax, Nova Scotia
Canada B3H 3J5
Phone: (902) 494-3656
http://www.mgmt.dal.ca/slis
Degrees accredited by the American
    Library Association (with date of next
    review):
    Master of Library and Information
        Studies (2005)

Other degrees or certificates:
    M.L.I.S./Bachelor of Laws
    M.L.I.S./M.B.A.
    M.L.I.S./M.P.A.
    Bachelor of Management

ONTARIO

University of Toronto
Faculty of Information Studies
140 St. George Street
Toronto, Ontario
Canada M5S 3G6
Phone: (416) 978-3234
http://www.fis.utoronto.ca
Degrees accredited by the American
    Library Association (with date of next
    review):
    Master of Information Studies (2003)
Other degrees or certificates:
    Ph.D.

University of Western Ontario
Graduate Programs in Library and
    Information Science
Faculty of Information and Media Studies
North Campus Building, Room 240
London, Ontario
Canada N6A 5B7
Phone: (519) 661-4017

http://www.fims.uwo.ca
Degrees accredited by the American
    Library Association (with date of next
    review):
    Master of Library and Information
        Science (2004)
Other degrees or certificates:
    Ph.D.—Library and Information
        Science

QUEBEC

McGill University
Graduate School of Library and
    Information Studies
3459 McTavish Street
Montréal, Québec
Canada H3A 1Y1
Phone: (514) 398-4204
http://www.gslis.mcgill.ca

Degrees accredited by the American
    Library Association (with date of next
    review):
    Master of Library and Information
        Studies (2009)
Other degrees or certificates:
    Ph.D. (Ad Hoc)—Library and
        Information Studies
    Graduate Diploma in Library and
        Information Studies
    Graduate Certificate in Library and
        Information Studies

Université de Montréal
Ecole de bibliothéconomie et des
    sciences de l'information
C.P. 6128, succursale Centre-Ville
Montréal, Québec
Canada H3C 3J7

Phone: (514) 343-6044
http://www.fas.umontreal.ca/EBSI
Degrees accredited by the American
    Library Association (with date of next
    review):
    Maîtrise en sciences de l'information
        (2007)
Other degrees or certificates:
    Doctorat en sciences de l'information
        (graduate)
    Certificat en archivistique
        (undergraduate)
    Certificat en gestion de l'information
        numérique (undergraduate)

APPENDIX III
U.S. LIBRARY TECHNICIAN PROGRAMS
(Includes Certificate, Associate, and Bachelor Degree Programs)

ARIZONA

Mesa Community College
Library Science Program
1833 West Southern Avenue
Mesa, AZ 85202
Phone: (480) 461-7686
http://www.mc.maricopa.edu/library/lbt.
  html
Degree/Certificate: AAS, Library
  Technician

Northland Pioneer College
Library Media Technology Program
1200 East Hermosa Drive
P.O. Box 610
Holbrook, AZ 86025
Phone: (520) 532-6120
Degree/Certificate: A.A.S., Library and
  Media Technician and Certificate,
  Library Assistant.

CALIFORNIA

Citrus College
Library Technology Program
1000 West Foothill Boulevard
Glendora, CA 91741
Phone: (626) 914-8643
Degree/Certificate: A.A. and Certificate
  in Library Technology

City College of San Francisco
Library Information Technology Program
50 Phelan Avenue
San Francisco, CA 94112
Phone: (415) 452-5519; (415) 452-5438
Degree/Certificate: A.A. or Award of
  Achievement

College of the Canyons
Library-Media Technology
26455 Rockwell Canyon Road
Santa Clarita, CA 91355
Phone: (661) 362-3362
Degree/Certificate: A.A. and Certificate
  in Library/Media Technology

College of the Sequoias
Library Technology Certificate Program
915 South Mooney Boulevard
Visalia, CA 93277

Phone: (559) 730-7349
Degree/Certificate: Library Technician
  Certificate

Cuesta College
Library/Information Technology Program
Route 1
San Luis Obispo, CA 93403
Phone: (805) 546-3159
Degree/Certificate: A.S. and Certificate
  in Library/Information Technology
Offers distance education option.

Diablo Valley College
Library and Information Technology
  Program
321 Golf Club Road
Pleasant Hill, CA 94523
Phone: (510) 685-1230 ext. 2241
Degree/Certificate: A.A. and Certificate
  in Library and Information Technology

Foothill College
Library Technology Program
12345 El Monte Road
Los Altos Hills, CA 94022
Phone: (650) 949-7086
Degree/Certificate: A.A. and Certificate

Fresno City College
Library Technology Program
1101 East University Avenue
Fresno, CA 93741
Phone: (559) 442-4600 ext. 8315
Degree/Certificate: A.A. or Certificate
Offers distance education option.

Hartnell College
Library-Media Technology Program
156 Homestead Avenue
Salinas, CA 93901
Phone: (831) 755-6872
Degree/Certificate: A.A. and Certificate
  in Library-Media Technology

Imperial Valley College
Library Technician Program
P.O. Box 158
380 East Aten Road
Imperial, CA 92251

Phone: (760) 355-6377
Degree/Certificate: Library Technician
  Certificate

Palomar College
Library Technology Program
1140 West Mission Road
San Marcos, CA 92069
Phone: (760) 744-1150 ext. 2848
Degree/Certificate: Certificate, A.A.,
  Library Technology

Pasadena City College
Library Technician Program
1570 East Colorado Boulevard
Pasadena, CA 91106
Phone: (626) 585-7837; (626) 585-7833
Degree/Certificate: Certificate Program
  in Library Technology

Santa Ana College
Library Technology Program
Nealley Library
1530 West 17th Street
Santa Ana, CA 92706
Phone: (714) 564-6717
Degree/Certificate: A.A. and Certificate
  in Library Technology

Sacramento City College
Library and Information Technology
  Program
3835 Freeport Boulevard
Sacramento, CA 95822
Phone: (916) 558-2186
Degree/Certificate: A.S. or Certificate in
  Library and Information Technology

San Bernardino Valley College
Library Technology Program
701 South Mount Vernon Avenue
San Bernardino, CA 92410
Phone: (909) 888-6511 ext. 1628
Degree/Certificate: Associate of Arts,
  Library Science; Certificate, Library
  Technology

COLORADO

Pueblo Community College
Library Technician Program
900 West Orman Avenue
Pueblo, CO 81004

Phone: (719) 549-3308
Degree/Certificate: Certificate and
  A.A.S. degree
Colorado Community College Online
  (http://www.ccconline.org) offers
  distance education degree option.

CONNECTICUT

Capital Community College
Library Technical Assistant Program
950 Main Street
Hartford, CT 06103
Degree/Certificate: Associate in Science
  in Social Service: Library Technical
  Assistant Option; Certificate: Library
  Technical Assistant

Southern Connecticut State University
School of Communication, Information
  and Library Science
501 Crescent Street
New Haven, CT 06515
Phone: (203) 392-5781
Degree/Certificate: B.S. with
  specializations in Library-Information
  Service, Information Science,
  Instructional Technology, Training and
  Development
Offers distance education option.

Three Rivers Community College
Library Technology Program
Mohegan Campus, Mahan Drive
Norwich, CT 06360
Phone: (860) 383-5260; (860) 465-5001
  (Director)
Degree/Certificate: Certificate, Library
  Assistant

DISTRICT OF COLUMBIA (WASHINGTON, D.C.)

USDA Graduate School,
  Correspondence Program
Library Techniques Program
South Agriculture Building, Room 1033
Washington, DC 20250
Phone: (202) 720-5885
Degree/Certificate: Library Techniques
  Certificate of Accomplishment
Offers distance education option.

FLORIDA

Indian River Community College
Library Technical Assistant Program
3209 Virginia Avenue
Fort Pierce, FL 34981
Phone: (772) 462-4757

Degree/Certificate: A.S., Library
  Technical Assistant

Hillsborough Community College
Library Technical Assistant Certificate
  Program
4001 Tampa Bay Boulevard
Tampa, FL 33614
Phone: (813) 259-6059
http://www.hccfl.edu/student/catalog/02_
  03/index.html
Degree/Certificate: Library Technical
  Assistant Certificate (30 credits)

IDAHO

College of Southern Idaho
Library Science Program
P.O. Box 1238
Twin Falls, ID 83303
Phone: (208) 733-9554 ext. 2504; (800)
  680-0274
Degree/Certificate: A.A. in Library
  Science

University of Idaho Independent Study
  Program
Education Media Generalist Endorsement
  or University of Idaho teaching minor
  in Library Science
Independent Study in Idaho, University of
  Idaho
P.O. Box 443225
Moscow, ID 83844
Phone: (877) 464-3246; (208) 885-6641
Degree/Certificate: Graduate and
  Undergraduate
In-state tuition applies to all; offers
  distance education option
  (correspondence and on-line).

ILLINOIS

College of DuPage
Library Technical Assistant Program
425 Fawell Boulevard
Glen Ellyn, IL 60137
Phone: (630) 942-2597
Degree/Certificate: A.A.S. and
  Certificate in Library Technology

College of Lake County
Library/Media Technology Program
19351 Washington Street
Grayslake, IL 60030
Phone: (847) 543-2551
Degree/Certificate: Certificate in
  Library/Media Technology
Catalog pdf file available at
  http://www.clcillinois.edu

Illinois Central College
Library Technical Assistant Program
One College Drive
East Peoria, IL 61635-0001
Phone: (309) 694-8504
Degree/Certificate: A.A.S., Library
  Technical Assistant

Wilbur Wright College
Library Technology Program
300 North Narragansett Avenue
Chicago, IL 60634
Phone: (773) 777-7900
Degree/Certificate: A.A.S., Certificate in
  Library Technology
Offers distance education option.

INDIANA

Indiana College Network
Library/Media Services Program
Indiana State University
Erickson Hall 210
Terre Haute, IN 47809
Phone: (888) 237-8080
Degree/Certificate:
  Undergraduate/graduate certificate
On-line program.

KANSAS

Emporia State University
School Library Media Certification
  Program
Campus Box 4035
1200 Commercial Street
Emporia, KS 66801
Phone: (800) 552-4770 ext. 5062
Degree/Certificate: Certificate.
  Additional degree programs in library
  studies are also available.

KENTUCKY

Lexington Community College
Information Management and Design
  Program, Library Information
Technology Option
201-I A/T Building
Cooper Drive
Lexington KY 40506
Phone: (480) 461-7686
http://www.kyvu.org
Degree/Certificate: A.A.S.
This is a Web-based on-line program
designed for Kentucky public library
employees who must meet state certifica-
tion requirements. Other students are
welcome.

MAINE

University of Maine at Augusta
Library and Information Services Program
Bennett D. Katz Library
46 University Drive
Augusta, ME 04330
Phone: (888) 850-5379 (toll-free nationwide); (877) UMA-1234 (toll-free in Maine); (207) 621-3341 (local)
Degree/Certificate: Certificate, A.S., B.S.
In-state tuition applies to all; financial aid is available. This distance education program includes national and international delivery via asynchronous technologies—computer, e-mail account, and access to the Internet are required.

MICHIGAN

Oakland Community College
Library Technical Assistant Program
2900 Featherstone Road
Auburn Hills, MI 48326
Phone: (248) 232-4100
http://www.occ.cc.mi.us
Degree/Certificate: A.A.S. or Certificate
For information about this program, contact the college directly or view their catalog via the college home page.

MINNESOTA

Northwest Technical College
Information Resource Specialist Program
Distance Education Office
150 2nd Street SW
Suite B
P.O. Box 309
Perham, MN 56573
Phone: (877) 598-8523
Degree/Certificate: A.A.S.
A distance education program.

NEW JERSEY

Rutgers University
Online Training Program for Library Assistants in Academic and Research Libraries
SCILS Professional Development
4 Huntington Street
New Brunswick, NJ 08901
Phone: (732) 932-7169

NEW MEXICO

Clovis Community College
Library Technology Program
417 Schepps Boulevard
Clovis, NM 88101
Phone: (505) 769-4081
E-mail: admissions@clovis.cc.nm.us
Degree/Certificate: A.A.S. in Library Technology

Dona Ana Branch Community College
Library and Information Technology Program
P.O. Box 30001
Department 3DA
Las Cruces, NM 88003
Phone: (505) 527-7567
Degree/Certificate: A.A.S. or Certificate in Library and Information Technology, Library Media Specialist Endorsement
Offers Distance Education option.

Northern New Mexico Community College
Library Technology Program
921 Paseo de Oñate
Espanola, NM 87532
Phone: (505) 747-2111 or (505) 747-2100
Fax: (505) 747-2180
Degree/Certificate: Associates degree or Certificate, Library Technology

NEW YORK

Long Island University C. W. Post Campus
Palmer School of Library and Information Science
720 Northern Boulevard
Brookville, NY 11548
Phone: (516) 299-2866 or (800) 548-7526
Degree/Certificate: B.S. in Information Transfer

Fulton-Montgomery Community College
Library Technician Certificate Program
2805 State Highway 67
Johnstown, NY 12095
Phone: (518) 762-4651

NORTH CAROLINA

Central Carolina Community College
Library and Information Technology Program
1105 Kelly Drive
Sanford, NC 27330
Phone: (800) 682-8353
Degree/Certificate: Two-year Associate in Applied Science; one-year diploma; Certificate of Public Services; Certificate of Cataloging
Library-related courses available through distance education only.

University of North Carolina at Chapel Hill
Information Science Program
Undergraduate Student Services Manager
School of Information and Library Science
100 Manning Hall
CB # 3360
Chapel Hill, NC 27599
Phone: (919) 962-0208
Degree/Certificate: B.S.

OHIO

Raymond Walters College—University of Cincinnati
Library Technology Program
9555 Plainfield Road
Blue Ash, OH 45236
Phone: (513) 745-5600
Degree/Certificate: A.A.S. or Professional Certificate in Library Technology
Offers distance education option.

OKLAHOMA

Rose State College
Library Technical Assistant Program
6420 SE 15th Street
Midwest City, OK 73110
Phone: (405) 733-7538
Degree/Certificate: A.A. and Certificate, Library Technical Assistant
Offers distance education option.

PENNSYLVANIA

Northampton Community College
Library Technical Assistant Program
3835 Green Pond Road
Bethlehem, PA 18017
Phone: (215) 861-5358
Degree/Certificate: Library Technician Certificate

UTAH

Salt Lake Community College
Library Technician Program
Miller Campus
9750 South 300 West
Sandy, UT 84070
Phone: (801) 957-3802
Degree/Certificate: No degrees or certificates issued at this time
Classes offered via Internet.

WASHINGTON

Highline Community College
Library Technician Program
2400 South 240th Street
P.O. Box 98000 MS 25-1E
Des Moines, WA 98198
Phone: (206) 878-3710 ext. 3259
Degree/Certificate: A.A.S. and Library
    Technician Certificate of Completion

Offers distance education option and
    Library Development Institute
    Certificates for managers of small
    libraries.

Spokane Falls Community College
Library Technician Program
Building 2, MS 3020
3410 West Fort George Wright Drive
Spokane, WA 99224-5288

Phone: (509) 533-3500
Degree/Certificate: A.A.S., Library
    Technician

APPENDIX IV
STATE LIBRARIES

ALABAMA

Alabama Department of Archives and History
624 Washington Avenue
Montgomery, AL 36130
Phone: (334) 242-4435
http://www.archives.state.al.us

Alabama Public Library Service
6030 Monticello Drive
Montgomery, AL 36130
Phone: (334) 213-3900 or (800) 723-8459
(within Alabama only)
http://www.apls.state.al.us

ALASKA

Alaska State Library
P.O. Box 110571
Juneau, AK 99811
Phone: (907) 465-2920
http://www.library.state.ak.us

ARIZONA

Arizona Department of Library, Archives and Public Records
1700 West Washington
Suite 200
Phoenix, AZ 85007
Phone: (602) 542-4035
http://www.lib.az.us

ARKANSAS

Arkansas State Library
One Capitol Mall
Little Rock, AR 72201
Phone: (501) 682-2053
http://www.asl.lib.ar.us

CALIFORNIA

California State Library
Library and Courts Building
914 Capitol Mall
Sacramento, CA 95814
Phone: (916) 654-0261
http://www.library.ca.gov

COLORADO

Colorado State Library and Adult Education Office
201 East Colfax Avenue
Room 309
Denver, CO 80203
Phone: (303) 866-6900
http://www.cde.state.co.us/index_library.htm

CONNECTICUT

Connecticut State Library
231 Capitol Avenue
Hartford, CT 06106
Phone: (860) 757-6500
http://www.cslib.org

DELAWARE

Del-AWARE: The Digital Library of the First State
43 South DuPont Highway
Dover, DE 19901
Phone: (800) 282-8696
http://www.state.lib.de.us

DISTRICT OF COLUMBIA

District of Columbia Public Library
901 G Street, NW
Washington, DC 20001
Phone: (202) 727-0321
http://dclibrary.org

FLORIDA

Florida Department of State
Division of Library and Information Services
500 South Bronough Street
Tallahassee, FL 32399
Phone: (850) 245-6600
http://dlis.dos.state.fl.us

GEORGIA

Georgia Public Library Services
http://www.georgialibraries.org

HAWAII

Hawaii State Public Library System
http://www.librarieshawaii.org

IDAHO

Idaho State Library
325 West State Street
Boise, ID 83702
Phone: (208) 334-2150 or
(800) 458-3271 (in-state toll free)
http://www.lili.org/isl

ILLINOIS

Illinois State Library
300 South 2nd Street
Springfield, IL 62701
Phone: (217) 785-5600; (800) 665-5576
(within IL only)
http://www.cyberdriveillinois.com/departments/library/home.html

INDIANA

Indiana State Library
140 North Senate Avenue
Indianapolis, IN 46204
Phone: (317) 232-3675
http://www.statelib.lib.in.us

IOWA

State Library of Iowa
1112 East Grand Avenue
Des Moines, IA 50319
Phone: (515) 281-4105
http://www.silo.lib.ia.us

KANSAS

Kansas State Library
State Capitol Building
Topeka, KS 66612
Phone: (785) 296-3296 or
(800) 432-3919
http://skyways.lib.ks.us/KSL

KENTUCKY

Kentucky Department for Libraries and Archives
Phone: (502) 564-8300
http://www.kdla.state.ky.us

LOUISIANA

State Library of Louisiana
701 North 4th Street
Baton Rouge, LA 70802
Phone: (225) 342-4923
http://www.state.lib.la.us

MAINE

Maine State Library
230 State Street
State House Station #64
Augusta, ME 04333
http://www.state.me.us

MASSACHUSETTS

State Library of Massachusetts
The George Fingold Library
State House Room 341
Boston, MA 02133
Phone: (617) 727-2590
http://www.state.ma.us/lib

**Massachusetts Library and
    Information Network**
Massachusetts Board of Library
    Commissioners
648 Beacon Street
Boston, MA 02215
Phone: (617) 267-9400; (800) 952-7403
    (in state)
http://www.mlin.lib.ma.us

MICHIGAN

Library of Michigan
702 West Kalamazoo Street
Lansing MI 48909
http://www.michigan.gov/hal

MISSISSIPPI

Mississippi Library Commission
1221 Ellis Avenue
Jackson, MS 39209
Phone: (800)-MISS LIB (647-7542);
    (601) 961-4111; (800) 446-0892
    (Blind and Physically Handicapped
    Library Service)
http://www.mlc.lib.ms.us

MONTANA

Montana State Library
1515 East 6th Avenue
P.O. Box 201800
Helena, MT 59620
Phone: (406) 444-3115
http://msl.state.mt.us

NEBRASKA

Nebraska Library Commission
The Atrium
1200 N Street
Suite 120
Lincoln, NE 68508
Phone: (402) 471-2045 (in Lincoln and
    outside Nebraska); (800) 307-2665
    (Nebraska only)
http://www.nlc.state.ne.us/index.html

NEVADA

**Nevada State
    Library and Archives**
100 North Stewart Street
Carson City, NV 89701
Phone: (775) 684-3360; (800) 922-2880
    (in-state only)
http://dmla.clan.lib.nv.us/docs/NSLA

NEW HAMPSHIRE

New Hampshire State Library
20 Park Street
Concord, NH 03301
Phone: (603) 271-2144
http://www.state.nh.us/nhsl

NEW JERSEY

New Jersey State Library
P.O. Box 520
Trenton, NJ 08625
Phone: (609) 292-6029
http://www.njstatelib.org

NEW MEXICO

New Mexico State Library
1209 Camino Carlos Rey
Santa Fe, NM 87507
Phone: (505) 476-9700
http://www.stlib.state.nm.us

NEW YORK

New York State Library
Cultural Education Center
Empire State Plaza
Albany, NY 12230
Phone: (518) 474-5355
http://unix2.nysed.gov

NORTH CAROLINA

State Library of North Carolina
1811 Capitol Boulevard
Raleigh, NC 27635

Phone: (919) 733-3270
http://statelibrary.dcr.state.nc.us

NORTH DAKOTA

North Dakota State Library
604 East Boulevard Avenue – Dept. 250
Bismarck, ND 58505
Phone: (701) 328-2492
http://ndsl.lib.state.nd.us

OHIO

State Library of Ohio
274 East First Avenue
Columbus, OH 43201
Phone: (614) 644-7061
http://winslo.state.oh.us

OKLAHOMA

**Oklahoma Department of
    Libraries**
200 Northeast 18th Street
Oklahoma City, OK 73105
Phone: (405) 521-2502
http://www.odl.state.ok.us

OREGON

Oregon State Library
250 Winter Street Northeast
Salem, OR 97301
Phone: (503) 378-4243 ext. 221
http://www.osl.state.or.us

PENNSYLVANIA

Office of Commonwealth Libraries
333 Market Street
Harrisburg, PA 17126
Phone: (717) 787-4440
http://www.statelibrary.state.pa.us

RHODE ISLAND

Rhode Island State Library
State House
Room 208
Providence, RI 02903
Phone: (401) 222-2473
http://www.state.ri.us/library

SOUTH CAROLINA

South Carolina State Library
P.O. Box 11469
Columbia, SC 29211
Phone: (803) 734-8666
http://www.state.sc.us/scsl

SOUTH DAKOTA

South Dakota State Library
Mercedes MacKay Building
800 Governors Drive
Pierre, SD 57501
Phone: (605) 773-3131; (800) 423-6665
http://www.sdstatelibrary.com

TENNESSEE

Tennessee State Library and Archives
403 Seventh Avenue North
Nashville, TN 37243
Phone: (615) 741-2764
http://www.state.tn.us/sos/statelib

TEXAS

**Texas State Library and Archives
    Commission**
P.O. Box 12927
Austin, TX 78711
http://www.tsl.state.tx.us

UTAH

Utah State Archives and Records Service
P.O. Box 141021
State Capitol, Archives Building
Salt Lake City, UT 84114

Phone: (801) 538-3012
http://www.archives.state.ut.us

VERMONT

Vermont Department of Libraries
109 State Street
Montpelier, VT 05609
Phone: (802) 828-3261
http://dol.state.vt.us

VIRGINIA

Library of Virginia
800 East Broad Street
Richmond, VA 23219
Phone: (804) 692-3500
http://www.lva.lib.va.us

WASHINGTON

Washington State Library
Point Plaza East
6880 Capitol Boulevard
P.O. Box 42460
Olympia, WA 98504
Phone: (360) 704-5200; (360) 704-5213;
    (360) 704-5221
http://www.statelib.wa.gov

WEST VIRGINIA

West Virginia Archives and History
The Cultural Center
1900 Kanawha Boulevard East
Charleston, WV 25305-0300
http://www.wvculture.org/history

West Virginia Library Commission
Cultural Center
1900 Kanawha Boulevard East
Charleston, WV 25305
Phone: (304) 558-2041
http://librarycommission.lib.wv.us

WISCONSIN

**Wisconsin Division for Libraries and
    Community Learning**
Phone: (800) 441-4563 (U.S. only) or
    (608) 266-3390
http://www.dpi.state.wi.us/dlcl

WYOMING

Wyoming State Library
2301 Capitol Avenue
Cheyenne, WY 82002
Phone: (307) 777-6333
http://www-wsl.state.wy.us

APPENDIX V
FEDERAL LIBRARIES

NATIONAL LIBRARIES

Library of Congress
101 Independence Avenue, SE
Washington, DC 20540
Phone: (202) 707-5205
http://www.loc.gov
The nation's oldest federal cultural institution, this library serves as the research arm of Congress. It is also the largest library in the world, with more than 120 million items on approximately 530 miles of bookshelves. The collections include more than 18 million books, 2.5 million recordings, 12 million photographs, 4.5 million maps, and 54 million manuscripts. The library's mission is to make its resources available and useful to the Congress and the American people and to sustain and preserve a universal collection of knowledge and creativity for future generations.

National Agricultural Library
10301 Baltimore Avenue
Beltsville, Maryland 20705
Phone: (301) 504-5755
http://www.nalusda.gov
The National Agricultural Library ensures and enhances access to agricultural information, and serves as a national library of the United States and as the library of the U.S. Department of Agriculture. The library acquires, organizes, manages, preserves, and provides access to information and provides quality stewardship of its unique collection. It also provides leadership in information management, maximizes access to information through collaborative efforts and utilization of technology, and enhances global cooperation through international exchange of information and the provision of services and technical assistance.

National Library of Education (NLE)
400 Maryland Avenue, SW
Washington, DC 20202
Phone: (800) 424-1616
http://www.ed.gov/NLE
The world's largest federally funded library devoted solely to education, the NLE is the federal government's main resource center for education information.

National Library of Medicine (NLM)
8600 Rockville Pike
Bethesda, MD 20894
Phone: (888) 346-3656
http://www.nlm.nih.gov
NLM, on the campus of the National Institutes of Health in Bethesda, Maryland, is the world's largest medical library. The library collects material in all areas of biomedicine and health care, as well as biomedical aspects of technology, the humanities, and the physical, life, and social sciences. The collections include more than 6 million books, journals, technical reports, manuscripts, microfilms, photographs, and images. Housed within the library is one of the world's finest medical history collections of old and rare medical works. The library's collection may be consulted in the reading room or requested on interlibrary loan. NLM is a national resource for all U.S. health science libraries through the National Network of Libraries of Medicine. For more than 100 years, the library has published the *Index Medicus,* a monthly subject/author guide to articles in 3,400 journals. This information is also available in the MEDLINE database, the major component of PubMed, freely accessible via the Internet. MEDLINE has more than 12 million journal article references and abstracts from the early sixties. Other databases provide information on monographs, books, audiovisual materials, and on such specialized subjects as toxicology, environmental health, and molecular biology.

CABINET-LEVEL LIBRARIES

Department of Commerce Library
Office of Administrative Services
1401 Constitution Avenue, NW
Washington, DC 20230
Phone: (202) 482-5511
http://www.osec.doc.gov/lib
The primary mission of this library is to provide service to all operating units in the Herbert C. Hoover Building, those Department of Commerce operating units and offices not maintaining their own libraries, other federal agencies, and the public. The collection consists of books and periodicals in business, economics, international trade, management, telecommunications, CD-ROM products (phone, disc, and major newspapers), and on-line resources (Knight-Ridder, NEXIS, Dow Jones, and Dun and Bradstreet). The library is a selective government depository, whose primary clientele includes all Department of Commerce employees and other government agencies. Assistance is provided to the academic and business communities.

Department of Defense
Pentagon Library
1155 Defense Pentagon
Butler Building
Washington, DC 20310-6605
http://www.hqda.army.mil/library
The Pentagon Library fosters excellence by fulfilling the research requirements of Department of Defense personnel serving at the Pentagon and in locations without library services in the National Capital Region.

Department of Housing and Urban Development (HUD) Library
Room 8141
451 7th Street, SW
Washington, DC 20410
Phone: (202) 708-1112
http://www.hud.gov/offices/adm/library
This library provides services for HUD staff, including database searches, answers to legal and general questions, program information and referrals to HUD specialists, periodical routing to authorized headquarters staff, loan of library materials, and help in borrowing from other libraries. Services for the public include ready reference answers to legal and general questions that do not require research, program information and referral to HUD specialists, loan of library materials through interlibrary loan via a requester's local library, and help in using HUD Library resources to walk-in patrons.

Department of Justice Library
Main Library
U.S. Room 5400, Robert F. Kennedy
    Justice Building (Main)
950 Pennsylvania Avenue, NW
Washington, DC 20530
Phone: (202) 514-3775
http://www.usdoj.gov/jmd/ls/index.html
The Justice Library System includes the main library, the Patrick Henry Library, and five branch libraries at various locations in Washington, D.C. The main library is a broad research facility with extensive legal and nonlegal holdings. Service is provided primarily to the offices, boards, and divisions of the Department of Justice. Branch libraries primarily serve the litigating divisions and maintain specialized collections of particular interest to the personnel of the divisions, in addition to essential legal materials. Most Justice Department libraries' resources are for the use of Justice Department personnel only. Libraries are open to the public for access to government depository items, Department of Justice materials, or unique titles.

Department of the Interior Library
1849 C Street, NW
Washington, DC 20240
Phone: (202) 208-5815
http://library.doi.gov
The U.S. Department of the Interior Library promotes the mission of the department by providing a full range of professional reference and research services, available to Interior Department employees in the Washington, D.C., area and nationwide. The library has collections centered on documents produced by or for the department, as well as a broad range of related books, journals, and other resources that support the department's efforts to protect and provide access to the nation's natural and cultural heritage and to honor its trust responsibilities to Indian tribes.

Department of Labor Library
Wirtz Labor Library
U.S. Department of Labor
200 Constitution Avenue, NW
Room N-2445
Washington, DC 20210
Phone: (202) 693-6600
http://www.dol.gov/oasam/library
The Department of Labor Library, established in 1917, is one of the oldest cabinet-level libraries. Large segments of its collection, which document the history of labor and labor unions and the growth and development of the labor movement in a national and world context, are unique either in their nature and content or in the length and completeness of their coverage. The library's large journal collection is predominantly historic. The library's on-line catalog includes about 67,000 titles. Not all catalog records, have been converted to electronic format, however, and a card catalog still provides access to most holdings acquired prior to 1975 (almost 248,000 records). On March 28, 2000, the library was dedicated in honor of former Secretary of Labor Willard Wirtz and Mrs. Jane Wirtz to become the Wirtz Labor Library of the U.S. Department of Labor. In the same year, it was designated a Millennium Library by the White House Millennium Council in recognition of its unique historical holdings.

Department of State
Ralph J. Bunche Library
A/RPS/IPS/LIBR, Room 3239
2201 C Street, NW
Washington, DC 20520
Phone: (202) 647-1099
http://www.state.gov/m/a/ls
The Ralph J. Bunche Library of the U.S. Department of State is the oldest federal government library, founded by the first Secretary of State, Thomas Jefferson, in 1789. It was renamed the Ralph J. Bunche Library on May 5, 1997, in honor of the Nobel Peace Prize recipient and United Nations secretary-general. The library has a large and important collection of unclassified and published information sources on foreign relations. The Bunche Library is a federal depository library, whose mission is to support the research needs of state department personnel. The library is not open to the public and does not lend books directly to members of the public, although the library will lend books, at its discretion, to other libraries. Members of the public must contact a library through which they may borrow books from the Ralph J. Bunche Library. Magazines, newspapers, and microfilm may not be borrowed from the Ralph J. Bunche Library.

Department of Transportation (DOT)
    Library
400 7th Street, SW
Room 2200
Washington, DC 20590
Phone: (202) 366-0746
http://dotlibrary.dot.gov

The DOT Library is one of the largest transportation libraries in the United States, with more than 300,000 titles and more than 1,200 periodical titles. The library collects materials related to all areas of transportation, in both print and electronic formats. The library's Nassif technical collection is the primary source for materials concerning general transportation, surface, and water transportation. Other special topics include bridges, driver studies, engineering (emphasis on civil engineering), highways and highway safety, history of transportation, land utilization, marine engineering, mass transit, merchant marine, navigation (except air), oceanography, pipelines, railroads, ships and shipbuilding, statistics, traffic engineering, traffic surveys and forecasts, urban transportation, and waterways. The Federal Aviation Administration technical collection contains materials covering the areas of general aviation, aviation safety, airports, airport access, human factors in aviation, aviation medicine, and selected materials in supporting sciences such as navigation, aerospace, and engineering. The DOT Library's three law collections contain general legal materials in addition to those specifically related to transportation law. Bibliographic records for the library's collection of print materials can be accessed through the on-line catalog. There are also separate lists of periodicals (currently being updated) and electronic databases held by the library. The library is open to DOT employees, contractors, and members of the public with transportation-related questions.

OTHER FEDERAL LIBRARIES

Department of the Army
Army Library
http://www.libraries.army.mil
The Army Library Program's worldwide network of academic, research, technical, general, and special libraries provides the army community access to a selected group of Web resources via the Digital Army Library Service.

NASA
The Goddard Space Flight Center
    Library
Code 292, Building 21
Greenbelt, MD 20771
Phone: (301) 286-7218
http://library.gsfc.nasa.gov

The Goddard library provides access to the library's resources, print and electronic, as well as tools, services, staff expertise, and the ability to search a wide range of Internet resources. The library is committed to providing timely access to scientific, technical, and management information. The library facilitates research in earth science, space science, and enabling technologies by stimulating discovery, creativity, and communication.

Environmental Protection Agency Libraries

EPA West Building
Constitution Avenue and 14th Street, NW
Room 3340
Washington, DC 20460
Phone: (202) 566-0556
http://www.epa.gov/natlibra
The EPA Library Network, established in 1971, is composed of libraries in the agency's headquarters, regional and field offices, research centers, and specialized laboratories located throughout the country. The combined network collection contains a wide range of general information on environmental protection and management, basic sciences such as biology and chemistry, applied sciences such as engineering and toxicology, and extensive coverage of topics featured in legislative mandates, such as hazardous waste, drinking water, pollution prevention, and toxic substances. Several of the libraries maintain collections focused on special topics to support specific regional or program office projects. The library network provides access to its collections through the Online Library System (OLS), a Web-based database of the library holdings. The OLS offers author, title, and keyword access to documents and makes it possible to retrieve information relevant to almost every request. The National Library Network Program provides leadership and direction for the libraries, ensuring their support of the agency's mission. The program provides a wide range of services to the EPA libraries, facilitating communications, networking and resource sharing, and provides technical assistance on all aspects of library management.

Federal Bureau of Prisons Library

500 First Street, NW
7th Floor
Washington, DC 20534
Phone: (202) 307-3029
http://bop.library.net

The Federal Bureau of Prisons (BOP) Library offers a wide variety of traditional and automated information services covering the field of corrections and related fields of study, including criminology, sociology, psychology, and business. The BOP Library has nearly 5,000 books, government documents, statistical and organizational publications covering all areas of corrections and other criminal justice topics. More than 70 periodicals, including journals, magazines, newsletters, and major newspapers, are found in the collection. The library's CD-ROM data bases include the National Criminal Justice Reference Service database, with more than 100,000 abstracts of books and articles about criminal justice topics; the Criminal Justice Abstracts, with more than 55,000 abstracts from both domestic and foreign periodicals about criminal justice topics; and the PsychLit Database from the American Psychological Association. The librarian conducts on-line database searches of the Dialog or Westlaw databases for Bureau of Prisons staff only.

National Oceanographic and Atmospheric Administration (NOAA) Central Library

Silver Spring Metro Center Building 3 (SSMC3)
2nd Floor
1315 East-West Highway
Silver Spring, MD 20910
Phone: (301) 713-2600 ext. 124
http://www.lib.noaa.gov
This library has an extensive collection of historical Coast and Geodetic Survey materials (from 1807) and Weather Bureau materials (from the 1830s), including foreign meteorological data. These materials include historical meteorological data, information on instruments, and metadata. Most of these materials are found nowhere else in the world. The NOAA Central Library's collection is multidisciplinary to serve the needs of NOAA, including information on oceanography, ocean engineering, marine resources, ecosystems, coastal studies, atmospheric sciences (climatology and meteorology), geodesy, geophysics, cartography, mathematics, and statistics. This library's mission is therefore different from that of other libraries, which tend to collect in only a single or limited number of disciplines. The collection enables one-stop reference service for ecosystems studies and other interdependent, multidisciplinary studies.

U.S. Agency for International Development (USAID) Library

Ronald Reagan Building
Room M.01-010
Mezzanine Level
1300 Pennsylvania Avenue, NW
Washington, DC 20523
Phone: (202) 712-0579
http://library.info.usaid.gov
The USAID Library serves as a point of access to the body of knowledge relating to sustainable development and USAID information for individuals interested in the field of international development. With a particular focus on international sustainable development and economic assistance, the library's collection supports the agency's development efforts in its strategic objective areas: democracy and governance, economic growth, education and training, environment and agriculture, humanitarian assistance, and population, health, and nutrition. The library's primary mission is to serve the information needs of USAID staff. The general public with an interest in researching USAID or development topics is also welcome to use the resources.

U.S. Geological Survey (USGS) Library

MS950 National Center
Reston, VA 20192
http://library.usgs.gov
Established in 1879 to build and organize a collection of scientific materials in the earth sciences, the USGS Library is now the largest library for earth sciences in the world. The library system includes four libraries and is part of the Geographic Information Office of the USGS. The original collection was based on exchange partnerships with domestic and international scientific organizations. Today the library holds more than 1 million books and journals, 450,000 maps, 370,000 microforms, 270,000 pamphlets, 250,000 black-and-white photographs, 50,000 color transparencies, 15,000 field record notebooks, and 250 videocassettes. Materials include USGS publications as well as those produced by state and foreign geological surveys, scientific societies, museums, academic institutions, and government scientific agencies. The libraries in Reston and Menlo Park are designated as official depositories for selected U.S. government publications. In addition to the four libraries of the Geographic Information Office, the USGS has other libraries associated with science

centers and field offices across the country with collections closely related to the specialized research of their local USGS scientists.

U.S. Naval Academy Nimitz Library
589 McNair Road
Annapolis, MD 21402

Phone: (410) 293-2420
http://www.nadn.navy.mil/Library
The Nimitz Library, completed in 1973, is named in honor of Fleet Admiral Chester W. Nimitz. The library offers comprehensive library services to midshipmen and faculty. Service is also provided to U.S. Naval Academy military and civilian staff,

to personnel attached to the other activities of the Annapolis Area Naval Complex, and to local retired faculty members and retired military personnel. Other residents of the Annapolis community and authorized researchers may make use of the library's resources under specific circumstances.

APPENDIX VI
PRESIDENTIAL LIBRARIES

The Presidential Library System is made up of 10 presidential libraries. Each presidential library contains a museum and provides an active series of public programs. Also included in the Presidential Library system is the Richard M. Nixon Presidential Materials Staff, which administers the Nixon presidential materials under the terms of the Presidential Recordings and Materials Preservation Act.

This nationwide network of libraries is administered by the Office of Presidential Libraries, which is part of the National Archives and Records Administration (NARA), located in College Park, Maryland.

Office of Presidential Libraries
National Archives and Records
    Administration
8601 Adelphi Road
College Park, MD 20740
Phone: (301) 837-3250
http://www.archives.gov/presidential_
    libraries

**George Bush Presidential Library and
    Museum**
1000 George Bush Drive West
College Station, TX 77845
Phone: (979) 691-4000
http://bushlibrary.tamu.edu
    Museum Hours:
    9:30 A.M.–5 P.M., Monday–Saturday
    12 P.M.–5 P.M., Sunday

**Jimmy Carter Presidential Library
    and Museum**
441 Freedom Parkway
Atlanta, GA 30307
Phone: (404) 331-3942
http://www.jimmycarterlibrary.org
    Museum Hours:
    9 A.M.–4:45 P.M., Monday–Saturday
    12 P.M.–4:45 P.M., Sunday

**William J. Clinton Presidential Center
    and Park**
P.O. Box 1104
Little Rock, AK 72203
Phone: (501) 370-8000
http://www.clintonpresidentialcenter.org

**Dwight D. Eisenhower Presidential
    Library and Museum**
200 Southeast 4th Street
Abilene, KS 67410
Phone: (785) 263-4751; (877) RING-IKE
    (toll-free)
http://eisenhower.archives.gov
    Museum Hours:
    9 A.M.–5 P.M., every day

(8 A.M.–6 P.M., Memorial Day–mid-
August)

**Gerald R. Ford Presidential Library
    and Museum**
The Gerald R. Ford Presidential Library and Museum are in two different locations. Despite the separation, the library and museum are a single institution sharing one director.

Ford Library
1000 Beal Avenue
Ann Arbor, MI 48109
Phone: (734) 741-2218
http://www.ford.utexas.edu

Ford Museum
303 Pearl Street, NW
Grand Rapids, MI 49504
Phone: (616) 451-9263
http://www.ford.utexas.edu
    Museum Hours:
    9 A.M.–5 P.M., every day

**Herbert Hoover Presidential Library
    and Museum**
210 Parkside Drive
P.O. Box 488
West Branch, IA 52358
Phone: (319) 643-5301
http://hoover.archives.gov
    Museum Hours:
    9 A.M.–5 P.M., every day
    (open until 8 P.M. Wednesdays in July
    and August)

**Lyndon B. Johnson Presidential
    Library and Museum**
2313 Red River Street
Austin, TX 78705
Phone: (512) 721-0200
http://www.lbjlib.utexas.edu

Museum Hours:
9 A.M.–5 P.M., every day except
    Christmas
Reading Room Hours:
    9:00 A.M.–5:00 P.M. weekdays
Closed on federal holidays

**John F. Kennedy Presidential Library
    and Museum**
Columbia Point
Boston, MA 02125
Phone: (617) 514-1600; (877) 616-4599
    (toll free)
http://www.jfklibrary.org
    Museum Hours:
    9 A.M.–5 P.M., every day

**Richard M. Nixon Presidential
    Materials Staff**
National Archives at College Park
8601 Adelphi Road
College Park, MD 20740
Phone: (301) 837-3290
http://nixon.archives.gov

**Ronald Reagan Presidential Library
    and Museum**
40 Presidential Drive
Simi Valley, CA 93065
Phone: (800) 410-8354
http://www.reagan.utexas.edu
    Museum Hours:
    10 A.M.–5 P.M., every day except
        Thanksgiving, Christmas, and New
        Year's Day
    Library Research Room:
    9 A.M.–5 P.M. Monday through Friday,
        closed on all federal holidays

**Franklin D. Roosevelt Presidential
    Library and Museum**
4079 Albany Post Road
Hyde Park, NY 12538

Phone: (845) 486-7770; (800) FDR-VISIT
http://www.fdrlibrary.marist.edu
   Museum Hours:
     9 A.M.–5 P.M., every day (open until
       6 P.M., April–October)

**Harry S. Truman Presidential Library
  and Museum**
500 West U.S. Highway 24
Independence, MO 64050-1798
Phone: (816) 833-1400; (800) 833-1225

http://www.trumanlibrary.org
   Museum Hours:
     9 A.M.–5 P.M., Monday–Saturday
      (open until 9 P.M. Thursday)
     12 P.M.–5 P.M., Sunday

APPENDIX VII
BEST LIBRARY SCIENCE
MASTER'S PROGRAMS, 2005

U.S. News & World Report ranked the 48 ALA-accredited master's degree programs in library and information science in the United States. The rankings are based on the results of a survey sent to deans, program directors, and faculty of accredited graduate programs in fall 1998. The questionnaires asked individuals to rate the academic quality of programs at each institution as distinguished (5), strong (4), good (3), adequate (2), or marginal (1). Individuals who were unfamiliar with a particular school's programs were asked to select "don't know." Scores for each school were totaled and divided by the number of respondents who rated that school. The response rate was 60 percent.

Library Science
1. University of Illinois–Urbana-Champaign
   University of North Carolina–Chapel Hill
2. Syracuse University (NY)
   University of Michigan–Ann Arbor
   University of Pittsburgh

Library Science Specialties: Services for Children and Youth
1. Rutgers–New Brunswick (NJ)
2. Florida State University
   Texas Woman's University

Library Science Specialties: Archives and Preservation
1. University of Texas–Austin

2. University of Maryland–College Park
   University of Michigan–Ann Arbor

Library Science Specialties: Health Librarianship
1. University of Pittsburgh
2. University of North Texas
3. University of North Carolina–Chapel Hill

Library Science Specialties: Information Systems
1. Drexel University (PA)
2. Syracuse University (NY)
3. University of Pittsburgh

Library Science Specialties: Music Librarianship
1. Indiana University
2. University of Illinois–Urbana-Champaign

Library Science Specialties: School Library Media
1. Rutgers–New Brunswick (NJ)
2. Florida State University
3. University of South Carolina–Columbia

BIBLIOGRAPHY

Bly, Robert W. *Careers for Writers and Others Who Have a Way with Words.* New York: McGraw-Hill, 1995.

Bopp, Richard E., and Linda Smith. *Reference and Information Services.* 2d ed. Westport, Conn.: Libraries Unlimited, 1995.

Carter, Robert A., and S. William Pattis. *Opportunities in Publishing Careers.* Rev. ed. New York: McGraw-Hill/Contemporary, 2000.

Crawford, Walt. *Being Analog: Creating Tomorrow's Libraries.* Chicago: American Library Association, 1999.

Degalan, Julie, and Stephen Lambert. *Great Jobs for English Majors.* New York: McGraw-Hill, 2000.

Eberhart, George M. *The Whole Library Handbook 3: Current Data, Professional Advice, and Curiosa about Libraries and Library Sciences.* 3d ed. Chicago: American Library Association Editions, 2000.

Eberts, Marjorie, and Margaret Gisler. *Careers for Bookworms and Other Literary Types.* 3d ed. New York: McGraw-Hill/Contemporary, 2002.

Evans, G. Edward. *Developing Library and Information Center Collections.* 2d ed. Westport, Conn.: Libraries Unlimited, 1987.

Evans, G. Edward, and Patricia L. Ward. *Management Basics for Information Professionals.* New York: Neal-Schuman Publishers, 2000.

Farr, Michael, and LaVerne L. Ludden. *200 Best Jobs for College Graduates.* 2d ed. Indianapolis, Ind.: JIST Publishing, 2003.

Flanagan, Alice K. *Librarians.* Minneapolis, Minn.: Compass Point Books, 2001.

Fourie, Denise, and David Dowell. *Libraries in the Information Age: An Introduction and Career Exploration.* Westport, Conn.: Libraries Unlimited, 2002.

Garoogian, Rhoda. *Careers in Other Fields for Librarians: Successful Strategies for Finding the Job.* Chicago: American Library Association Editions, 1985.

Gisler, Margaret M. *101 Career Alternatives for Teachers: Exciting Job Opportunities for Teachers Outside the Teaching Profession.* Roseville, Calif.: Prima Lifestyles, 2002.

Goodman, Leonard. *Alternative Careers for Teachers, Librarians, and Counselors.* New York: Hungry Minds, 1983.

Gorman, Michael. *Our Enduring Values: Librarianship in the 21st Century.* Chicago: American Library Association Editions, 2000.

Katz, William A. *Introduction to Reference Work.* New York: McGraw-Hill, 1978.

LaGuardia, Cheryl, and Christine K. Oka. *Becoming a Library Teacher.* New York: Neal-Schuman, 2000.

Larsgaard, Mary. *Map Librarianship: An Introduction.* Westport, Conn.: Libraries Unlimited, 1999.

Leone, Laura. *Choosing a Career in Information Science.* New York: Rosen Publishing Group, 2001.

Massis, Bruce. *The Practical Library Manager.* Binghamton, N.Y.: Haworth Press, 2002.

McCook, Kathleen De La Pena. *Opportunities in Library and Information Science Careers.* Chicago: VGM Career Books, 2002.

McDermott, Irene E. *Librarian's Internet Survival Guide: Strategies for the High-Tech Reference Desk.* Medford, N.J.: Information Today, 2002.

Nardi, Bonnie, and Vicki O'Day, eds. *Information Ecologies: Using Technology with Heart.* Cambridge, Mass.: MIT Press, 2000.

Nesbeitt, Sarah L., and Gordon, Rachel Singer. *The Information Professional's Guide to Career Development Online.* Medford, N.J.: Information Today, 2002.

Newlen, Robert R. *Writing Resumes That Work: A How-To-Do-It Manual for Librarians.* New York: Neal-Schuman, 1998.

Rubin, Richard. *Foundations of Library and Information Science.* New York: Neal-Schuman, 2000.

Shontz, Priscilla, K., Steven J. Oberg, and Robert Klob. *Jump Start Your Career in Library and Information Science.* Lanham, Md.: Scarecrow Press, 2002.

Siess, Judith A. *Time Management, Planning, and Prioritization for Librarians.* Lanham, Md.: Rowman & Littlefield, 2002.

Singer-Gordon, Rachel. *The Accidental Systems Librarian.* Medford, N.J.: Information Today, 2003.

Stripling, Barbara. *Learning and Libraries in an Information Age.* Westport, Conn.: Libraries Unlimited, 1999.

Wilkinson, Frances C. and Linda Lewis. *The Complete Guide to Acquisitions Management.* Westport, Conn.: Libraries Unlimited, 2003.

INDEX

ABOUT THE AUTHOR

School librarian Linda Carvell, M.A., M.L.S, is a former head librarian at the Lancaster Country Day School and a former president and current board member of the Pennsylvania School Librarians' Association. She holds a B.A. in English from Albright College, an M.S. in library science from Drexel University, and an M.A. in English from Temple University. She also holds an instructional certification (K–12) in library science from Millersville University.

Carvell's past library experience includes working as a science reference librarian at the Los Angeles Public Library for two years, in business reference and as head of popular library at the Cleveland Public Library for two years, and as assistant children's and adult librarian at the Cherry Hill Public Library in New Jersey for three years.

In addition to her library background, Carvell has served as editor of the library journal *Learning & Media* for six years, writing a column in each of the quarterlies. As an affiliate representative, she has continued to write a column for each issue. An assembly delegate of the American Association of School Librarians since 1996, she also has been a member of the Commonwealth Libraries, Youth Services Task Force of Commonwealth Libraries, the Lancaster-Lebanon School Librarians Association, and the Lancaster County Library Association.

Attending national, regional, and state conferences and workshops in addition to serving on various state-level committees has kept Carvell aware of current trends in school library management and in teaching information literacy.